The Life of Music
in North India

Boredom is the dream bird that hatches the egg of
experience. A rustling in the leaves drives him
away. His nesting places—the activities that are
intimately associated with boredom—are already
extinct in the cities and are declining in the country
as well. With this the gift for listening is lost and
the community of listeners disappears.

Walter Benjamin,
"The Storyteller"

Wayne State University Press

Detroit, 1980

The Life of Music in North India

The Organization of an Artistic Tradition

by Daniel M. Neuman, DARTMOUTH COLLEGE

Library of Congress Cataloging in Publication Data

Neuman, Daniel M   1944–
    The life of music in North India.

    Bibliography: p.
    Includes index.
    1. Music, Hindustani—History and criticism.
    2. Music—India. 3. Musicians, India. 4. Music
and society. I. Title.
ML338.N44   781.7'54   79-16889
ISBN 0-8143-1632-8

The costs associated with the publication of this volume were
supported through a grant from the National Endowment for the Humanities,
an independent federal agency.

Photograph Credits: Photographs unaccompanied by a credit line were made by the author.

This book is dedicated to my parents: not only because of the special nature of such a kinship relation, but because it is they who led me into the very special world of music.

Contents

Illustrations

Preface

It has by now become a cliché to refer to India as vast, ancient, and highly diverse, which of course does not deny the reality of India's complexity. But scholars concerned with other cultural areas point with some justification to the weakness of generalities about India following the catalogue of caveats Indianists are constrained to generate as they explain one or another facet of Indian civilization. The culture of North Indian (*Hindustani*) art music in some respects presents no such problem, since—and this itself is an important datum—it is a historical and performance tradition remarkably uniform throughout the northern part of the subcontinent, including Pakistan and Bangla Desh. Yet by virtue of this very extensiveness, Hindustani music culture is an enormity and it becomes necessary therefore to specify the perspective taken and the sources of knowledge.

This book is not about Indian music *per se*: rather it is about the cultural and social world in which Hindustani music is nurtured, listened and attended to, cultivated and consumed. It is about Hindustani musicians; their ideas and actions about music and musicianship, making a living through music and living a life of music. It is in short an anthropological account of Hindustani music culture, with the inaudible yet everpresent background of the music itself.

From the beginning of 1969 until the middle of 1971, and again for briefer periods in 1973–74, 1976–77, and 1978, I was engaged in the anthropological enterprise of fieldwork: interviewing musicians, collecting their genealogies, attending concerts, learning the Indian fiddle, having tea with musicians and listening to their gossip, becoming a source of gossip, speaking with connoisseurs, and eventually becoming part of the scenery—although never completely blended in—of the world of music in North India. Most of my time was spent in Delhi, although I made several short visits to Bombay, Calcutta, Banaras, Jaipur, Lucknow, and several other smaller towns, where I also met and interviewed musicians. The data I have gathered are, accordingly, not limited to Delhi, but the perspective of my book is largely filtered through what I learned in Delhi. I have consequently made claims about the North Indian music tradition which probably overemphasize the Delhi reality and take insufficient cognizance of other musically important areas of North India, principally Maharashtra, Bengal, Rajasthan, and the Banaras region.

One of the consequences of my Delhi focus is that the majority of musicians I interviewed are Muslims. Friendly critics of the earlier manuscript version of this work have commented on the Islamic cultural and Delhi regional bias inherent in it. I have attempted here to provide a more balanced picture in response to the helpful comments I have received, but the reader should be forewarned that my perspective continues to be informed by my unyielding, though not irrational, conviction that Delhi is the birthplace, ancestral home, and historical center of North Indian music culture. Other areas, important as some have now become, are nevertheless derivative from the Delhi tradition.

Without the help of scores of musicians and their families, many of whom remain anonymous here, this work obviously could not have been started. To those singing but unsung heroes of contemporary Indian music I give my deepest thanks. I would especially like to acknowledge my teacher in India, Ustad Sabri Khan, who first pointed the way to an understanding of Indian music. In addition, special thanks must be given to Ustad Yunus Hussein Khan and Ustad Zia Mohiuddin Dagar for the many hours they have so kindly given to me.

During my initial sojourn in India, several people not directly connected to my research illuminated, in their own manner, my understanding of India. Two who always had, and have, light to provide are Harbans Mathur and D. P. Sen.

At various stages of my writing, Joep Bor, Joseph Casagrande, Harold Gould, T. N. Madan, Naomi Owens, Jennifer Post, Mark Slobin, and Manon Spitzer read all or parts of the manuscript and I have truly learned much from their suggestions.

As with music, every scholarly work arises out of a tradition, and I have been especially fortunate in having two such traditions. My colleagues in the Department of Anthropology at Dartmouth College, Hoyt Alverson, David Gregory, and Kenneth Korey, have provided a continually active intellectual environment from which I have benefited invaluably. Not only are they excellent anthropologists, but by happy coincidence, they are authentic music devotees as well. The other tradition consists of a small circle of scholars in North America concerned with the music culture of India. Peter Row and Brian Silver, as close friends and colleagues for several years, have been particularly helpful in providing a constant source of insight into the workings of Hindustani music. The conceptual refinements I have been able to incorporate in this book are due in no small measure to their wisdom and knowledge.

In a similar fashion, I have benefited from my relationships, as student and colleague, with William Kay Archer and Bruno Nettl. What I know of ethnomusicology can be traced directly to them. Bill Archer first introduced me to ethnomusicology, Indo-Iranian civilization, and the delights of talking about both through many nights. Bruno Nettl guided me with wisdom and patience for many years, and he continues to be a source of much reflection on music and culture in my thinking.

My initial research support was provided by a grant and fellowship from the National Institute of Mental Health, augmented by a grant from the Department of Anthropology at the University of Illinois. For subsequent research in India I have received generous support from the American Institute of Indian Studies, whose director in India, Mr. Mehendiratta, aided me there as he has many others. Dartmouth College has been equally generous in providing several small grants to enable me to conduct short-term research in India.

It has somehow become a tradition of the structure of acknowledgments that one's spouse occupy the "last but not least" position. If this position be understood as the epitomizing symbol of gratitude, the reader will have a true understanding of the importance my wife, Arundhati, has had in the formation of this book. As field assistant, as translator, and above all as critic, her presence has been crucial.

Note on the Text

Most of the Indian vocabulary used here is ultimately derived from either Sanskrit or Persian and Arabic. The language spoken in Delhi, where most of my research was conducted, is there referred to as Hindi, Urdu, or Hindustani. These three terms are often considered synonymous in India. Or they may be considered as variants of one another. Hindi has a vocabulary derived primarily from Sanskrit and is written in the same script, known as *devanagari*. Urdu has a vocabulary that borrows heavily from Persian and Arabic and is written in the Arabic script. Hindustani is the generic term for either or both of these variants.

In addition to alternative vocabularies available to speakers of what I shall refer to as Hindustani, there are often alternative pronunciations, particularly of words derived from Persian and Arabic. Thus the *kh* of the word *khāndān* can be pronounced as an aspirated *k* (particularly by one who claims Hindi in contrast to Urdu as his mother tongue), or it can be pronounced as a fricative (as it typically will be by Urdu speakers). Because of the numerous alternatives in both written and spoken language, the effort to construct a consistent system of transliteration encounters difficulties that require compromises. A consistent system of compromises is available in *A Practical Hindi-English Dictionary*, compiled by Mahendra Chaturvedi and Bola Nath Tiwari (2d edition, 1975, National Publishing House, Delhi). Because it is consistent, and because it transliterates Hindustani as spoken in the Delhi area, I have based my own system of transliteration on this work, with the following modifications:

15

(1) A macron indicates a long vowel (ā, ī, etc.).
(2) No symbol is used to indicate nasalization.
(3) For consistency with common usage, a transliteration other than the one found in the dictionary is occasionally provided. The dictionary transliteration is furnished in the Glossary, in parentheses, following the form used in the text, for example: shaikh (shekh).
(4) Transliterations in direct quotations from sources are not changed. To avoid ambiguity, both forms are included in the Glossary.
(5) Personal and place names are transliterated according to common usage and without diacritical marks.
(6) Plurals of nouns are formed by the addition of *s* to the singular.

Complete transliteration, including diacritical marks, is provided for all non-English words on first mention in the text and for all words listed in the Glossary. Diacritical marks are subsequently not inserted, except in the words *rāg* and *bīn,* because of the too familiar orthography they otherwise have for the general reader of English.

1. Introduction

This is an inquiry into the relationship between a people and their music. It sets out to explore this relationship by interpreting the art, or classical, music of North India as a cultural phenomenon and reporting its connections to a number of social domains it calls its own. Specifically, it is an anthropological account of the culture of North Indian (Hindustani) music and the changing social context of which it is part, as expressed in the thoughts and actions of its professional musicians. As an analysis of musical life in North India, it is also intended to reveal part of a major drama being unfolded in India today: a great musical tradition engaging a modern world.

The music culture of India is the only major system, outside the West, that has succeeded in maintaining its traditions largely unmarked by the West and a colonial past, and that has also journeyed away from its cultural home to be welcomed elsewhere. Indian art music, to use Gerald Abraham's expression about Western music, has generated a "dynamic nucleus" of listeners in North America and Europe (Abraham 1974:124). This spread of Indian music beyond its cultural boundaries suggests that, as with biological species, the ability to thrive in an expanded ecological niche is a positive adaptive response; and, as with other cultural phenomena flowing over traditional boundaries, it has something to say, and something to do. The question here, however, is not so much what it says and what it does but

17

how such a characteristic, yet elusive and ephemeral, cultural phenomenon continues to maintain its integrity and autonomy in a world so vastly changed from that which gave it birth.

Many Indian musicians see in this integrative process the central problem for Indian music today: it is the unbalanced phasing between social and technological changes, on the one hand, and the cultural structures through which we organize our experience and give it meaning, on the other. Certainly in the West, with current notions such as "future shock," and in other parts of the world, where cultural traditions often appear ill-prepared for the technological revolutions they engage, the problem of a harmonious interlinking of both seems paramount.

A century or so ago, when India was first becoming truly unified through the world of ideas and the new technologies enabling their swift and inexpensive communication, the social world of Indian music was markedly different from what it is now. Musical events, which took place in the courts of the nobility and in the homes of the wealthy, provided opportunities for private patronage rather than public appreciation. Musicians were commonly attached to households as respected artists and artisans. By the third quarter of the nineteenth century, when communication and travel were improved, artists also journeyed from one court to another, often for extended sojourns. Master musicians, as in earlier times, were very much in demand, with princes outbidding one another to attract the luminaries of the day. Sometimes rulers went to great lengths—and deeply into debt—to sustain a top-ranking musical establishment, as did their eighteenth-century counterparts in Europe. Lesser musicians—accompanists of dancing and singing girls—were the artisans of the musical community: craftsmen, commonly organized into guild-like brotherhoods and living in particular urban wards, they formed the musicians' pool of the day, available when needed for a performance. Courtesan vocalists often had their own favorite accompanists who, in such cases, were regularly employed in the salons of Delhi, Calcutta, Bombay, Lucknow, Banaras, and other towns and cities of North India.

Toward the end of the first quarter of the present century, the social basis of music making began to be redefined by the

18

The grand masters of the past: musicians at a conference in Nepal circa 1900. *Photograph from the collection of Yunus Hussein Khan.*

tastes and economic power of the rising middle class and by the search for a national identity. In theory and in practice, music was celebrated as an artistic heritage transcending caste, religious, ethnic, and linguistic boundaries, an especially salient cultural phenomenon at a time when few other expressions, aside from the shared desire to rid India of the British, could claim to be of national relevance. V. N. Bhatkhande, the father of modern Indian musicology, in a speech in 1916, even expressed the hope that the Hindustani and Karnatak systems, which distinctly separate North and South India, would merge to become a truly national music.

The new middle class, which played an important role in the incipient nationalistic movement, was born and bred in the cities of India. A product of British colonial enterprise, it initially shared with its mentors a Victorian antipathy toward India's traditional performing arts. It disapproved in particular of the tradition of temple dancing, performed by specialist communities of dancing girls (*devadasis*), which was gradually prohibited in many provinces during the early part of the century. The courtesans' salons and their musicians, who were also associated with the developing theater in West India, remained active but also were socially (and morally) suspect for the respectable middle class.

By the 1920s, however, middle-class attitudes toward *learning* classical Indian music began to change. Historically, the profession of music had been hereditary, dominated by Muslim families whose knowledge of the art was a jealously guarded secret sanctified by similar traditions of caste specialization in other communities. Then in Maharashtra and Bengal, later in other regions, high-caste Hindus, usually *Brāhmans,* apprenticed themselves to Muslim masters and became master musicians in their own right, eventually performing in public at musical conferences. These provided a platform for learned papers on music and history as well as a stage for the performing artist.

The social conditions prompting the transformation of Brahman interest in music from an avocational status to a professional one have yet to be systematically explored, but certainly it was a part of the cultural florescence accompanying the development of nationalism and the emergence of a public celebration of Indian civilization. Bengali middle-class interest in art music, for example, was decisively influenced by the views of Rabindranath Tagore. Whatever its genesis, however, Brahman attention to Indian art music gave it a respectable place in middle-class culture.

Much as in nineteenth-century Europe, music making became one of the social graces of the bourgeoisie. Young girls especially were expected to learn at least enough music so that when it came time to arrange a marriage, the parents could assert their daughter's musical accomplishments and the future husband could dream of being serenaded by his bride. (Curiously, the

20

wives of the bourgeoisie were expected to assume this part of the traditional courtesan's role at a time when keeping a mistress was increasingly frowned upon.) Even now, women form the vast majority of students in music colleges in both North and South India.

The social and cultural need for music was not limited to celebrations of a national Indian consciousness or to a young woman's kit of social graces. Classical Indian music provided much of the programming for the new radio stations from the 1930s onward, and for the film industry, now the second largest in the world. In the film industry's early days, composers and performers with a classical background created music that combined classical, light classical, folk, and theater forms. Later, Indian film music became a distinct genre—a new medium creating a new music. Today it is a social phenomenon of great but unstudied significance.

The remembered past which contemporary musicians evoke is not the immediate past but a world that to the modern sensibility seems like something from the Arabian Nights. It was a world in which the nobility were men of high learning and deep sensitivity; men who apprenticed themselves to their own musicians and called them masters, where music contests could destroy in a single night a reputation built over four decades of hard work, and award to the victor his weight in gold and jewels. This was a world where musicians practiced unceasingly until practice itself became a form of worship and its own objective, where listeners were a rare and delicate species, having the leisure to cultivate an art from early youth, to mature with age into true connoisseurs; a world, in short, where musicians of excellence flourished, being, as they were, measured only by listeners of excellence.

If all this seems a trifle romanticized, it is nevertheless what the musician wistfully imagines and is probably truer as an affective reality than our contemporary sceptical sensibilities would allow us to believe. It is a truth, however, which attaches solely to the music; it can only be made convincing through its own voice, and perhaps that is the very special appeal it holds for us.

The grammar of that appeal remains to be outlined for the Western reader, although I am cautioned by A. H. Fox-Strangways' admonition concerning generalities about India (in his classic work, *The Music of Hindostan,* first published in 1914). "There is, it is said, no statement which will apply to the whole of India except the geographical one that it is east of Suez. But three statements can be made about it which no one will be disposed to deny—that it is old and large and hot. India has had time to forget more melody than Europe has had time to learn" (1965:7). It is Strangways' fourth statement that points to a key idea of Indian music.

Hindustani music is a *melodic* system, and in this sense the relationship between tones is linear and horizontal in contrast to the Western harmonic system in which the relationships between tones could be said to be governed by the hierarchical and vertical. The performance of art music in North India is largely soloistic. A vocalist or instrumentalist is accompanied by a drummer, and the vocalist is also usually joined by another melodic instrumentalist who provides a heterophonic accompaniment. Sometimes two (rarely three) soloists will perform together, either in complete unison or in alternating sections, in which one soloist and then the other take their separate turns.

Perhaps the most striking difference between Hindustani and Western art music traditions that lends itself to a verbal description is in the conception of composition. The Hindustani system is fundamentally an oral tradition—that is, actual performances are derived not from written scores but from remembered repertoires. The relationships between what we can call the model *for* performance—the score in Western music, the remembered repertoire in Indian music—and the actual performance are of a substantively different kind. In Western music the relationship between the score and the performance is isomorphic; the score is not only a model *for* performance, but it can also be used as a model *of* the performance, when following a performance by reading the score. The score is also isomorphic with the composition, the score being the material object and the composition being the idea of a given performance.

In the Hindustani system, there is no score. The compositions—known as *chīz* for vocal music, *gat* for instrumental music or *bandish* for both—are set to a recurring rhythmic cycle, but comprise only a relatively small portion of the total performance, the rest of which is improvised.[1] As Nazir Jairazbhoy characterizes it: "The composition serves as a spring-board for these [extemporizations] and a frame of reference to which musicians periodically return. Thus the form is similar to that of the Rondo, the composition alternating with the improvisations" (1971:31). The improvisations themselves are usually made up of previously worked-out phrases, musical elements put together in unique ways for each performance. The intricacy of the structure of these musical elements and the ingenuity of the architectural assembly establish the degree of creativity and inspiration in a performance.

Improvisations are not generated on the basis of the composition as such, but are elaborations of the *rāg*. The rāg, which has no conceptual analogue in Western music, has been defined by Peter Row "as a set of musical materials that together form a unique modal identity that serves as the basis for composition and improvisation" (1977:104).[2] The significance of the composition then is not in exhibiting itself, but rather in exhibiting the rāg; it is an instance of the rāg in both a miniature and template sense, as microcosm and as generator of authentic versions. This is why the quality of a composition is determined by its success in expressing the essence of a rāg and inspiring elaboration of it. This would be equivalent in the Western tradition to saying that a composition—a late Beethoven quartet, for example—was written and is performed to demonstrate the quality of its key.

The identity of the composer of Hindustani compositions is usually unknown because the compositions themselves, notated in a solfège system, were, until this century, not only unpublished but also largely kept secret within the household traditions of hereditary musicians. It was and still is the identity of the performer that is of key importance, because it is he or she who is penultimately responsible for the quality of a performance. (Ultimate responsibility comes from the Divine.) The identity of a composer may be important to establish the authenticity of a performer and his performance, but such identity is significant only if the composer and thus the composition are very old; in such cases the contemporary performer authenticates himself by exhibiting the antiquity of the musical tradition he claims.

The theoretical orientation that underlies my analysis is based on a consideration of three types of phenomena: the cultural structure, social organization, and adaptive strategies of musicians.

The cultural structure is the system of symbols and meanings which musicians utilize and exhibit with reference to their music and their being musicians. This is the subject of the opening chapters; it constitutes only an initial analysis of what is an incredibly rich and complex world of meaning. I have focused on concepts which the musicians themselves believe to be of primary importance: the meaning of practice, the affective relationship between master and disciple, and the role of the Divine, as these pertain to the making of a musician and the creation of music. My concern in these chapters is with an indigenous perspective of the music culture. From interviews, gossip, conversation, and discourse, I have attempted to construct a Hindustani interpretation of what it means to become and be a musician. These interpretations should be loosely understood as "norms," in the way that David Schneider uses the term to refer to a pattern for action: "The phrase 'for action' in my definition of norms is meant to imply that norms entail the clear mandate of legitimacy, propriety, appropriateness, moral authority" (1976:200). If the description I present appears at times to be too idealized, it is because I am elucidating the system as a code *for* behavior, not as a systematization, description, or celebration *of* it.

I also examine the social organization of musicians from an "outside" perspective. No individual within the system would understand (or seek to understand) the totality of the social system as I have presented it. When I brought my detailed formulation to the attention of informants, however, my own teacher responded that, although he had not thought of it that way before, he instantly recognized it as "making sense." The basic data for the construction of the social organization of musicians were numerous genealogies collected over a period of eight years, and it is only by using this classic anthropological method that I was able to conceptualize their social organization as a system.

In describing the social organization of professional musicians, I am guided by Milton Singer's formulation for the study of cultural specialists in India, which, beyond performance, includes "his recruitment, training, remuneration . . . his relationship to his audience, patron, other performers and his community" (1972:73). The term *professional musician* here refers to a member of an occupational category which includes a variety of performing specialists. The occupational category itself, however, raises many provocative questions within the Indian context, for professional musicians do not originate, as do so many other occupational specialists in India, from a common social pool—a caste—but rather from a variety of social groups. They are recruited from castes of musical specialists and from matrilineages of courtesans, from Brahmans and from Untouchables, from Muslims and Hindus, from members of the ruling class and from the ruled. The music culture which classical musicians share, despite these diverse origins, implies that there is a social organization transcending those ordinarily encountered on the basis of caste, class, ethnicity, and religion. The interaction among different social types for the learning, transmission, and creation of Hindustani music also suggests that Indian social and cultural boundaries are more permeable than commonly believed. Regardless of the affirmed social constraints, particularly the system of castes, there is good evidence that, when necessary, India's social structure has been more labile than we are accustomed to think.

The recent findings of social scientists working in India corroborate the view that India's traditional culture is not nearly as static as was once assumed. The caste system, that symbolic bulwark of tradition, has clearly evolved over time and is doing so even now. Castes have been able to change their social identity, history, and rank. They have been able to organize themselves into larger social blocs when politically expedient and have splintered into smaller factions when grown too complex (Singer

1972; Silverberg 1968; Rudolph and Rudolph 1967; Dumont 1970; Srinivas 1976; Bailey 1957). My own interest in the persistence of Indian music culture—its ability not merely to survive but to thrive—has led me to investigate its adaptive strategies. Here also, as in other areas of Indian civilization, the evidence is that traditional modes are not being abandoned; rather, they are reinterpreted so as to preserve the core by adjusting their articulation with the changing shapes of Indian civilization.

The concluding part of this work leans obviously and heavily on another extrinsic interpretive frame, that of cultural ecological theory, albeit of a rather special sort. It is directly inspired by William Kay Archer's exploratory essay, "On the Ecology of Music," which asks of the ethnomusicologist that music be considered a cultural artifact of the larger environment (1964). But music is also, among many things, a system of ideas, and my own thoughts about how these flourish from, transform in, and relate to the sensibilities of a people have been informed by the writings of Gregory Bateson (1972) and Clifford Geertz (1972).

One of the adaptive strategies has been the urbanization of music culture. Indeed, the consideration of an urban environment as a special niche for music making has been considered in recent studies in a number of music cultures (Nettl 1978). In contemporary India, performances of classical music typically originate from cities. As the patronage base has become increasingly dependent on the heterogeneous many of the city rather than the homogeneous few of the court, professional musicians have situated themselves in areas of high population density where they can attract a large listening public.

The media through which music performances are communicated have also become more diversified than in the past, and are similarly concentrated in urban environments. Radio, public music conferences, music schools, and more recently television are all primary means by which performers can be patronized. For a musician to utilize these media—and to be utilized by them—he must work and live where they originate, with relatively easy and regular access to the media brokers.

The problem for the musician (and in microcosm perhaps for India as well) is to adopt a strategy that does not negate his musical heritage, deny him the present, or spoil the future for his children. A more general dilemma confronting us all is embedded in a specific question we have sometimes been discouraged from asking: "Can a traditional music survive in a world that appears to undermine the basis upon which it existed?" The answer, in India at least, depends on what happens to her musicians.

Practitioners of the art and purveyors of its heritage, musicians are the mediators of their music culture. They are shaped by and give shape to the social and cultural environment of which they are part. How we are to interpret their role as mediators depends, in the final analysis, on the kind of relationship we assume between music and culture.

This book rests on the assumption that music, culture, and society are somehow interrelated, a view that is now commonplace among ethnomusicologists. In his pioneering work, *The Anthropology of Music,* Alan Merriam writes that music is "the result of behavior which is shaped by the society and culture of the men who produce it" (1964:25). Bruno Nettl, in *Theory and Method in Ethnomusicology,* devotes two chapters to music in culture and more recently has addressed himself to the explicit relationship between the music structure and social structure of Iran (1964, 1979). Mantle Hood also affirms that music "cannot be isolated from its socio-cultural context and the scale of values it implies" in his book, *The Ethnomusicologist* (1971:10). The nature of the relationship between music and culture (or music and society or sociocultural system) has been expressed in a number of ways, but is based always, I believe, on one of three primary metaphors of relationships, which need to be made explicit.[3]

First, music can be conceived as a component of a sociocultural system, one of a large number of artifacts existing among a people. As an element in the system, it both affects and is affected by other elements. To take a simple example, a repertoire of flute music is tied to the fact that materials are available for making the flute, or a repertoire of men's music is tied to an ideology which requires women be excluded from certain musical performance. Most ethnomusicological studies assume such a component relationship between music culture and the larger sociocultural system.

27

Second, music can be considered as a model, microcosm, or reflection of a sociocultural system. David McAllester's monograph on Navaho music and culture, published over twenty-five years ago, is still the standard work for this type of analysis (1954). Alan Lomax's wide-ranging research is the most ambitious attempt at relating musical phenomena isomorphically with other social and cultural phenomena (Lomax 1968). The assumption that music reflects its culture derives from the more general notion in Western society that the arts are comprehensive expressions of their sociocultural milieu.

Artistic performances can also be said to be reflections *on* or *about* cultural systems; that is, music provides a commentary, reading, or exegesis of a sociocultural system. It speaks to the members of a society and constructs part of the meaning or set of meanings about being a participant. In this sense music transcends the cultural system from which it derives—as component and model—and provides a metacommunication about the totality of a people, just as Bateson claims art does for the individual (1972:145). As commentary, music is to be distinguished from its relationship as model; in the latter case, music is the passive result of existing in a sociocultural system; in the former, music is an active force, speaking to and about a people, shaping the very characteristics it "only pretends to display" (Geertz 1972:28).

These three interpretations concerning the relationship between music culture and society are examples of theoretical emphases; they are not mutually exclusive. In one context, I speculate on Indian music as a model of Indian civilization; in another, I provide examples of how it is interpreted as a commentary on Indian society. But the primary focus in this inquiry is on the way Indian music articulates with the broader structure of civilization.

Another way of putting this is to say that the music culture of North India is presented to the reader as a Wilson cloud chamber, in which the actual phenomena—the music sounds—are only perceived in the wakes and trails they leave behind. This is as it must be since music exists essentially in the moment of its own making and any kind of recording of it—on tape, in transcription, or in memory—is a phenomenon not to be confused with it. And since music, as Claude Levi-Strauss avers, "is the only language with the contradictory attributes of being at once intelligible and untranslatable, the musical creator is a being comparable to the gods, and music itself the supreme mystery of the science of man" (1970:18).

The ambitions of the present work are not to investigate the mystery so much as to illuminate the creators of it; the wakes and trails which are their thoughts, values, organization, and actions, and only through these perhaps to be guided toward a glimpse of the mystery itself.

2. Becoming a Musician

Ideas and beliefs that musicians have about becoming and being a musician are shared to a large degree by all kinds of classical musicians in India, whatever their social background and performance specialty. This is not to say that they all have a set of identical values. There is, for example, the concern and the respect an instrumentalist has for his instrument—an attitude of which the vocalist is aware, but which for him is largely irrelevant. What is shared, however, is a belief that there are three elements required to become a performer of art music in India: (1) one's will or discipline, (2) one's teacher or perhaps—more properly—one's guide, and (3) one's spiritual status or divine intercession or grace. These elements derive from ideals regarding *riaz,* or practice; the *guru-shishya* institution, and the world of Supreme Being.

Riaz refers also to a rather extensive complex of ideas which provide a standard for individual responsibility and achievement. Riaz is the measure and the mark of the role of the individual in becoming a musician. The way one does (or is said to do) riaz expresses symbolically the way one is as a musician and reflects in this manner the relationship and effect of the other two elements here presented.

The guru-shishya institution is a relationship between master and disciple. Thoughts about what constitutes the proper nature of their relationship and the consequent results form the subject matter of many conversations heard in musical circles.

For the individual as a musician it is the primary social relationship, and it provides the continuity of the musical tradition between generations. In addition to guiding his disciple in his musical training, the guru guides his disciple in learning the role of the musician. As important as his function of teaching is his function as a model for his disciples. And in addition to perpetuating the tradition through time, the guru embodies in his "space" an identity which his disciples will assume and transmit to their disciples. A musician's identity is always defined in part by the identity of his teacher who, in turn, is identified by the identity of *his* teacher back through the line. This taken as a whole comprises a given "school," called a *gharānā* (*lit.*, "of the house"), distinguished from other gharanas on the basis of its unique history, pedigree, and style of performance.

The final element, one's spiritual status or Divine Will, is one which I shall treat first as a constant. It is a subject about which musicians have much to say and will be explored more fully in relation to the conditions of being a musician.

Riaz

If a musician wants to celebrate the genius of another musician, he will do so not so much in terms of musical accomplishments, which are taken for granted (and do not easily lend themselves to verbal description), but in terms of practice habits. The amazing feats of a musician's accomplishments are described not so much with reference to pyrotechnics, but with respect to accomplishments of discipline and perseverance in practice. My knowledge of this aspect of musicianship is necessarily subjective because descriptions and stories about riaz are very often given to students with a moral function in mind, and it is in this vein that they were undoubtedly often given to me.

Often when I met musicians, the first thing they asked me was whether I had been practicing hard; and while saying this, one would take my left hand and look at my nails and cuticles for the "hard" evidence. If the cuticles were built up into a horny ridge, and if my nails had grooves at the point where the nail

31

meets the cuticle, then the evidence was there. If it showed that I had practiced diligently, they would, so to speak, pass the hand around for other musicians to inspect. There were times when my practice was less than perfect, and I sometimes seriously considered cutting grooves in my nails with a file, so that I would look more accomplished than I was. The evidence was rarely in the hearing, because at the propaedeutic stage there was little I had to offer that would indicate what I knew, since real "knowing" was still far away, and what was important at the beginning was acquiring the basic technique.

One can ask, though, about listening for accomplishment of technique. This was done from time to time, more out of politeness than from any genuine interest; for genuine interest I had to rely on the condition of my nails, and this puzzled me. It also disturbed me, because I was proud of what I had learned, and, although I would be reticent about performing for others, I was also very flattered when asked and rarely protested with any conviction. But the fingernails were the real proof, and my aesthetic sensibilities were not attuned to a fingernail performance. I had yet to learn the beauty of mutilated cuticles, because I did not understand that it was this which constituted evidence of the student's dedication to his art. The practiced eye could gauge very accurately how much practice had been accomplished and from it—a measure of meaning—the degree of dedication, for this last is having and understanding meaning.

Dedication and Discipline

The following story, which I heard in several versions from different musicians, illustrates the kind of description given to communicate the greatness of another musician. The story is unusual in that it was told about someone who was still performing. Having interviewed him myself, I was able to get his own—and unsolicited—version. The subject is Ustad Ahmed Jan Thirakwa, generally conceded to be India's greatest *tabla* (drum) player, until he died in 1975. The first version was told to me by my own *ustād* (teacher):

Where would he sit when he practiced? Where bugs and insects and scorpions used to bite. He used to sit there so he wouldn't feel sleepy and go to sleep. He is about ninety years old and still very healthy. He used to practice the whole night. In the morning his brother would get almonds and raisins and that sort of thing and put it in his milk and mix it up nicely. [His brother] used to tell him to go to sleep. This is for strength and then he would make him go to sleep. He would go to sleep about six in the morning and wake up about one in the afternoon. At this time he would be very hungry and they used to make him very good meat with very good *ghī* [clarified butter] and give it to him and tell him to go for a stroll and come back and sit with his friends and have a good time. At nine in the evening he would eat his meal and go out for another walk. He would return at eleven and sit down at the tabla. At twelve o'clock he would tie his hair to the ceiling and stay awake, and he would play till six in the morning. He continued like this for one or two years. Now he doesn't need to do this any more. Now he practices for about an hour or two a day.

A similar story is told by Pandit Ravi Shankar about his guru, Ustad Allaudin Khan:

Sometimes when he practiced, he tied up his long hair with a heavy cord and attached an end of the cord to a ring in the ceiling. Then, if he happened to doze while he practiced, as soon as his head nodded, a jerk on the cord would pull his hair and awaken him. [Shankar 1968:51; cf. also Naomi Owens 1969:33]

Ahmed Jan Thirakwa's recollections of his own practice habits are illuminating, if only because he was truly a living legend. The point is the same, even though the schedule is different:

I used to practice for sixteen hours, with half or one hour gap in between. If I started at ten in the morning, then at twelve I took a rest, took lunch. After lunch I practiced again till seven at night and then had an interval of an hour. . . . I even practiced when I traveled by train. There was less crowd in the train then.

Whereas in the first version, practicing through the night and under somewhat extreme conditions constitutes the main theme, the second "autobiographical" variation emphasizes the number of hours expended. In these, and indeed in most stories about riaz habits, the characteristics of discipline and dedication

33

are the essential features, illustrating simultaneously what it means to be a great musician, what great musicians have had to do in order to become what they are, and, by implication, what is a necessary condition for anyone aspiring to a similar standard. Other stories are about, for example, one musician (Ustad Bundu Khan) who would take his instrument with him when he went to bed, playing on his back, while another practiced so rigorously that he has permanent marks on his thighs as a testimonial.

Scars, scorpions, and sleepless nights; the image emerges and the idea of riaz as it is so stunningly elaborated serves to convey the seriousness with which music is taken and instructs the uninitiated of what is to be required of him. Having understood this, one is still struck by the amount of attention given to what seems, after all, to be merely the preparation as opposed to its performance, particularly as it serves as an evaluative procedure. We learn not only that a musician *becomes* great by submitting himself to a very rigorous practice schedule, but also that, in part at least, the evidence for his genius lies in this very rigor. Clearly then, the concept of riaz encompasses more than its translation as "practice" would suggest. It is not only a preparation for performance, but also a preparation for an unattainable perfection. It is a learning experience for which there is never an end, only successive stages. As we shall see, one has to practice in order to learn how to practice, and practicing sixteen hours a day exemplifies a sense of scholarship and a level of learning which it inevitably generates. The concept of riaz symbolizes a certain accomplishment of one's inner development. Seen in this way, sixteen hours of riaz a day are symbolically equivalent to the high quality of the music that would inevitably result. To say, then, that Ahmed Jan Thirakwa practices sixteen hours a day is another way of saying that he produces great music and is consequently a great musician, *and* that he is a great musician and consequently produces great music.

Not all musicians can or will claim an extraordinary history of riaz, but most of them have a fairly extensive range of ideas associated with practice habits. What we can call the ideology of riaz refers not only to its symbolic attributes, but—in its more conventional sense—also to a set of associated values.

Maintenance

Practice as an ordinary feature of a professional musician's daily life is no less significant a concept than its symbolic attributes, although its orientation is along somewhat different lines. Riaz is held to be important as a source of ideas, an institution of continuing discipline, a route for continual refinement, and a way of maintaining a level of performance. Most musicians do not practice as much as they think they should. In evaluating their own practice habits, they always distinguish between a period of intensive riaz undergone sometime in the past, and what seems to be a holding action in the present. Their reasons for this are varied, and not mutually exclusive, since one musician may give several.

Perhaps the most common, as well as the most reasonable explanation given is the lack of time, often attributed to the demands of living in a world vastly different from that of the recent past. The leisure of the idealized village of the past or the princely patronage system is replaced by the scramble to earn a living. The comment of a renowned sitarist from Delhi is typical:

> I used to start [practice] at six in the morning and continue without a minute's gap till twelve noon. The evening riaz was not fixed. I used to go to my guru for lessons in the evenings. On the whole I practiced for about eight to ten hours a day. . . . There is no limit to riaz, but I would say that a minimum of five to six hours would do. Our ustads used to practice for twelve hours together. Nowadays one cannot afford so much time for practice. Now if a person practices for five to six hours continuously without fail, then after a few years he may become a good musician. . . . Now I am rather busy and don't have much time to practice; still I manage to sit down for riaz two, two-and-a-half hours a day.

Several things about this quotation invite examination. The sitarist's earlier years, a period of intensive riaz, contrast with a marked attenuation in the present. The ideal is "no limit"; ustads of the past practiced for twelve hours, the respondent for eight to ten hours formerly, and still fewer now. In one way, this pattern can be seen as three generations being covered, leading to decreased time for the intensive riaz pursued while one is still in the process of preparing to become a performer.

The distinction between riaz during one's discipleship and riaz during one's professional career is not often explicitly made, especially by younger musicians, who will acknowledge their still living gurus and ideally consider themselves ongoing disciples. Occasionally, however, a musician will make the distinction and separate explicitly what is required during the years of learning and what is required to maintain a professional standard. The standard is determined sometimes relative to other musicians—at least sometimes admitted as such—and more often as a self-defined measure of what is acceptable. As one sitarist of Delhi candidly described it:

> To maintain my standard it happens like this. When I have listened to all the other artists and I see that my standard is here, then I see that I am almost there; and the standard of the man who practices a lot is there, and I have reached here and I am all right. I have made this standard and it can't go. Now to improve further than this, at least five hours practice [daily] is required.

In order to reach "there," that is, a high standard defined not by a musician who is famous, or reputed to be a fine musician, but by one who "practices a lot," one then has to make an extra effort similar to that made by a disciple who is still in the process of learning. One reaches a certain plateau which, if it is to be passed, requires an extra effort. Why then is the extra effort not made? Here again the explanation offered is in terms of time—there never is enough time.

Another explanation is offered for practicing less now than before, the focal point of which is the art of riaz itself, and not performance capabilities. This explanation stresses the quality of riaz; that knowing how to practice is what must be learned, after which many hours of practice are no longer necessary. The renowned *sārangī* (bowed fiddle) artist, Pandit Ram Narayan, described it to me:

> I used to practice very hard, practicing many hours a day and into the night. Then one day my ustad [with whom he had just recently begun to study] asked me, "Why do you practice so much? Learn to practice correctly and then all you need is an hour or two a day." Now I only practice about two hours a day, because I have learned how to do correct riaz.

Indeed, Ram Narayan is well-known among his peers as being one who made special sacrifices to be able to practice a great deal. As others have told me, he would practice through the night in an empty musical-instrument shop, when everyone was asleep. He is now one of the top performers in India who, besides being an exceptionally sensitive musician, is a phenomenal technician. When he made this statement, I inquired further to find out what doing "correct" riaz means. "You will learn that by practicing," he replied. It is something, he went on, which one must discover for oneself, which will be accomplished when one seriously concentrates on his riaz. As Latif Ahmed Khan, the eminent tabla player, so succinctly put it, "You can't practice without practice."

Having learned how to practice correctly implies a certain level of achievement which I suspect is not different from the kind of practice accomplished musicians say they pursue to maintain their standard. When Ahmed Jan Thirakwa says that now he has to practice only an hour or two a day, he means that he knows how to practice.

The association between knowing how to practice well and being an already accomplished musician (that is, someone who is prepared to the extent that he or she will be, at the minimum, competent in a public performance) is perhaps an apparent one, although again it is not usually explicit in the conversations of musicians. The sitarist quoted above suggests that accomplishment as a musician depends not on how much one practices but on one's technique of practice, taking into account the extent to which one is already an accomplished musician.

> Here the thing [riaz] is such that it depends on technique. One musician practices for six hours and one [other] musician practices for one hour. But the one who practices for six hours cannot come near the one who practices for one hour. It depends on his technique. *It is dependent on the way he practices.* [Emphasis mine]

The Proper Context

There are certain ideals concerning what constitutes a proper environment for riaz in the sense of internal states and external surroundings. Part of knowing how to practice is knowing how to create the proper atmosphere and the proper discipline, so that practice becomes not only a habit, like going through the ritual of the morning toilet, but a directed process which requires above all else deep concentration. Riaz, if it is to be correctly done, is described as being very difficult to learn because the doing of it requires extended periods of extreme concentration:

> The more you practice the sooner you will be able to play well, but you need to concentrate. You can't keep your mind on several things at the same time. You can't think about other things and then try to practice also. You have to keep your mind concentrated on one place. You can't play for ten minutes then get up and do something and come back and start playing again.

So said my own teacher, Ustad Sabri Khan, many, many times.

Another important element is the notion of continuity and discontinuity. Practicing for two hours in thirty-minute units is very different from practicing two hours continuously. The former accomplishes little, since it takes that long just to "warm up." Whatever is accomplished by riaz, part of its importance lies in its continuity over long periods of time, that is from day to day, building little by little, and part is the process of continuity within a session, the beginning of which serves to establish the connection with the end of the previous day's riaz. The importance of having a sustained practice session is demonstrated in Ahmed Jan Thirakwa's comment and that of the sitarist.

However, there should be rest periods. Practicing without rest for extended time periods may lead to riaz being done mechanically, merely going through the process without having the requisite concentration. This is considered wasteful of time, besides being debilitating. It is better to have, for example, three two-hour sessions or two three-hour sessions, than to have one five-hour session and then another one- or two-hour session at some later time. The extent to which one practices depends on the individual. Some are able to maintain their concentration for long periods, whereas others may require short intervals of rest between practice sessions.

The same kind of emphasis is not placed, however, on the continuity of practice from day to day. Missing one or more days of practice, although undesirable, is not disastrous. This is perhaps truer for the already accomplished musician who can regain his technique readily (if he conceives of having lost some), compared to the student who is building on his previous work in order to achieve a certain standard. The distinction between the ideal and the real can sometimes be captured in a single statement, as one musician so poignantly illustrates:

> I think there should not be such gaps (of a day or two) in the riaz, and I myself have *never failed to practice every day.* Since my father and grandfather were musicians, it has been a part of my upbringing. The *days I failed to do riaz,* I felt that the food I ate was not deserved and I promised to do double riaz on the next day. [Emphasis mine]

This is the sort of thing a student may hear from a teacher and perhaps believe. As a performer, one views things rather more pragmatically since there can be a number of reasons why practice must be skipped. The most notable reason, for Muslim musicians who observe it, is the prohibition against producing any kind of music during the holiday of Muharram. Many neither perform nor practice during this period. It is a difficult time for All India Radio, in which scheduling time has to be filled by Hindu musicians. There are also fewer planned public events during this period.

Other reasons for skipping a day from time to time are illness, the long train journeys to music conferences (although as we have seen, Thirakwa claimed that he used to practice on the train), and being just too busy. Although it is impossible to determine how much time is spent on practice, I strongly suspect that most professional musicians often do not practice for extended periods of time, and that when they do, they will usually be so motivated because they are scheduled to give a public performance. I have known a few musicians who admitted not having done any serious practice in weeks, and in one case, months. Yet a good musician will be able to regain his technique in one day's sustained practice. It all depends, as one musician— our candid sitarist—phrased it, on "will power":

> To become an artist the first thing you need is will power. This is very necessary for artists. So if I don't practice for two days, and

suddenly I have to go play somewhere, then there the artist's will power will work. He will play like he plays every day. It will be the same, no difference.

Will power does not refer here to discipline in practice but to the discipline or knowledge to play up to par even though some days of practice have been skipped. Thus, although continuity in practice is said to be very important, one can skip days and even longer periods of time and still depend on one's technical reservoir, as it were, which can be recalled when necessary. Developing the reservoir as well as utilizing it depends ultimately on one's powers of concentration. But how does one learn to concentrate? For the student at least, an outside environment is required which allows no disturbances, no interruption of his concentration during riaz.

In India, especially in urban areas, a quiet environment is not easily available; hence, practicing during the night is highly valued. As the reader may already have noticed, practicing through the night is a theme common to many descriptions of practice habits. In addition to presenting the ideal context, practicing through the night conveys a sense of devotion, discipline, and sacrifice, the necessary ingredients for becoming a good, perhaps great, musician. One sets oneself apart at night, free from the intrusions of the day and other people. One is alone; and solitude, which is usually impossible during the day, allows one totally to immerse oneself in riaz.

Another reason for practicing alone, or at least with only well-defined kinds of people being present, is that practice and performance will otherwise become confused. During the day there is an unavoidable audience: friends and relatives drop in, before some of whom there will be a tendency to perform instead of to practice:

> At the time of practice we want to be alone, we don't want others to listen to our music. . . . While I practice I have a separate style and while I perform on the stage I have another style. . . . When I practice I don't know what I am practicing [so] I don't want others to listen to my practice.

The context of an event will define it, and if there are other people present who are not part of the inner circle of a musician's close relatives and students, then aside from not really being able to concentrate, he will have to be conscious of what he is playing, or rather conscious of the difference between what he can do during riaz and what he would not be able to do in a performance. During practice, many liberties can be taken. One can practice a rāg outside its set time period, and can experiment and try out new ideas, one can play scales continuously, jump from one kind of style to another, or one kind of music to another and, most comforting of all, make mistakes with impunity:

> Whenever we play at home, it is for riaz. Then we are practicing in order to improve ourselves. Then we are at liberty to make as many mistakes as we like. But in a public performance we have to adjust ourselves according to the tastes of the audience. Then we have the fear in our minds of being criticized. At the same time we crave applause, so we perform with more seriousness. It is different from riaz.

There is still another kind of environment, a combination of the inner and outer environments known as *chillā*. Chilla has the connotation of a discipline which is undertaken for forty days without a break. A chilla then is a vow that one assumes, to concentrate on whatever one is desirous of achieving. This discipline is not limited to musical objectives alone. Individuals will meditate next to the tomb of their saint as a spiritual discipline and call this a chilla. The chilla can have this-worldly functions as well: "If you want to control a woman, keep thinking about her regularly at the same time every day. On the fortieth day this woman will herself come to you."

Chilla, as we will see later, is a technique that musicians utilize for a variety of objectives, not only for riaz. The important point is that the discipline is constant, with practice, for a certain time, place, and duration. If one practices at different times of the day, even if the amount is the same in terms of time, then one is not doing chilla, and the effect of the chilla will not be realized. I am not certain whether the rule regarding the same place so stringently defines a chilla; but the principle, however realized, is that the condition for chilla requires replication of environment and minimally forty days.[1] Replication of the outer environment by creating a constancy in time, space, and duration creates a constancy in the inner environment, a focused concentration during riaz. Forty-one days would not be a better chilla than forty days, unless it was the beginning of another cycle. According to one musician, if one performs one chilla and then follows it by three others continuously (i.e., four chillas in a row for a total of one hundred and sixty days), "there can be no defect in your performance as a musician."

Riaz in some cases means neither practice nor performance but simply worship. Musicians who are known to be saintly or otherworldly are said to practice as their way of doing music in order to "reach" God or achieve a state of supreme bliss. Purnima Sinha recounts one story about the famed Imdad Khan which makes this point. "There is a story about Imdad Khan that when he was practicing music one evening his daughter died, and people came to call him to take care of the funeral. He said, 'Please wait for a while, I am not through my prayers yet. You arrange for the funeral' " (1970:45,46).[2]

I have said that the ideal of intense riaz is a common if not universally felt requirement for becoming a musician and that an important part of one's ability as a musician is a function of the quality and quantity of riaz performed. These ideals of riaz are not limited to musicians alone, but form a part of the generally felt values about music held by professional, amateur, and layman alike. In the public media, for example, accounts of famous musicians will characteristically include descriptions of their extensive riaz habits.[3]

That musicians consider riaz important and even fundamental is not particularly surprising. What invites our attention is the special uses to which the concept of riaz is put: riaz as a means of devotion and a measure of dedication, riaz as an explanation of success, and—by extension—riaz as a pedagogical device with a moral. Riaz as a concept becomes a symbol which conveys qualities about music making in a variety of contexts, giving values to those contexts while it takes its meaning from them. This interpretation is corroborated etymologically, because the word *riaz* itself, coming from the Arabic, connotes abstinence, devotion, discipline, and hard labor.[4]

The difference between the condition of an ideal state

which is rarely, if ever, achieved and the mundane riaz of the ordinary musician's experience has its counterpart in Indian society as a whole, between the achievements of saints and kings and the unrealized aspirations of ordinary people. The pervasiveness of caste organization and its fundamental ascriptive characteristics often make the observer lose sight of the fact that within a particular category much can be achieved through one's own efforts.

The musician often describes himself as merely the instrument for what is in essence the will and thereby the music of God. Without riaz the instrument is itself incapable of expressing everything. Riaz by itself will not automatically make one a great musician; it is, however, a necessary if not complete requirement. Of course, given Divine Will anything is possible, even dispensing with the requirement of riaz. I heard an account of one musician whose mother correctly recognized a disguised saint; the latter as reward fulfilled the mother's wish that her son become a great musician. This was indeed accomplished without any riaz efforts on the part of the musician: an exception which demonstrates the rule.

There is basically one other component, aside from the absolute of Divine Will, which is a prerequisite for becoming a musician. Along with riaz, which is ultimately the responsibility of the individual, there is the guru-shishya relationship, which is the responsibility of two individuals.

The Guru-Shishya Parampara (The Master-Disciple Tradition)

If the requirement of riaz in its literal sense seems self-evident for becoming an accomplished performer, so also is the requirement of having a teacher. Yet the concept of the guru is, as in the case of riaz, a highly elaborated one. Insofar as musicians are concerned, it is a topic of even greater significance, encompassing a still wider domain of symbolic referents and associations than does riaz.

Basic to the characterization of any musician is his sociomusical identity, that is, a social identity based on his musical heritage. Whether a musician is considered great, good, or even mediocre, he will (in the absence of anyone else) establish—so to speak—his credentials as a musician on the basis of whom he has studied with and whom he is related to. "My name is so and so and I have studied with so and so," might be a musician's most common introduction if he presumes these facts to be unknown. He will also usually mention his gharana or stylistic school. Some musicians, however, eschew the whole concept of gharana and do not publicly identify with any, but they must always have a guru or an ustad.

Guru and *ustad,* used interchangeably here, are in practice virtually synonymous, the former being used for Hindu and the latter for Muslim musicians. Etymologically, however, the terms have a different history of meanings and this difference encapsulates different social constructions of the musician's role. *Ustad,* a Persian-derived Urdu word meaning "master," is used as a term of reference and of address in occupational contexts. For example, a motorcycle repairman who is acknowledged as a master mechanic will be addressed as *ustadji* (the *ji* being another honorific tag usually translated as "sir"). *Guru,* derived from the Sanskrit, has traditionally been reserved for learned men who are teachers or, perhaps more exactly, preceptors, and who are thus usually Brahmans. Such an individual can be addressed as *guruji* or *panditji* (*pandit,* "learned man"). However, whereas a Muslim musician can append *ustad* to his name, a Hindu musician will always add *Pandit,* not *guru,* to his name. The Urdu equivalent of *guru-shishya* is *ustad-shāgird,* but the more literal gloss in Urdu would be *shaikh-murīd,* a relationship which exists between a *Sūfī* master and his disciple. The use of *ustad-shagird* by musicians, however (instead of *shaikh-murid,* which is never used in this context), illustrates the professionalization of the occupation of musician, which Muslims initiated and developed in India. The Muslim custom contrasts with that of Hindus, or perhaps more correctly Brahmans, who did not professionalize this specialty, a point which will be developed more fully in later chapters.

The guru-shishya parampara, or the master-disciple tradition, provides for the continuity of the system. Indeed, the relationship between the guru and his shishya is seen as homologous to the relationship between father and son, and, in fact, the roles are often combined in the same persons. Where they are not, a musician will say of his guru that "he is like a father to me," and will refer, when he translates into English, to the father of his guru as his "grandfather" or "grand-guru." Two disciples of the same guru will refer to each other as *guru-bhāi* ("guru-brother") and will address each other as *bhai* ("brother"). Disciples of the same guru are ideally expected to behave towards each other as if they were brothers, but in practice this does not always occur. If a teacher has many pupils and he initiates all as disciples, then these "disciples" may very well be strangers to each other. If, on the other hand, an ustad has only a few disciples and they spend a great deal of time with him, it is more likely that "brotherly" relationships will develop. The homology extends to sex as well. Only men can become gurus or ustads. A woman can be a disciple and, in some cases, an unofficial teacher, but she can never assume the status of guru or ustad.

The status of the guru is distinct from that of father in several ways. An individual need not be an actual father or be married in order to assume the status of guru. What the guru transmits to his disciple or what the disciple receives is not conceptualized as biological. Musicians do not seem to regard music as something biologically inherited, although they do appreciate the importance of a musical environment such as is found in musical families.[5]

Love and Devotion

The relationship between the guru and his disciple in its ideal form and essential nature is described and expressed by the devotion of the disciple to his guru and the love of the guru for his disciple. Without love and devotion there can be no communication, and communication is the fundamental requisite of this relationship—the communication of a tradition.

What does it mean for a disciple to be devoted to his guru? Primarily, it means being devoted, in this instance, to music, which implies that the disciple has an understanding and perception of music as fundamentally significant. The disciple will be described as having a "good brain" or a "good ear" or—as we might put it—"being talented." The guru does not consider any disciple devoted to him as automatically being talented. There are examples where the disciple is seemingly devoted, and yet in the judgment of the guru is far from talented. But in the ideal situation, the devotion of a disciple carries with it the implication of a musical sensibility which can be developed and refined by proper training.

Being devoted to one's guru also implies obedience to him and, as the musicians put it, giving "respect" (*izzat*). Being obedient refers not only to matters of music such as doing riaz, and playing what one is told; the disciple must be obedient in his life style as well. In the ideal system, the disciple, whether he is related or not, lives with his guru as part of the household. As a member of the household his position is like that of the guru's own son, although again there are differences in role-playing. The most important of these is that the disciple considers it his duty to provide services for his guru and make life generally as comfortable as possible for him. The disciple will massage his guru's legs (in general a symbol of subordination and respect), bring his tea, provide him—if he can afford it—with *bīrīs* ("cigarettes"), and, if the guru has the propensity, with opium and other pleasures which he may enjoy.

The disciple will also treat his guru to meals in a restaurant and try to provide other services for his guru. If the guru is traveling, the disciple will arrange for the tickets (*not* paying for them, however), and if he accompanies his guru, will see to it that the luggage is properly stored on the train, get tea at the station, order the meals, unroll the bedding, and solve any other small problems. The sure sign of a disciple is that he will carry his guru's instrument, wherever he goes, all the way to the stage platform.

The behavioral repertoire that is usually manifest in a situation of social subordination will also be performed by the shishya. Like a son, younger brother, or woman, the shishya does not smoke, drink alcohol, sit higher, or talk more than his guru. A sober demeanor is the rule and the model.

The shishya treats his guru with a respect and loyalty which extend even after personal contact ends. If the shishya mentions the name of his guru, he will—at least if he is a Muslim—touch his right ear with his right hand. This is done, as I have been told, out of respect for one's guru. To demonstrate any disrespect whatsoever is tantamount to a termination of the relationship, which on occasion does happen.

The shishya will never say bad things about his guru; and ideally he should never think bad things. If he hears derogatory comments, he should either remove himself from the company or rise to the defense of his guru. The shishya represents the guru, is a part of him as, in the same sense, the guru is part of him. Even after death, the shishya should honor the memory of his guru, continuing to acknowledge his debt in terms of what he has learned and what he is as a musician.

For his part, the guru must have some feeling of affection for his shishya before he will teach him anything. As one musician put it, the disciple must win his ustad's heart in order to learn from him. If the guru has reservations about his disciple, then he will hold back on the more subtle aspects of his art. The following words from my own ustad are particularly illuminating and include an exchange with another musician who was sitting with us:

> Music lessons were not given as freely [in the past] as I give my pupils, like I give to Daniel and others. They were taught separately in secrecy. Especially the traditional things which have come from the great grandfathers [ancestors] like the way to teach *sthāī*, *khayāl*, *ṭappā*, *tarānā*, *dhrupad*, *tirvat*, *thumrī*, *dādrā*, and *gīt-ghazal* type: all the traditional things which have come from our elders are still with us. These things will be taught to a special student, the one I like the most and the one whom I have controlled and the one who likes me and takes care of me. These things cannot be imparted through money, even with Rs. 1000/-. But you can buy it with your heart, love, and care of your teacher. The teacher and student relationship is such that the teacher won't teach all his pupils with love. I have fifty pupils. These fifty aren't the same for me. Why? Because of their different temperaments; their way of thinking is different and their playing and singing are different. I don't know whether we reciprocate the same way, but if I love one of them and he loves me

the same way, I think he is good and I can give him everything if he lives with me. I can tell him as much as I know. Why? Because I love him.

To the other musician's comment, "Either you like him or he likes you very much," my ustad replied, "No it doesn't matter whether he likes me or not, or it is because of his love. But I like him. I am talking about myself, how do I know about him?"

The feeling that in order to give something to the disciple, the guru must love him—or at the very least like him—is, I think, universally felt to be true (see, e.g., Shankar 1968:51–58, 69–75). This is not an all-or-nothing relationship but rather one of degree, which grows with time, with the disciple's learning increasing proportionately.

In addition to affection for his shishya, the guru also maintains discipline, as a figure of authority for the disciple. It is not clear whether this in fact constitutes a definitive element of the guru role, but there are many descriptions of gurus being stern taskmasters (alternatively with gentle dispositions). Having a shishya "whom I have controlled" is probably an important prerequisite for both the guru and his shishya. If there is no control, that is if the guru has little or no authority over his disciple, then probably nothing can be learned.[6]

From his point of view, the guru can only transmit his knowledge through the medium of his students, who are, in many cases, his sons and other relatives—especially nephews. But a guru will not transmit his knowledge promiscuously. The transmission must be pure; that is, it must not be distorted so as to reflect negatively on himself. The guru would rather have no students, or perhaps more precisely, would rather not transmit those aspects of his knowledge which may become distorted through the medium of his students, but let them die with him, than be witness and accomplice to their degeneration. The guru communicates something of his being, and this must remain true and immutable.

If an ustad feels that he has no disciples who are worthy of receiving the more subtle aspects of his art, then he will limit his teaching. This can range from withholding a rare rāg to refusing to teach a special kind of instrument. For example, in response to an inquiry about the possible demise of the *surbahār* (a bass sitar), a venerable and highly respected ustad, with many students of sitar said:

> You think that the ustads want to keep surbahars to themselves. It is wrong to think in that way. We do want to teach, but who is going to learn? It is such a big science, and if anybody asks for it and we give it then it would be like playing *vīnā* [the *bīn*] in front of a water-buffalo, so we only play for those who understand.

This ustad has several well-known musicians as his disciples, and had at least one student who studied with him for twenty-six years. Nevertheless, not one of his students has yet qualified—in his opinion—to learn the surbahar. The last sentence in the quotation refers to listeners rather than students, but illustrates vividly what an ustad considers his knowledge to be with respect to those who are not musically informed. This knowledge is something which cannot be acquired solely by spending many years in learning. The ustad has to perceive that his disciple has what it takes to understand in depth.

From the guru's point of view, he—to borrow a phrase used of Charles Dickens—"communicates with posterity," and it is supremely important to him that this communication is not distorted. This is not to say that it is specifically the "purity" of his music which he is transmitting and which should not be changed, although it is often spoken of in these terms. It is rather, I would suggest, the integrity of his message to posterity which must remain undistorted: it is better to communicate the message of silence than to allow something that is not his own to be perpetuated through time. The medium for the guru's message is not a written system (notations are considered ineffective for any but the most rudimentary lessons) but his own disciples, their message and remembrance.[7] The ustad then has to be sure of his medium, and since the medium is not an artificial one, the ustad has to evaluate the capability of this highly unpredictable medium to reflect, in himself, the "true" message of his mentor.

This evaluation is in large measure subjective, necessarily so since it involves another human being, and a prediction about him. In part, the judgment is determined by the student's devo-

tion to his teacher as well as to his music. And although not in
substance separable, the teacher's love for his student constitutes
the ultimate verification procedure. The guru may love the student, who may in fact be his son, but if the son is not devoted to
his father and to his music, then there is no point in teaching
him. Conversely, even though a student may be devoted, he
must "win his ustad's heart." There is no other condition:

> Only love and understanding are the keynotes, not even money. If
> the ustad really loves a pupil, only then will he teach him the finer
> points of his art, that includes these secret rāgs. Even a king or
> maharaja cannot persuade a teacher to do this.

Things and Ways

The majority of musicians, especially those who have been shish-
yas to their gurus, will say that Indian classical music cannot be
thoroughly or completely learned in schools or from books. In
order to understand the subtleties of the art and become a professional performer, some period of intensive training with a
guru is considered mandatory. If one asks what it is that a guru
can give that a music college cannot, the answers provide us with
a partial theory of musical inheritance, while the *kinds* of answers
provide us with clues for a more comprehensive theory. The
following paragraphs outline what is transmitted from guru to
shishya, indicating the importance of this relationship.

The guru enculturates the shishya into musical life. He
transmits two elements, neither of which is available through any
other medium of instruction: a body of knowledge which is both
secret and esoteric, and the way a musician must lead his life.
This total musical life provides important evidence that social
relations between musicians are indeed systematic. It compre-
hends a subculture in India which cuts across the boundaries of
sex, religion, age, caste, territory, language, as well as time, yet
includes all these as internal categorical distinctions.

The first and explicit element, the fund of knowledge
which the ustad possesses and which he can pass on to his disciples, is to a certain extent unique to him and not replicable

either with another ustad or in a music institution. Typically, this knowledge includes secret or rare rāgs, compositions, and techniques. The ustad also imparts *tālim,* which connotes the substantive training or instruction in technique. Talim refers also to the initial training an individual receives from a guru. A musician usually receives his talim from only one guru, or if from two or more sources, they will be separate specialties, such as vocal music from one guru and sitar from another.

Many descriptions of the guru-shishya relationship are couched in terms of winning the guru's attention and affection, perhaps giving him little gifts and providing services for him in the hope that he will reciprocate with a rare rāg or a secret asthai:

> I have learned [music] by spending a lot of money. I have given gifts to my gurus and all this has cost money. I. Khan Sahib, one of my gurus, was addicted to opium but he was poor. I used to invite him for lessons and I used to give him a little opium; he used to bless me and was very pleased. This was the way he used to teach me. I also used to give cash—twenty, twenty-five [rupees] for his pleasure, too. . . . Some gurus neither took money nor had any addiction. Such people I took to restaurants for special treats. A special hotel I used to go to was the Hakim Hotel[8] with A. Khan Sahib. He liked having his legs massaged. A. Khan Sahib used to like a dancing girl named G.B.P. where he stayed. From there I took Khan Sahib for treats. Time and again this way I learned from Khan Sahib.

What is important here is not only the means by which one learns things but also the variety of gurus a musician may have. Although musicians typically learn from a number of gurus, often only one is acknowledged as *the* guru.

This quotation may be misleading if it conveys the impression that a shishya pays for his learning, that is, buys his knowledge. Ideally, a disciple never pays tuition. In a formal sense, money is presented only on certain ritual occasions and constitutes an offering, not a payment. What the guru gives to his pupils is invaluable; it is an exchange in which the guru gives knowledge and the student reciprocates with services and gifts. It is, however, an unequal exchange; the student forever owes a debt to his guru, which he can never completely fulfill or repay.

Giving a guru gifts and treating him to a meal at the Hakim Hotel are interpreted as providing a basis for an affectionate relationship which might otherwise be difficult to initiate. It is exactly because the guru-shishya relationship must be based on affection that the introduction of money is discouraged or forbidden. Otherwise, the relationship might be suspect, from both points of view. The disciple might think that whatever he receives cannot be worth much, since it is being exchanged for money, and the guru might think that the shishya is taking things from him for selfish purposes; that is, having paid for it, he need not acknowledge its source. If payment is understood at all in the ideal system, it is conceived as carrying the name of the guru forward through another generation. In the event that the student becomes renowned, his fame will reflect on his guru, and it is mandatory that the shishya always acknowledge his guru.

The value of inherited things depends on who the guru is, how distinguished and old his particular tradition, and how rare or scarce the thing being transmitted. If the guru is very distinguished, the fact that he is doing the transmitting makes the transaction valuable. This is particularly so if he comes from a long line of distinguished musicians, which if authentic will suggest that he is in possession of old—thereby rare—as well as genuine or pure musical knowledge.

What makes musical elements scarce "commodities" is that few people know of them and they are rarely performed. A rāg such as *Ratnai Malhar* is said to be *acchop* (*lit.,* "hidden") because it is only known to some musicians of the Agra gharana. An acchop rāg will be reserved for a select, musically informed audience—connoisseurs who can appreciate the value of what is being presented to them.

> Every gharana has some acchop, secret rāgs. I usually do not play these acchop rāgs. If there is a specially learned audience, then I may play a secret rāg. Chances are even these learned men will not identify this rāg because this is a secret rāg. So every gharana has a secret rāg, sthayis and khayals which are only played before a very distinguished audience. . . . If you play something unheard of, the audience will give special attention to your performance and will really appreciate and try to understand this new item.

Esoterica are valued for two reasons. First, they imply learning and knowledge. There is a high premium on musical knowledge, and the more esoteric, the more it is valued. Part of the prestige that a musician may enjoy comes from demonstrating what is distinctive and perhaps unique to him. The second reason is explicit in the last sentence of the quotation. Something old but unknown is something new, and as such is an important source of musical innovation. Whether such esoterica are authentically traditional or not, they appear to be a legitimate way of introducing "innovations."

Disciples not only learn secret and esoteric musical knowledge, they also inherit a style of playing from a guru which, while distinct and different from other styles of playing, is yet recognized as coming from a particular tradition. Some musicians are said to be able to play in several styles, although they are often not associated with a particularly renowned guru. Styles can be copied, and they often are, but there is a difference between the copy and the "real thing," as Radika Mohan Moitra, the esteemed *sarod* player, says:

> I play in the style of Ustad Hafiz Ali Khan because I belong to his gharana, but I won't play or copy Allaudin Khan because that would be improper, because I don't know and I might play it all wrong. Of course I know how he plays. But it is a different thing to know and how to express it. There are many things you know but you can't express . . .

Thus, in addition to learning a corpus of material, one learns a style from a guru, and each guru's style will be representative of the style of a gharana. This style will be reflected in technique, repertoire, and stress. For example, Ustad Allaudin Khan put more emphasis on rhythm than other musicians do, and this emphasis is reflected in his students' performances as well as his own. His technique of sarod playing required that the fingertips be used to press the string to the fingerboard. Students of Hafiz Ali Khan utilize the tip of the fingernail for the same purpose.

These details represent the tangible knowledge that a disciple receives from his guru. But just as significant—though only implicit—is the musician's way of life that the disciple learns from his guru.

In the ideal context, the musician—in this case the guru—lives, eats, breathes, and sleeps music. He will get up in the morning, usually very early, say his morning prayers, have some tea, and start practicing. After a few hours' practice he will eat breakfast, perhaps go out to do some errands and then return home. As he goes about, he will often be observed humming to himself, singing some *tāns* (musical phrases), perhaps also beating out a rhythmic pattern with his fingers. Often he will be joined by friends or close relatives for lunch, and their discussion may often center around musical topics or other musicians. After an afternoon nap, tea will be served and then it is again time for practice or teaching, either or both of which will last into the late evening. A guru or an ustad tends to have a circle of friends, relatives, and acquaintances around him. In this circle, topics unrelated to musical concerns are seldom discussed. If they are, the discussion will not last long, for the guru is inclined to be silent; it is out of his universe, and to talk around him would be disrespectful. The point is again that music forms the basis of his being, his thinking, and his relationships, and the picture drawn above may even be an understatement if we consider stories told about deeply committed gurus. The revered and saintlike Ustad Bundu Khan carried his sarangi wherever he went. If someone came up to him on the street, he would sit down right on a main thoroughfare in Delhi and start playing. For some musicians it is not merely rhetoric to say that music is a way of life.

It is exactly this overwhelming involvement with music and musically related activities which the disciple is at first exposed to and then, ideally, becomes a part of. He does not just enter into the environment as a casual observer only to leave it quickly, return to his family, and live an "ordinary" life at other times. This is why the disciple is encouraged to live with or near his guru. He must be an integral part of his guru's life, becoming immersed in music. He must learn not only the subtleties of the art, but also the subtleties of being an artist. Thus a guru will take a favored disciple with him when he is to perform, have him on the stage with him, and, if he is advanced, allow him to sing or play a little while the guru takes a break. A disciple will, in addition, learn the folklore of the past, the amazing feats of great musicians, the power of rāgs, the contests between musical giants, and, in particular, the traditional history of the gharana.

It is far from an easy matter to have an ustad accept an individual as a disciple, especially if there has been no basis for a relationship in any other social sphere. An ustad might be very reluctant to take a person for a disciple, but rather would attempt to discourage him unless he could demonstrate his sincerity. One test of such sincerity is a trial period in which he has to perform the duties of a disciple without having much—if any—of the reward of being one. In other words, the disciple will serve his ustad, wait on him hand and foot, but receive no talim from the ustad.

The trial period is partly a test of devotion to the guru, and it eliminates those who are not truly sincere. It has another very important function, however, the learning of obedience—total obedience—to the guru. What this implies is a subordination of one's self to another person. The trial period may be seen as a rite of passage in which the old self is abandoned in order to allow the new to emerge. The disciple enters as a child—whatever his age—and assumes a status and performs a role which, in the beginning, is a basic one: being subordinate and keeping his mind open to learning, starting again from the beginning, to become musically enculturated (Shankar 1968:11, 12).

The guru does not always discourage a candidate from becoming his shishya. The trial period is the theme of many stories about musicians, however, and represents a more extreme experience of the first stage of being a shishya. Formally, there are two stages to being a shishya. In the first, the disciple is only a pupil—he is only beginning, and it remains to be seen in what direction he will go. Only after this initial period does the shishya go through a formal ritual of being "tied" to his guru. He then becomes a *khās shāgird,* a genuine, fully accepted disciple.[9] The period between the first acceptance and the second initiation may last from a few months to many years. The implication of becoming a khas shagird is that he is a special disciple who will be given particular attention and will be, in theory, treated as the guru's own adopted son.

Guru in the Hindu sense of the word denotes someone

Ustad Bundu Khan with one of his unique sarangis. *Photograph from the collection of Yunus Hussein Khan.*

The formal initiation of a disciple: Ghulam Sabir garlands his ustad, Sabri Khan.

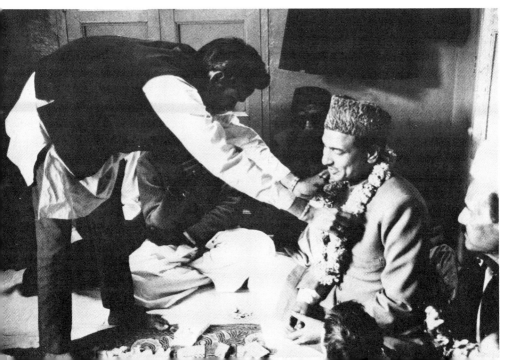

The formal initiation of a disciple: Ghulam Sabir requests permission to perform.

The formal initiation of a disciple: Ghulam Sabir performs before his ustad, Sabri Khan, and other members of the brotherhood of musicians. The young musician began his study of the sarangi with his father, who lives in Moradabad, the ancestral home of this brotherhood. Ustad Sabri Khan is also Ghulam Sabir's mother's brother.

who is not one's father, someone who is in fact not a member of one's family. To become a disciple, one temporarily suspends family ties. Ideally, that is what is said to occur with a shishya, since he is to live with his guru. Muslim musicians, as we have said, almost always come from musical families. Those musicians who do come from hereditary musician families are referred to as *khāndānī,* that is, musicians who come from a "genuine" tradition that is passed on from father to son. A piece of music can also be referred to as *khās khāndānī,* something that is the speciality of hereditary musician families. It is assumed the ustad will pass the best and the most on to his own son or sons, and only if the ustad loves his disciple as his own son will he treat him as such. The father-son relationship thus provides, at least among musicians, the model upon which the guru-shishya relationship in its ideal form should be based. If the guru has no sons, but does have nephews, sons-in-law, or other relatives, these will be typically favored over other disciples from outside the family. But if there is a son, ideally he will be the one who will carry on the tradition.

The guru-shishya parampara thus provides for the inheritance of a musical tradition and often is the cultural model of the natural relationship between father and son. The disciple learns not only the craft, but also the trade secrets. He learns how to behave as a member of the artist's community and how to become a professional performer on stage—and accordingly learns not only the art of making music but of being a musician.

3. Being a Musician

It is said that once Akbar asked Tansen to bring him to his guru, Swami Haridass. The Saint, who had his hermitage in Nidhban, by the river Yamuna, was singing with such fervour and devotion that Akbar felt enchanted. When the emperor returned to his court, he asked Tansen to sing the same bhajan as had been sung by his guru. Tansen obeyed, but Akbar did not feel the same ecstasy as he had experienced when he heard Haridass sing. Tansen humbly explained that he as a musician sang before a king, while the Saint poured out his soul to God, so his bhajans had an uplifting power that a mere musician could not be expected to produce.

P. N. Mathur, "Tansen"

 Tansen and Haridas are pivotal figures in the history of Hindustani music. They represent the two aspects of music, forming its fundamental concept for the contemporary musician. Swami Haridas, the Brahman saint for whom music is a way of life, a means for devotion and a path to the Absolute, represents the performer with only himself for an audience and the Divine as patron. Tansen, his disciple, and the ancestral guru for descendant generations of musicians, is the "mere musician" who brings music to a public, establishes it as an art, and begins the tradition of the profession.

The antiphony of music as a way for and a way of life is expressed by musicians as juxtaposed themes in their discussions; by the former as the reality of their condition, and by the latter as its ideal form for which all strive. This double dimension of music is important to understand because it balances the image of music as it is typically presented to the outsider. Music as sacred endeavor comprises a significant part of the musician's conception of what he is doing, but typically it does not dominate the view of himself as artist or craftsman.

To gain insight into these interrelated concepts of music, I shall present each more or less independent of the other, with the caveat that although they are thought of as distinct conceptualizations, as well as analytically separate types, they are actually more like two mirrors that, when held up to each other, reflect each other's image.

Music as Divine Expression

Writings on Indian music abound concerning the relationship between music and the supernatural. The importance of sound (*nada*) as a primeval organizing principle has its roots in the Vedic texts and the chanting of the *Samveda*. Music is a means of acquiring and expressing power; it is a method for achieving Supreme Bliss; it is also a means of devotion. This last idea has been popular since at least the eighth century A.D., when the devotional movements sprang up in the South and spread throughout India (Raghavan 1966:20–32; cf. also Krishnaswamy 1968:passim). That music is a means of devotion is perhaps the most common idea expressed by musicians. For Sufis and the Muslim musicians today, music as a form of devotion to and worship of God is the rationale given to explain the performance of music in the light of its discouragement or prohibition in Islam.[1]

Interestingly enough, although music and God are closely connected, music and religion are not. That is, all musicians, whatever their particular religious background, agree that one's personal religion has no effect on the performance of music. One musician, a Hindu, went so far as to say that all musicians have one religion, music, and that a religious man cannot also be a musician. What he meant by this rather enigmatic statement is that if one is a religious Muslim or a religious Hindu, one will be blinded (or deafened) to a perception of Supreme Being through music.

No musician with whom I have talked utilizes music regularly as a form of devotion. Virtually all, in one way or another, earn their living because of their musical knowledge (the few who do not are independently wealthy). Almost without exception, they put a premium on the devotional aspects of music. However, in practice, this devotional aspect is left as the concern of the saintly ones who are known from the past. It is sometimes assumed that such saintly musicians are living today, but by virtue of their devotional practice they stay out of the public eye and are consequently unknown.

Some musicians claim to have had religious experiences through their music, but these all have the characteristic of happenstance. Such experiences can also occur in seemingly unlikely contexts:

> One day I was playing in Studio One [at All India Radio] with no one around. I felt myself crying, tears flowing down my face. I did not know why; but all of a sudden I realized this was something Divine. I said "O God, this is the time you have done something for me. You have given me the power to create this music."

Many musicians have special musical experiences, although the source is not always divine, at least directly. Musicians often have spiritual figures to whom they are devoted and who guide and inspire them in turn. There are also historically important personages who are patron saints to musicians, especially to those who are Muslim. These saints, called *pīrs* or *auliyās,* were typically Sufis instrumental in utilizing music as a source of devotion and in defending its use against the more orthodox in Islam. Two of these are especially important in North India.

The first is Khwaja Mu'inuddin Chisti (A.D. 1143–1234), who introduced the Chisti order of Sufism into India. He entered India in 1190, and by way of Lahore and Delhi finally settled in Ajmer. Once a year there is a memorial anniversary (*urs*) when devotees from all over India gather in Ajmer, including numbers of musicians who go there on an annual pilgrimage.

The other saint is Shaikh Nizamuddin Auliya (A.D. 1236–1325), a native of Budaun who lived most of his adult life in Delhi, witnessing the reign of seven sultans. He persisted in using music for his devotional gatherings in spite of much pressure brought to bear by the orthodox *ulamā,* including a call before a tribunal of fifty-three theologians (Husain 1957:36–41). His tomb, across the road from one of India's most modern hotels, is in a residential area of Delhi named after him. Here a large urs is held once a year for several days, during which *qawwālī* (a Muslim devotional song type) is sung and a general fair is set up.[2] Some musicians live in Nizamuddin while others from Old Delhi come from time to time to pray there.

Nizamuddin Auliya can also be a source of inspiration. Ustad Wahid Khan, a vocalist living in Old Delhi (now moved to Pakistan), described his own experience of Nizamuddin's force. He was asked to sing at the wedding of one of his relatives. Because he was out of practice, his father was concerned about whether he would be able to sing. Wahid Khan insisted that he could sing and that if his father, who was also his ustad, would pray for him, he would surely be successful. He climbed onto the dais and faced the direction of Nizamuddin Auliya's tomb ("because he is our pir") and started with an *alāp* (introductory movement), which he continued for forty-five minutes. After that he gained control of his voice and started the khayal in rāg *Gujari Todi* called "Merī naiyā pār karo, Ustad Nizamuddin Auliya" ("Let my boat cross, Ustad Nizamuddin Auliya"). After that his music was so inspiring that "ninety-nine percent of the audience was moved to tears. Everyone was equally affected, irrespective of their taste and attitude towards music."

This same vocalist also had a pir who was personally known to him, although he met him only three times. The first time they met was when, as a young child, he accompanied his father (who was one of India's greatest vocalists) on a visit to the pir. The second time the pir "allowed me to take an oath of allegiance over his hand." On the third and final visit, the pir told him "henceforward do not come until you are a great man." Meanwhile the pir has died, and the vocalist still feels that he does not qualify for a visit:

After that I could not go to him. . . . I felt a longing so many times to visit his tomb, despite the fact that I failed [to become a great man]. I go to Bihar twice a year. Haswa Fatehpur [where the tomb is located] is on the way. I wanted to get down at the station but I could not dare. How can I disobey my pir? I am looking forward to the promised day when I become a great man and thereby present myself at the tomb of my pir.

A pir, even after he has died, can have the power to affect men's destiny. Inspiration is one way, but sometimes the method can be more direct, as in the following case which resulted from doing chilla.

Hyder Baksh used to play at the tomb of his Auliya. Now the person whose tomb this was, Hazrat Bu Ali Shah Kalandev Rahamatallah Auliya, appeared to him on the fortieth day and asked him, "Hyder Baksh, what do you desire?" Hyder Baksh replied, "Sir, let there be such power in my hands that whenever I play the sarangi, I play with such sweetness that people will have nothing but praise for me." And so it was done.

Many anecdotes are related about musicians in the past who are considered saintly in some way. These stories serve to demonstrate the power of a spiritual force in the formation of a particular musician's genius. This saintliness is the element beyond riaz and the guru-shishya tradition which sets apart exceptional figures of the past, and—rarely—a few ancient musicians of the present. A good example of it is found in the story about Ustad Bande Ali Khan, a great bīn player, who is described as a very saintly person. It is said that he used to play his bīn next to a holy man who never acknowledged his presence. The ustad would come every day, but still there would be no response. This went on for fourteen years. One day while he was playing, the sound of his music sent the holy man into a meditative state (*tapasyā*). After this he told Bande Ali Khan to leave, as he was finally ready and, wherever he played, people would honor him for his music. Bande Ali Khan himself is said to have similarly inspired a musician, in this case a woman named Gokibai, who studied with him for many years and eventually went on to fame herself.

63

There seems generally to be a matter-of-fact attitude about the various relationships between music and spiritual development among Muslim musicians. This attitude extends to a common belief in spirits, especially *jinns* (from which we derive our notion of genii).

Jinns, in contrast to pirs (who are sometimes thought to be immortal in the sense that their souls continue to exist after their physical death), do not have their origins in human beings. They may, however, manifest their presence by assuming the form of a man, woman, or animal. What makes them interesting here is that they enjoy good music and even have their preferences for rāgs.

These spirits are morally ambivalent. Jinns can be either malevolent or benevolent, although usually they are merely capricious. They come most often in a variety of shapes and forms late at night when one is playing alone. Sometimes they are invisible and one can only sense their presence. As one instrumentalist described their effect (and possibly their motivating nature for riaz), "The invisible kind sit beside you and listen to you. You can't see or hear them, you can just feel their presence. If you stop playing they may beat or even kill you."

Jinns, when benevolent, will bestow rewards on persons whom they favor. If a musician plays well, they will come to listen and will show their appreciation in a number of ways, but always as a material reward. The following story, which I heard from Ustad Wahid Khan, exemplifies in summary fashion some of the concepts which we have been considering, and suggests the relationship between a court musician and his patron, all within the theme of a jinn story.

> Certainly the jinns exist. But I must say I have not seen them. But then there are clear references about jinns in the holy Koran. That proves the existence of jinns. Let me cite here an example, related by my father. Once when he was at the court of the Raja of Purnia in Bihar, he observed something that would interest you. He would practice for long periods of time. Sometimes he would begin from seven or half past seven in the evening and continue up to nine or half past nine in the morning. The whole night would pass almost unfelt. Often the Raja, the late P. C. Lal, would himself come and

knock at the door and say, "How long will you continue practicing? After all there is a limit to everything," and my father would answer, "My Lord, I was in a trance. I never knew the night passed and the morning came." My father told me (and there are people who are witnesses to it) he felt as if a roller was rumbling on the roof of his room through the night. And you know what this roller meant to him? He meant by it the joyful movement of the jinns. Moreover he said he could smell the fragrance of various incenses in the room so much as if the containers of them were opened. It reflects the interest the jinns take in music. To come to the main incident, my father would perform the exercise of chilla, and it is a common belief that if you entertain the jinns for forty days, the jinns bestow a reward. Sometimes they bestow wealth; sometimes they give a clue to find buried treasure. But when the fortieth day of my father's exercise came, the Raja had to go to Calcutta, and he insisted that my father should also go with him, and they went. If my father had stayed there and exercised on the fortieth day also, he said, the jinn definitely would have given him some reward.

There is general agreement among musicians that jinns are especially attracted to rāg *Malkauns,* a rāg frequently performed in India. It is played late at night and is considered one of the more important and serious rāgs. Because jinns are attracted to *Malkauns,* some musicians are afraid to practice it at night:

One night, when everyone was at home sleeping, I was playing *Malkauns.* Suddenly I felt frightened. I heard footsteps and someone approaching. My heart started pounding. I got scared and stopped playing and went to sleep. In the morning I discussed this with my father. My father asked me whether I was playing *Malkauns,* and then explained to me that *Malkauns* was one such rāg that jinns love.

Another musician who has heard about jinns from his father but has never actually experienced their presence, will nevertheless not play *Malkauns* alone at night:

I never play it when I am alone. I never play it for a long time. Even if I play it, I play it before ten o'clock at night. I never play *Malkauns* between two and three [in the morning]. I don't have the guts to play. I can play it in front of an audience.

The attraction that rāg *Malkauns* has for jinns presents a good example of the magical nature of music generally and rāgs in particular. Musicians have a large fund of lore describing the magical effects of rāgs, and those musicians who could make it work. Indeed the most articulate expression of the power of music is revealed through anecdotes, assertions, and stories about the magic potential of rāgs. It is a theme common to both musicians and musicologists, and few if any works on Indian music do not at least refer to it.

Sometimes rāgs are discussed in general terms, that is, without specifying a particular one, but attributing characteristics said to be common to all. Such statements vary from person to person, suggesting that they are primarily metaphoric, or they may be dictated simply by varieties of belief. For example, one musician claimed that he could tell the exact time after listening to a given rāg, because rāgs are performed according to certain prescribed periods of the day and night. Since these periods encompass a range of four or five hours, the precision claimed is difficult to understand. Another musician claimed that if a rāg were performed by a spiritually devoted individual, the rāg could be weighed.

At the other extreme are certain rāgs which have myths attached to them and which constitute a body of knowledge shared by all musicians. Foremost among these is rāg *Dīpak*, a rāg known more for its power to produce heat than for its musical qualities.

> If you sing *Dīpak* rāg in a house regularly it will be bad for the house, it will be destroyed. If you play it for eleven days you feel it in your body. My eyes will start burning. I'll get pimples and boils.

Some musicians still believe this, and the musician just quoted said that although he knows rāg *Dīpak* he never performs it (cf. Kaufmann 1968:12,13). Other musicians are skeptical, but always with a qualification. One musician denied the effect of rāg *Dīpak*, because he had heard it performed in the studios of All India Radio, and the building did not burn down. But it was not because the rāg did not have the inherent power; there just were no longer any musicians who had the power to generate this kind of magical effect from a rāg.

Another standard magical rāg is *Mian-ki-Malhar*, which is

associated with rain; and indeed, during the monsoon season, one commonly hears it performed. *Malhar,* if it is correctly performed, is said to have the power to bring rain. Some musicians claim or imply that they have produced such an effect, although always referring to it as an accidental occurrence, never a consciously planned one. The performance is, as it were, "accidentally perfect." "I was playing *Malhar* and it was a cloudless day. All of a sudden as I was playing, clouds began to appear, and after some time it started raining."

Music also has healing powers, according to some musicians. One artist told me that any rāg which is played correctly will reduce a fever, while another musician was more specific as he had—again accidentally—caused a cure:

I have heard stories of curing diseases with rāgs ever since my childhood. Even while learning music I heard such references. . . . The Nawab had a very high fever one day. . . . Just by chance I was present at the moment here and singing *Gujari Todi,* and you know *Gujari Todi* can cure even the severest temperature if sung with perfection. . . . I proceeded and sang this khayal. "Oh you curer of all pains and anxieties, take care of Tanras Khan, you are the darling of Ganj-Shakhar." Ganj-Shakhar was the pir of Nizamuddin Auliya. Mind well, I was not asked by anyone to sing it. Only I was in a trance. I sang with all my heart. After the song was over, the Nawab came to me and said, "You sang excellently. May God reward you. I haven't heard such a song for a long time. The song has cured me of my fever." Now when I thought of the minutest detail of the song, I found I was quite justified. No doubt this was the blessing of God.

Not all music results in healing, of course, as the following anecdote of Hazrat Inayat Khan suggests:

Once the Maharaja of Baroda, on hearing that healing could be accomplished through music, introduced concerts in certain hospitals, and the amusing result was that all those who were suffering began to cry out, 'For God's sake, keep quiet! Go away!' That was not the music to soothe them. It only made them suffer more; it was like giving a stone for bread. [Khan 1973:145]

The idea that a rāg must be correctly performed in order to achieve its effect, whether it be magical or purely aesthetic, pervades the literature and conversations with musicians. Most musicians do believe that under certain conditions rāgs have these powers. The magical feats of musicians in the past are coextensive with their spiritual nature and power. The knowledge that music and the Divine are related is the underlying principle which yields a rich tradition not only about the magical powers of music, but also about the personification and deification of rāgs, and a whole, complex aesthetic of music about which many volumes have been written.

Not all musicians are conversant with the aesthetic theories that abound in the history of Indian music. For example, the concept of *ras* (affective states) is something of which many musicians are only dimly aware, even though it has been elaborated, in the context of the dramatic arts, since the *Natyashastra* (ca. 200 B.C.–A.D. 400).[3]

Whatever supernatural theories a musician may have, there is a sense that magical music is something of the past; that the times today do not provide the proper environment in which the art can be cultivated or, perhaps more precisely, in which the artist can be cultivated. The truly great musicians live in the distant past, as heroes of a Golden Age. Even Tansen, who became a court musician, inherited a spiritual sensibility which enabled him to produce magical rāgs and pass this tradition on to his descendants.

Where Tansen represents the movement from the temple to the court, Ravi Shankar today perhaps best of all represents the movement to the concert stage. It is from this platform that music is most often heard today. Musicians are, in a sense, now twice removed from the sacred and magical. They believe in the power of music, but rarely seem to experience it. Like riaz as a sacred duty and the guru-shishya system as a hallowed relationship, musicians as magical performers are becoming a thing of the past. "It is the common man," as some musicians are fond of putting it, "that calls the tune." The piper's patron which has emerged is a very complex mixture of people, and musicians are now listening carefully so that they know which tune to play.

The Listening Public

Musicians recognize that as professionals they are not, in any but the most ideal sense, engaged in sacred activity. The most distinguishing manifest element in the secularization of music performance is that it is addressed to other people—the audience—not to one's self or to God.

Musicians are particularly sensitive to the nature and movement of their listening public, responding to what they perceive to be its sensibility. The relationship between the artist and his audience is often acknowledged as a significant one, but it has as yet been little explored by scholars. This is partly a problem of providing an adequate conception of what constitutes an audience.

Performers claim that they can "come to know" what the audience understands and adjust their programs accordingly. With the increased size and heterogeneity of the listening public, this has had the apparent effect of making musicians less specialized than they were in the past. Musicians now can and will perform in a variety of styles and forms when the occasion demands.

Musicians distinguish essentially two kinds of listeners: those who are connoisseurs (*samajhdār log*, "people who understand") and those who are musically unsophisticated, for which there are a variety of epithets. Audiences now usually include both kinds of listeners, in marked contrast to audiences in the past when all were connoisseurs, members of a highly educated and refined nobility.

Another kind of samajhdar audience is one made up of other musicians. It is perhaps the most discriminating audience and one for which the artist will presumably do his best. For example, in 1976 the celebrated Ustad Vilayat Khan gave a private performance in honor of D. T. Joshi, before a select group of India's finest musicians. I was told by one musician, senior in age to Vilayat Khan and not easily given to praise, that this performance was so outstanding that it excelled anything he had ever heard, even that of his own guru, heresy as that might be to believe, let alone say. There are other kinds of occasions when one has virtually an all-musician audience. When an ustad has a birthday, all his disciples and other admirers will come by his house, give him gifts, and perform for him. *Saraswatī Pūjā* (a celebration in honor of Saraswati, goddess of learning and music) provides still another occasion when disciples will gather to perform and then listen to their guru perform. Sometimes a whole extended family of musicians will provide an audience. When the son of the late Ustad Karamatalla Khan was first engaged to the daughter of Ustad Sabri Khan, the occasion was celebrated with a gathering of about fifty musicians to listen to the son play. He played solo tabla for about two hours, showing in effect what he knew, and the heritage of his house.[4]

In the past, solo performances on the tabla and sarangi, the two major accompanying instruments, were heard only in such intimate gatherings of a musical fraternity. Ustad Ahmad Jan Thirakwa, the venerated tabla player, already famous in the early part of this century, recalls the situation during his youth:

> When I was young, tabla solo wasn't very common. We played solo only in *mehfils* where only our brother musicians were present. That is why we really had to practice. And after many years of practice we played solo in front of musicians. The same with sarangi. Only a good sarangi player could play solo. . . . we used to play things which were taught by our ustad, things which belonged to our gharana.

Another musical event in which many musicians and other musical connoisseurs are present is a concert presented as an homage in memory of some distinguished musician of the past. Members of his gharana, or immediate descendants, give performances, while other members, disciples, and interested informed listeners round out what is considered a desirable audience from the artist's point of view.

The importance of "kinship" with the audience can hardly be overestimated. For the artist, nothing is as gratifying as a sympathetic and understanding audience, for whom his art is not performed in vain and his product not merely a commercial phenomenon. A good audience, it is believed, will always generate a good performance. If the artist is in a bad mood, a good audience will bring him out of it. (If he is in a good mood, a bad audience will bring him out of that!) Sometimes a musician will be accused of manipulating the audience. As an example, I heard one instrumentalist explain the success of a rival by the fact that he would "plant relatives in his audience" to initiate and exaggerate applause. (Perhaps the claque is a music universal!)

There are also musical events which are not open to the general public, but are patronized by subscribers to a musical society. The purpose of these events is to support traditional art music by simulating the atmosphere of the mehfil, where the listeners sit on the floor, creating an intimate gathering of connoisseurs. *Pān* (betel nut and leaf) is passed around to musicians and onlookers alike. There is, above all, a sense of mutual appreciation between the artist and his audience, in which music serves as a serious vehicle for communication.

For musicians this is aesthetically, although usually not remuneratively, the most desirable context for a musical performance. The homogeneity of the audience suggests that the program has a minimum of constraints. The musician does not have to serve a variety of tastes, aiming for a middle ground so as to satisfy high-, middle-, and low-brows together. In the mehfil, the atmosphere is relaxed. The artist can tune at his own pace; he will be at his place for some time before beginning, exchanging anecdotes with listeners whom he knows from other events, and getting into the mood, as musicians themselves put it. There will also be other musicians present, some part of his own retinue and others who have come to hear him and perhaps to pay their respects. When he begins, he can do so leisurely, without the impatience characteristic of a large gathering waiting for the next performer; at the mehfil there is typically only one principal performer. This is important because he knows the listeners have come to hear only him; and he need not feel pressed, as happens at music festivals, because a more famous artist is waiting in the wings.

The mehfil thus provides a most satisfying kind of musical event, for musicians and listeners alike. Accordingly, the common sentiment heard in the West concerning the primacy of chamber music is similarly expressed in India with regard to music in the mehfil. It is in the context of the mehfil that the artist best reveals what he knows, and it is against this that all other events are measured and upon which they are occasionally modeled.

When a musician is faced with a large number of listeners, the highly prized intimate quality of the mehfil is lost, although attempts are made to simulate its atmosphere. At large music festivals, which are typically held outside under a *shāmiyānā* (a large tent), there is usually a space in front of the stage which is reserved for listeners who want to sit on the ground rather than on chairs or couches where the others sit. A musician is sometimes accompanied by disciples, who sit with him on the stage, providing an immediately responsive circle.

Because there are so many listeners, the musician has no way of evaluating the audience on the basis of who they are individually, so that he makes an evaluation in terms of the context of the event. For example, All India Radio sponsors an annual series of concerts, the Radio Sangeet Sammelan, which are held in a number of cities throughout the country. Performances in Delhi are held in an auditorium, broadcast live, and taped so that they can be aired by other stations at a later date. The audience, consisting for the large part of musically interested individuals, is there by invitation only. Although the performances are limited by time and the event does not have the intimate quality of a small gathering, the audience, being select, is a good one, and musicians consider it an honor to be included on the program.

The better-known musicians take numerous trips to perform in music festivals, which are held throughout India. Those who have had a certain amount of experience outside Delhi are able to offer their evaluations of the quality of regional audiences. Among Delhi musicians, audiences of other cities are more highly regarded than their "home" audience. The people of Calcutta are thought to be a much better audience. Although they may not understand as much as would be desirable, they sit quietly and listen with an attention which is generally appreciated by musicians. Interestingly, Hindustani musicians universally appear to rate South Indian audiences as the best in India. It is a well-established stereotype that listeners in Madras, for example, are sophisticated as a group, polite in their responses, and a model of what audiences in North India should be. Audiences in the North are generally louder and inattentive and through this behavior communicate the lack of that respect which musicians feel they deserve. No explanation is readily offered as to why South Indian audiences are better behaved, except that "they like music" even though they are not familiar with the Hindustani style.

In certain other regions, associated primarily with important music festivals, the audiences are also highly regarded. One of the most important festivals in North India is the Hardballabh conference, held annually in Jullunder (Panjab) towards the end of December. The audience is enthusiastic and musicians come there annually, so that even some accompanists, as I was able to witness, are well-known and appreciated.

Delhi itself has different kinds of audiences, defined in large part by the particular nature of the musical occasion and the place in which it is held. For example, until recently the most prestigious concert hall was Sapru House,[5] which seats about six hundred people and is centrally air-conditioned. This hall is rented by a variety of organizations sponsoring musical events. The audience is composed typically of a socially select group, which, in terms of its status, is said to be a desirable audience. Since the organizations book well-known artists as box office attractions, to perform at Sapru House, even as an accompanist (who is usually chosen by the soloist), is a prestigious accomplishment.

The audiences at this sort of affair are considered musically somewhat naive, and artists have to modify their presentations in order to communicate at a middle-brow level. The problem is well exemplified in a review of a concert sponsored by the Gandhi Centenary Celebrations Committee:

Finally came the young maestro . . . who refused to warm up before an impassive, unresponsive audience. But this he could realize only when he had selected a wrong rāg, *Sugrai Kanhra.* Simple [rāg] *Desh* was the melody meant for this audience. . . . [He] too, thought it better to drop the *vilambit* [slow movement] and went all out in his crisp composition in *teen tala* to move the audience out of its inertia by throwing in a few robust strikes and sequences. In such an eventuality he could naturally not pay due heed to the values of serious classical music. [*Times of India,* Delhi, February 5, 1970]

Musicians are often faced with the difficulty of merely being heard at a large gathering. Consequently, microphones are ubiquitous although excellent quality of sound is not. Musicians have a curious disregard for the quality of their output over the loudspeakers. There are several reasons for this attitude. The musician on stage often hears primarily his own unamplified sound so that he is unaware of the distortion heard in the audience. Also, the responsibility for the amplifiers is not considered to be the performer's but the engineer's. On only very few occasions have I witnessed a musician instructing the sound controllers to make some kind of modification, and the musicians on these occasions were always celebrities, presumably experienced in the ways of performing before large audiences.

Although the quality of amplified sound should be the responsibility of the engineers, supervised by the organizers of the performance, it is often left for someone in the audience to complain. Music critics sometimes bring this problem to the attention of their readers. Concerning a performance at Sapru House, where the sound was bad (and there it is usually good!), a critic indicates the extent to which this problem is merely ignored.

The [amplifier] sets are no doubt bad, but worse still is human negligence. I found no responsible acoustics expert in their control room. Instead there were two urchins who sat smoking biris, know nothing to balancing and turned the wrong key when asked. [*Times of India,* Delhi, April 14, 1969]

The aesthetic problem involved in the use of the microphone has been outlined by Menon:

[While the microphone] has made good music accessible to large audiences, [it] has had a serious detrimental effect on the performance of Indian music. It has led to carelessness in voice production, increase in falsettos [and] encouraged crooning, because the microphone is there to do the work for you. [1963:19]

Instrumentalists with whom I have spoken do not feel that amplification has much effect one way or the other. They point out that qualities as well as defects are amplified, and the only difference is that more people can hear the performance.

Amplified or not, the sound of music is not the only medium that an artist utilizes in order to communicate with his listeners. Often he will tell anecdotes to his listeners and perhaps talk a little about what he will perform. Usually this occurs before the performance proper, although on occasion, while retuning the instrument for instance, the performer will also use the time to communicate verbally to the audience. An artist may even interrupt his performance in order to say something. Once, for example, a private concert featured Ustad Ali Akbar Khan and Ustad Vilayat Khan in a *jugalbandī* (a duet with, in this case, the overtones of a duel). As this was the first time these two giants had performed together in something like fifteen years, the atmosphere was electric. The concert had barely begun when the tabla player, Pandit Shanta Prasad, who was sitting between them, said to the audience, "I feel like a lamb sitting between two tigers." The listeners laughed, acknowledging the now public definition of this concert as a duel and the role of the tabla player as performing mediator. In spite of this definition, however, the concert, which began at nine in the evening and ended at three in the morning, was so outstanding that there was no talk about the superiority of either soloist. Musically it had turned out to be a genuine duet.

Another kind of stage performance with extramusical features is exemplified in the following account. Bhimsen Joshi, a very popular vocalist, was giving a concert at the aforementioned Hardballabh conference in Jullunder. It was cold out, and the listeners were huddled under blankets, scarves, and heavy coats. Bhimsen Joshi entered the stage, sat down, tuned the two tanpuras, and before proceeding further began to take off his wraps. First he took off his long scarf with a flourish. Then he slowly unbuttoned his jacket all the way, after which he unbuttoned his shirt, exposing his neck and chest to the cold. As the huddled audience sat quietly murmuring and muffling their expectant laughter, the artist began very slowly and quietly to sing. The eyes and ears of the whole audience (which I estimated roughly at well over a thousand persons) were riveted on him, and a hushed silence reigned. His action had the desired effect, and the performance was a grand success.

Kinaesthetics is also an important part of a musician's communicative repertoire. Vocalists, especially, will move their arms, heads, and hands during the performance. Sometimes the artist traces out the melodic movement with his hands, moving the ascending sound with his right hand and following with his head as he sings up the scale. In a fast tan with *gamak* (a shaking ornamentation), his hand waves quickly back and forth, simulating in action the movement of the sound. At other times, following the words of a devotional song, he holds his hands in supplication as a sign of intense devotion.

Instrumentalists are also able to communicate with their hands, essentially by *not* using them. A sitarist playing a long *mīr* (i.e., portamento glide, made by pulling the string laterally) with one stroke, will raise his right hand in a wave to indicate that the tone is still being maintained without any additional strokes. This visual translation of an aural phenomenon is quite effective for instructing listeners unfamiliar with the subtleties of instrumental technique.

The more traditional musician, or rather musicians who conceive themselves to be more traditional, will eschew showy visual virtuosity of this sort. Vocalists are often criticized for making funny faces and movements—antics that do not properly belong with serious music. Older musicians especially tend to sit solemnly and seriously during their performances, imparting their art without adding anything extra, thus letting the audience find its way through the music alone.

The response of members of the audience is expressed in certain stereotyped ways, although the kind of response and its intensity depend again on the nature of the musical event, and the audience. Although audiences do indeed differ according to the region and event, audible responses during the music are everywhere acceptable and, if done with restraint, are even encouraged. "Vah-vah," "kyā bāt!" (*lit.*, "what a thing") and "javāb nahī" (*lit.*, "no answer," signifying it is so good there is nothing that can respond to it, except of course that response itself) are typical utterances heard from the ranks of the listeners. Naive listeners, it appears, also respond, and their naiveté is revealed by inappropriately timed responses. Musicians say that one of the ways by which they can tell what the audience knows is not only how it responds but when.

Responses are not random. Usually they appear at the *sam*, the point where the instrumentalist and tabla accompanist meet together at the end of a phrase (and which is also the beginning of the rhythmic cycle). Audiences sometimes respond with clapping, if a particularly well-executed series of tans has been completed or the tabla player has presented an exciting solo improvisation. An ill-timed response is one that occurs before the completion of a given musical unit, that is, a complete cycle or a complete set of tans. This is akin to the inappropriate applause at the end of a first movement of a concerto in the West.

Because many in a large gathering are not musically so-phisticated, several cues operate to signal when responses are appropriate. The soloist may compliment his accompanist with a "bahut achchhā" ("very good!") or the accompanist may respond to the soloist by a lateral shaking of his head. This lateral move-ment, a general Indian gesture signifying assent, is utilized by listeners as well, indicating that one is following and appreciating the performance. Connoisseurs usually sit up front on chairs, or on rugs in front of the stage. Their responses also serve as a cue to those behind them, educating the rest of the audience about appropriate gestures and timings (Joshi 1963:78).

Both verbal and kinaesthetic communication is regarded as important by the artist. On his part, it is a way of communicating to the audience at more than one level; he is saying something about the music through other means. The performance as a whole can be interpreted as an attempt on the part of musicians and listeners alike to establish a personal framework. The music does not speak to a crowd but to individual sensibilities, and individuals respond with their individual acclamations.

The importance of stage appearance is stressed by some musicians, who are known for the elegance of their dress and their bearing as they sit on the stage. One musician told me that he used to practice in front of a mirror to rid himself of funny expressions, to learn how to smile, and thereby "look nice" while performing. Although older musicians usually wear very serious expressions during their performances, younger musicians sensitive to the importance of visual communication smile from time to time, especially at the end of a particular musical elaboration, as if in anticipation of (or even to cue?) the audience's response.

Radio performance involves communication with an unseen and unheard audience, a dimly conceived, necessarily imaginary, and very little-understood group. Yet certain kinds of radio performance carry enough prestige to overcome this limitation. For example, performing on the national program of music, broadcast every Saturday night over the entire network throughout India, is an accomplishment of which musicians are justifiably proud. Only the best artists of the country are said to be invited to perform. But, according to one unofficial estimate (based on a private survey of All India Radio), fewer than one percent of the listening public tunes in to the national program.

Some artists, aware that the radio audience is small, uninfluential, and for the most part inattentive and naive, say that they find it difficult to perform well under such conditions. Yet very good audiences will sometimes gather in the station itself. For ordinary programs, friends of the performing staff artist drop by the studio to listen and hence to provide an audience, which may also include other staff artists and music producers who are themselves artists (see Chapter 6). If there is a special program with a renowned artist, many at the radio station drop by just to see, if not actually to listen.

The only regular public response to radio performances comes from the music and radio critics writing in the newspapers. The national program is reviewed weekly in all the major newspapers. *The Statesman,* one of India's prominent dailies, has a weekly section called "The Listening Post," in which selected radio programs, including musical ones, are reviewed. The only other public response is an occasional letter to the editor.

For the national program, a policy of having an invited audience in the studio was instituted in 1969. Many times, however, programs are taped in advance so that the performance, when broadcast, is not live and usually has no audience. When asked, musicians always indicate a preference for an audience, but they also add that it is not crucial. Sometimes, of course, there is no choice.

One way in which Indian musicians seem to be adapting to a heterogeneous listening public is by providing different levels of music for different listeners, all within a single performance. The alap and vilambit are considered relatively highbrow music. The *drut* (fast movement) which follows allows the performer to show his virtuosity in speed, which seems to communicate more immediately to less refined sensibilities. The alap itself is divided into three major sections: first the alap proper—slow, arhythmic, ideally the most serious and profound section (the one also performed exclusively for national mourning periods); then the *jor* and *jhālā* sections, both rhythmic and capable of allowing demonstrations of high technical virtuosity. By balancing the duration of these movements, artists are able to tailor the performance to the level of the audience.

The organization of a whole evening's program at a music festival also follows this pattern. Several musicians are presented in sequence, usually on a popular ascending scale, so that the "star" performs last. Each performance averages between an hour-and-a-half and two hours in length (although some are longer) and begins typically with a khayal, or an instrumental piece, which lasts from forty-five to seventy-five minutes. Then follows a shorter piece, perhaps half an hour long. The last piece is always "lighter," such as a thumri or a *dhun*. This, so musicians say, is to keep the less sophisticated listeners interested in classical music and to allow them to leave with a feeling which, if not joyous, is still good.

There are also recent innovations which owe their continued existence to popular taste. The *sawāl-jawāb* (*lit.,* "question-answer"), essentially a call-and-response pattern between soloist and accompanist, is often decried by traditionalists as being vulgar and playing to the gallery. Nevertheless, it is widely performed and very popular.

These views of the audience from the stage comprise some of the aspects which govern a musician's aesthetic decisions. The changing contexts of music events are an area which will be explored in more detail in a later chapter. Here it is appropriate to consider the musician's own aesthetics, his set of values about music itself, viewing it first as a cultural phenomenon, and then as a set of statements about the social system of musicians.

Evaluations

A complete analysis of the aesthetics underlying contemporary performance practices would confront a fundamental problem: the myriad of micro-traditions of the various specialties and schools of different performers. A sitar player usually knows very little about sarangi technique, and a representative of one gharana can only speak to a limited extent about the characteristics of others. A musician's social and cultural background also influences his judgment of a musical performance. As a result, the form and content of an evaluation depend as much upon the one who is offering it as about whom it is offered.

Musicians discuss their evaluation in terms of three criteria: competence, appropriateness, and affect.

A performer's theoretical knowledge and technical capabilities are important in establishing a reputation. There are certain minimal technical requirements which an artist must master in order to become accomplished, but once this threshold has been reached, musicians often say that they are a secondary consideration, as illustrated in the comments of musicians and other critics about a young performer embarking on his or her career. If the performance is appreciated, they will say that he is *bahut tayār hai (lit.,* "very ready"), signifying that he is competent and that he has the requisite technique and knowledge at hand. As one would expect, this phrase is rarely if ever used of a veteran performer.

Comments about particularly polished techniques are made, but musicians and connoisseurs alike say that these are only of secondary significance. They will say of a performer that he is *bahut tez* ("very fast") or his intonation is very precise (*bahut sūr ka hāt, lit.,* "very in-tune hand," i.e., for an instrumentalist). Occasionally an outstanding artist like Vilayat Khan, known for his exceptional virtuosity on the sitar, will elicit praise from younger sitarists who can appreciate the technical subtleties of his performance. But usually the celebration of virtuosity is minimized and only the qualities of intonation, if anything, will be commented upon.[6]

Musicians are extremely polite about one another's performances, and it is rare to hear explicitly negative comments made in public. If a performance has been obviously bad, a polite—or perhaps more correctly a euphemistic—response would be that it was "ṭhīk hai" ("O.K."). The appropriate comment on a mediocre performance might be "achchhā hai" ("it's good"), which means more precisely in this context that it is merely all right or that it will do. These comments are restricted to private situations, however, and are rarely if ever addressed to the performer concerned.

Evaluations of musicians and their music are largely based on social criteria and as such are better understood as social statements. Musicians who are members of high-ranking social groups or categories will tend to express sentiments about socially lower-ranked musicians and their performances in terms of their very ranks. More specifically, accompanists, who are usually recruited from social groups which traditionally have enjoyed only a very modest position in the larger social framework, are often thought of by others as having only a partial knowledge about the theory of classical music. Evaluations of their musical performance, if they are made at all, are characteristically made with reference to essentially technical considerations concerning their supporting role in a given performance. Put another way, an accompanist will be complimented because he played in tune, or did not exceed the limits of his performance role as the soloist perceives it to be; but it will be uncommon to hear that an accompanist increased by his performance the value of the performance as a whole. This limited evaluative paradigm is constrained in part by the accompanying role itself, which is by definition not central to the total performance. At the same time, because of the accompanist's modest social background, conceptions about his musical knowledge and capabilities are sometimes articulated within the framework of his social standing.

Aesthetic evaluations between equivalently ranked performers are expressed through a vocabulary of style and heritage, this last however being determined and thus defined by membership in certain social groups. For example, a critic, being a member of one stylistic school, will frame his comments about another artist in a vocabulary of technicalities—the composition is not authentic, the rāg is rendered incorrectly, and so forth. To the outside observer, however, this comment is explained as a criticism of a stylistic school; it may also represent implicit criticism of the social group which originally gave rise to that school.

This sort of evaluation is apparent even in writings about contemporary Indian classical music, where one finds students of one school paying homage to their own tradition while giving only a cursory mention of others. Occasionally, one finds a critic who acknowledges possible biases in the evaluation of other stylistic schools and then attempts to judge them objectively. Deshpande's study of the major vocal styles is both a description and a critique of the major schools. In his assessment he finds that his own school represents the ideal balance of melody and rhythm, whereas other schools suffer from too much stress on one or the other (Deshpande 1973).

A more general area of evaluation, and one which invites the participation of less specialized connoisseurs, is the appropriateness of elements of a performance. A musician can be criticized for introducing innovations of dubious merit. Examples are performing a rāg which the artist has created, or holding the instrument in a new way, or taking the techniques of one instrumental style and utilizing it for another style. In one instance, a surbahar player was criticized because, rather than staying with the traditional performance practice of that instrument (which is closely allied to that of the bīn tradition), he utilized techniques borrowed from the sitar style. In one review quoted above, the critic found the rāg inappropriate, as being too esoteric for the audience. Musician-critics often have a similar but opposite reaction, namely, that a performance is oriented merely "to the gallery," to please the crowd, exhibiting at the same time little of aesthetic value.

Onstage one often finds disagreements between the soloist and accompanist. The soloist monopolizes the performance and does not allow his accompanist adequate time for his own expression. Or the accompanist is thought to impinge on musical rights which are normally the soloist's. Vocalists sometimes complain, for example, that the sarangi accompanist anticipates incorrectly what the vocalist intends to do, thereby introducing elements in the performance over which the vocalist has no control.

Perhaps the most surprising aspect of evaluations is the limited expression given to affective results in spite of the high premium put on this aspect of music in the literature and in general conversation. The theory of ras, as I have mentioned, is little understood by many musicians. When asking questions about ras, responses were typically vague and often obviously extemporized. In discussing other living musicians, critics who are themselves musicians do not usually speak about an artist's ability to evoke emotional response. The reason for the limited discourse about affect is that this aspect of a performance is most eminently within the domain of music sound itself, not touched by verbal statements, except by poetry. However, a critic might refer to the effectiveness of an artist in producing the emotional valence of a given rāg.

What *is* discussed is not so much what a given performer can create in a performance, but what he can produce as part of his traditional repertoire. One of the less understood aspects of Indian classical music is the high premium placed on the bandish, or composition. This can be, for example, an astayi, or antara, or a khayal, or a gat. Although these are relatively short pieces, connoisseurs talk about what a beautiful or rare composition they have just heard. Indeed, an experienced performer is congratulated as much or more on the choice of his composition as his rendering of it, even though the composition, including repetitions, may constitute only a small portion of the total performance. When asked about its significance in relation to the total performance, musicians usually do not understand the reason for the question, and naturally enough. If they give an explanation they may define the importance of the piece in terms of its ability to capture the essence of a rāg and generate elaborations on it in a manner which will further enhance that essence.

Evaluations of compositions must also be considered social statements. Each stylistic school and the families representing it have a repertoire of set pieces which are considered the creations of that particular tradition. In producing a set piece for the listener, the performer often states, if it is not well-known, that it is something old and by implication authentic. This claim, made by an artist coming from a recognized social background and an established tradition, can be particularly convincing. Hereditary musicians therefore tend to speak from a more authoritative position, with regard to performance practices, than do non-hereditary musicians. To more fully understand evaluations and concepts about music and musicians as social statements, we have to understand how music as a specialized body of knowledge and as performance is socially organized.

4. The Social Organization of Specialist Knowledge

The history of Hindustani music and its practitioners can be traced back to Amir Khusrau (A.D. 1253–1325), and to Nizamuddin, who was his contemporary, close friend, and spiritual mentor. Both spent much of their long lives in and near Delhi. Khusrau is credited with the introduction of many new ragas, musical forms, and several instruments. He is also claimed as a direct ancestor by at least one contemporary family of hereditary musicians in Delhi; and as Wahid Mirza notes, "Qawwāls [singers of Muslim devotional music] all over India recognize him to be their master even today" (1974:239). Although there is uncertainty about his exact contribution, he was a formidable influence beyond whom Hindustani music history and virtually all musician pedigrees do not reach. Nizamuddin is important as a spiritual force which provided a rationale for the performance of music despite Islamic prohibitions.

The relationship between the two men anticipates that of Tansen and Swami Haridas. Khusrau, like Tansen, was lionized at court; Nizamuddin, like Swami Haridas after him, kept his distance in spite of repeated invitations from the court.[1] These relationships are also an expression of that attitude about music in India which alternates at the extremes of considering it sacred activity and everyday entertainment. Bards and minstrels as specialists in entertainment have been documented for early and medieval South India (Kailasapathy 1968:94–134 and passim), but similar traditions for the North are not in evidence until the establishment of the Delhi Sultanate in the thirteenth century. It is from this period of history that we read of patronage and celebration of outstanding musicians, of their being granted money, land, and titles, and often being lured or stolen from other courts. The number and quality of musicians in a court is part of the aura of court life and a measure of its ruler's prestige. Sometimes musicians can also be a symbol of a king's authority. For example, a major war was actually initiated by Mohammad Shah Bahmāni against the Raja of Vijayanagar in the fourteenth century because the Raja refused to remunerate three hundred musicians who had come down from Delhi to entertain Moham- mad Shah (Briggs 1966: II,190).

Although Amir Khusrau is generally credited with having created a true Indo-Persian synthesis in music and poetry in the thirteenth century, musicians were still being imported from out- side India for several hundred years thereafter. Abu'l Fazl, Em- peror Akbar's court chronicler and author of the sixteenth-cen- tury *Ain-i-Akbari,* listed thirty-six musical specialists in Akbar's court, of which at least nine were from outside India. Even today there are still musicians who trace their ancestry to Afghanistan and Arabia.[2]

We do know, however, that indigenous musician commu- nities already existed by Akbar's time. For example, from the names of musicians listed by Abu'l Fazl some indication of a musical specialist typology emerges. Two surnames of particular interest are *Kalāwant* and *Dhāri* because these turn out to be terms for Indian musician communities for several hundred years after.

Dhari are also found mentioned in the *Kitab-i-Nauras,* written soon after the *Ain-i-Akbari* by the ruler of Bijapur, Ibra- him Adil Shah. Adil Shah, who was a serious musician himself and a great patron of the arts, divided his court musicians into three categories, in ascending order of rank: (1) *Gunijan,* those who know some theory; (2) *Dhadhi* (Dhari) the average musi- cians; and (3) *Atai,* the highest-ranked artists in the court. All these musicians were also collectively referred to as Kalawant. Later in his reign, Ibrahim substituted three other categories (or terms for categories) of musical specialists, this time in descending order of rank: (1) *Huzuris,* master musicians; (2) *Darbaris,* also court musicians but not as accomplished as Huzuris; (3) *Shahis,* disciples of the Darbaris, but not yet court musicians. All received stipends from the court (Ahmed 1965: 46–55,143).

The most detailed historical information about musical specialists is found in the *Mādanul Mausiqi* written by Mohammad Karam Imam in mid-nineteenth century Lucknow. In this account, Imam lists many Dhari musicians, claiming that they are the oldest musician community in India.

> By tracing their history we know that they were originally Rajputs. They sang Karka. During the Muslim rule of the past, they embraced Islam. . . . Now, for all practical purposes the serious type of music has left this community. Most of the Dharis earn their living by accompanying dancing girls. [1959a:18]

Imam's work, brief though the translated parts are, is particularly revealing since the typologies of musicians which he provides us are still relevant. The following is a summary of Imam's classification of musicians:

1. *Gandharva:* "The one who knows both Desi and Marga ragas, i.e., both the new and the old ragas."

2. *Gunkar* or *Guni:* "The one who knows only Desi ragas."

3. *Kalawant:* "If a Gandharva and Guni knows Dhrupad, Trivat and other such things he is called a Kalawant."

4. *Quawwal:* "The one who knows Khayal, Quaul, Qualbana Naksh-o-gul and Tarana. . . ."

5. *Pandit:* "The one having a theoretical knowledge only."

6. *Nayak:* "The one who is a master of theory and an expert expōnent of both vocal and instrumental music and also a master of dancing and a composer." [1959a and 1959b]

In this classification Imam mentions Dharis as a side note in order to contrast their heritage with that of Quawwals. He

87

does not consider them part of this typology, but rather as followers of Amir Khusrau, who is said to be the creator of quaul, from which qawwali is derived.

The title Kalawant, conferred by Akbar, continues to be employed even today. According to Imam, it was granted to four musicians who were Gandharvas (1959a:14): Tansen, Brijchand, Samokhan Singh, and Srichand. The first two were originally Brahmans and the last two Rajputs. They originated four styles of music called *bānīs,* known as *Gorari, Dagari, Khandari* and *Noohari.* For Imam only the descendants of these four musicians are qualified to call themselves Kalawants. But just as some musicians today complain, Imam in his time states:

> There are many musicians who call themselves Kalawants but their claims are baseless. It is interesting to note that in practice they do what is taboo in a Kalawant family, i.e., they openly accompany the dancing girls thus putting even the devil to shame. [Ibid.]

In Imam's opinion there were no Nayaks, even at the time of Akbar:

> By stating this fact I do not mean to demean Tansen, who is considered by many as one like whom a musician was not born for a thousand years. Tansen was a singer of *unequal* [sic] merits, no doubt, but he was not a scholar. He was only a practical exponent. [Ibid.]

Kalawants and Qawwals were distinguished according to their performance practices as well. The former performed exclusively Indian music, the latter in both Persian and Indian styles.

> Qawwals . . . render the ragas of India and also the muquams [mode] of Islamic countries, and Kalawants are those who practice the Indian ragas originated by the rishis [sages]. Whereas the Kalawants begin with alap, the Qawwals create an effect without alap with the help of sacred names. [1959b:12]

Imam presents a different typology in his section on musicians of Lucknow (1959a:passim). He discusses first "professional musicians," who are implicitly defined as musicians coming from hereditary families of musicians and who perform music for an income. Non-professionals, according to his classification, do not come from hereditary families of musicians, and do not receive incomes. Musicians who are also nobles are treated by Imam as a separate category as well. His next category is women singers, some of whom come from musician families. One, Bi Rehman Bai, is considered by Imam (and Haddu Khan, one of the founders of the Gwalior gharana) to be the best singer of her time. Female singers were employed like men, at royal courts, with a regular salary. Imam lists most of them as disciples, with specific and named ustads. Some are listed as specialists in thumri and ghazal, two forms of music that are "in vogue now." Imam then lists instrumentalists such as *bīnkārs, sitariyās, sārangiyās, sarodiyās, shahnāī* players (one of whom doubled on the clarinet), tabla and *pakhāwaj* players, and dancers. These classifications provide a point of reference for a contemporary typology, corresponding as they do to the historical beginnings of modern Hindustani music culture and to historical personages whose direct descendants are alive today.

In contemporary North India, there are a wide variety of ways in which musical specialists are differentiated and identified. A classification of such specialists must, however, take into account the degree of inclusivity intended by a particular observer. The problem is more than merely one of a hierarchy of classes, because the basis of classification and social identification is not uniform. Musicians are identified by ethnic origins, community or caste; by the particular form of music they perform, the extent of their musical knowledge, and their instrumental specialty; and by sex, residence, and age, in addition to other criteria.

Given all these criteria, it is perhaps not surprising that there exists no commonly used word in Hindustani to refer to "musician" as an occupational category. There is, to be sure, the *sangīt ke kalakār (lit.,* "artist of music") of Hindi, or the Persian-derived *mūsīqār* of Urdu, but these terms are not commonly used. Instead, in the vernacular Hindustani of Delhi, one finds terms used which indicate the particular specialty of the performer, such as *gawaiyā* (vocalist), *sitariyā, tabliyā, bīnkār, dhrupadiyā,* or *khayāliyā.* This is not to say that there is no conception of the category "musician." However, except for the anthropologist asking questions about "musicians," and in certain other instances, people tend not to subsume very different social entities under one rubric, or within one category. Thus, that very distinctive characteristic of Indian civilization, a highly refined sense of taxonomy, extends to the musical world as well. Where in the West the social identity "musician" will usually be an adequate enough response, in India that category would tell us little about an artist's *social identity,* and at best make his *status, role,* and *social rank* ambiguous. A word should be said here about how I am using these terms.

Social identity refers to any marker such as Hindu, Panjabī, disciple, woman, Brahman, *tabalchī* which is socially significant. Social tags are the names given to social identities. Thus the conceptions about being a tabla player constitute the social identity and *tabliya* is the tag. Sometimes a single social identity can have more than one tag. Thus *tabalchī* and *tabliya* are both tags referring to tabla players, but the former is derogatory while the latter is not. Social identities can contextually imply others. For example, the social identity *tawāif* implies in the context of music making a female vocalist or dancer. Some social identities, such as *Mīrāsī,* Kalawant, and Dhari, are specific to musicians; sociomusical identities are a subcategory of social identities and refer to musical stylistic social identities.

Role refers to the corresponding behavior of a particular social identity or clusters of social identities. In the context of musicians, *role* refers to the musical behaviors of given categories of musicians, for example, what the tabla player does during the performance.

Status refers to the rights and obligations associated with a given social identity. Thus for example, an accompanist can perform the role of a soloist—a sarangi player giving a solo recital— but he still has the social identity of an accompanist and the rights and obligations concomitant with that identity.

Social rank is used here in the way that *status* is ordinarily used. A social identity is always situated in a social hierarchy in some position (e.g., high, middle, low), which is its social rank.

The relationship between an individual's occupation on the

one hand and his social identity, role, status, and rank on the other has characteristically been very close in India. This is, after all, the way the caste system is often conceived. In the previous chapters, which have dealt explicitly with the cultural structure of musicians, occupation and social identity have been treated within the single category "musician." Actually, there is no such unified social category as "musician," although the evidence points to a closely shared system of knowledge and values about music. The product seems to be essentially the same but, so unusual in India, the producers are not.

Although I will define the particular types of musicians in their own contexts, at this point I would like to define briefly what I mean by *professional classical musician.* By *professional,* I mean someone who recognizes his primary vocation as the performance and/or teaching of music. With a few exceptions, it is implied that knowledge and performance of music are the major means of livelihood. This definition of *professional* is essentially analytic; it does not necessarily imply a measure of competence. I recognize that there are non-professionals who achieve a high degree of skill in music making. There used to be, as I shall show later, a high correspondence between the concept of a "professional" and the concept of a "hereditary" musician, but this is increasingly not the case.

By *classical* musician, I mean specifically one who plays music set within the framework of rāgs, and compositions set to tals. In practice this means that the individual musician performs in dhrupad or khayal or corresponding instrumental styles as the primary classical forms, in addition to such styles as thumri, ghazal, and tarana, as auxiliary forms.

As with musicians, there are a bewildering variety of nomenclatures and their uses for musical forms, sometimes with very distinct lacunae. For example, although *khayal* and *dhrupad* refer to the major forms of classical vocal music, there is no corresponding term for instrumental music, which is derived, but conceptually distinct, from vocal music. An announcement for a vocal recital over All India Radio, for instance, can be phrased: "Ustad Fayyaz Khan will sing a khayal in rāg *Todi.*" For an instrumentalist the announcer will have to refer to the particular move-

ments of the performance without reference to the whole: "Ustad Imdad Khan will play on the sitar, rag *Yaman,* alap, jor, jhala,
and a gat in *tīntāl.*"

Soloists and Accompanists

To be complete, a performance of art music requires a minimum
of two individuals—the leader and the accompanist. With rare
exceptions, the leader, whom I here call the soloist, provides the
melodic line, and the accompanist the rhythmic component.[3]
When the soloist is a vocalist, there will be one, sometimes two,
or even three *tānpūrās* (strummed lutes) providing drone accompaniment. Sometimes the vocalist will strum one of the tanpuras
as well. A vocal performance, other than dhrupad, includes a
melodic accompaniment. The melodic accompaniment has traditionally been performed on the sarangi, although the harmonium
is perhaps now even more commonly used. When the soloist is
an instrumentalist, there is often, but not always, drone accompaniment by a tanpura. When not, the instrumentalist uses side
strings called *chikārī* for this purpose as well as others. An instrumentalist will not be furnished melodic accompaniment by
another instrumentalist. However, one sometimes hears a performance by two instrumentalists, which is called jugalbandi (*lit.,*
"to tie a pair"). The two soloists usually play alternately; neither
is considered the accompanist of the other. They are both soloists, and in our terms the performance is a duet.[4]
    The roles of soloist and accompanist—the minimal re-
quirements for a musical performance—provide the basis for the
two major categories of musicians to be considered. There are
other reasons for their significance aside from the required functions of musicians in performance. Perhaps most importantly,
soloists and accompanists *tend to see themselves* and are conceived
by others as having fundamentally different social identities.
    The most apparent evidence for this difference is that a
musician's sociomusical identity is one or the other, but never
both. A vocalist or a solo instrumentalist will not be perceived as
an accompanist, and a sarangiya or tabliya will not be perceived

as a soloist.[5] This is not to say that the roles are not at times interchangeable. Accompanists will occasionally give solo performances on their instruments, but such an event is clearly exceptional. Ram Narayan is the only performer of an accompanying instrument (the sarangi) who has become exclusively a solo performer. He has within the last few years given up accompanying, a decision that initially was made with some risk.[6]

Soloists virtually never perform in public as accompanists, absolutely never on an accompanying instrument, and only exceptionally on their own instruments. Occasionally one hears a solo instrumentalist accompanying a vocalist—an event I have heard only twice, and in both instances, it was the bīn accompanying a vocalist singing dhrupad, in which style accompaniment had traditionally been practiced. The only other example I know is the occasions when Ustad Vilayat Khan accompanies himself on the sitar as he sings.

Individuals can and do move from one category to the other—only in one direction, however, and then only rarely. An accompanist will attempt to become a soloist, usually a vocalist, sometimes an instrumentalist. If he attempts to establish himself as a vocalist, he will abandon his role as accompanist.[7] A soloist does not attempt to become an accompanist.

Other differences emerge between soloist and accompanist as well. Not surprisingly, there is a marked difference in rank between soloists and accompanists. As we shall see, there is a stigma attached to the latter, just as there is prestige for the former in being the leader. It is also unlikely that intermarriage will occur between the offspring of accompanists and soloists, although there are some important exceptions.

There are two subclasses for each of the major categories presented above. Among soloists it is necessary to distinguish between vocalists and instrumentalists, for a variety of important reasons, some of which have already been indicated. Accompanists are also of two major types, according to their specialty: those who perform the role of melodic accompanist, the sarangiya, or harmonium player, and those who provide rhythmic accompaniment, the tabliya.

The distinction between vocalists and instrumentalists is

substantively one of the medium through which music is generated—voice the natural instrument, and other instruments which are "cultural." The distinction among accompanists, in contrast, relates more directly to the elements of musical expression: melody and rhythm. Social recruitment of soloists and accompanists works in the opposite manner, as we shall see. Soloists, unified musically, are recruited from a variety of groups, whereas accompanists, diversified musically, are recruited from identical groups. The most distinguishing characteristic of the soloist is that he is identified and identifies himself with an established, recognized, and named musical lineage. Accompanists, although coming from musical families and identifying themselves with musical lineages, are generally not so recognized by others.

From the external perspective of the larger society, there is little that distinguishes a solo vocalist socially from a solo instrumentalist. Both are musical artists of the tradition. Internally, they comprise largely separate but by no means exclusive groups. Groups identified as vocal include among their members solo instrumentalists. Similarly, groups that are defined by instrumental traditions have related vocalist members.

Vocalists

The thirteen vocalists whom I interviewed (see below, Table 1) all exhibit features which are included in the definition of vocalist. He or she: (1) has been trained in the tradition of classical vocal music and has performed in public; (2) is recognized by other musicians and musically knowledgeable individuals as a vocalist to the exclusion of other musician categories; (3) is primarily occupied with the performance of vocal music and/or derived vocations. Four vocations derived from and associated with the profession vocalist are (a) music teacher, (b) music scholar, (c) music producer (administrative position at All India Radio), and (d) tanpura player (a common activity for vocalists at A.I.R.). This definition excludes, for example, one man interviewed who had his training as a vocalist, but whose primary occupation is music scholarship. The reason for this exclusion is that he is not generally regarded as a vocalist, probably because he never performs in public. There is one music scholar on my list (No. 3), but he was considered a professional vocalist as well.

Given this definition, three kinds of vocalists can be distinguished on the basis of socially significant criteria. First are those who come from hereditary musician families whose members are mainly vocalists. Second are those who come from families of musicians, which, however, are not identified as originating in a vocal tradition. Third are persons who do not come from musician families, whom I refer to as non-hereditary musicians.

From the first type there are two musicians in Table 1, listed as Kalawants by caste. Their identity as Kalawant is used in at least two distinct ways. In the most general, it is translated as artist, and any musician can call himself a Kalawant by this definition. More precisely, however, the title Kalawant refers to members of certain established families of musicians who are defined by their descent from a well-known ancestor, and in whose pedigree there is no evidence of sarangi or tabla players.

Nowadays, Kalawant as a formal identity is largely restricted to families whose major specialty is vocal music. Formerly, instrumentalists descended from Tansen were also called Kalawants, but this custom ceased when Ustad Dabir Khan, the last descendant who practiced music, died in 1972. There are also certain families specializing in the dhrupad form of Indian art music who occasionally are referred to as Kalawants. In this sense, the title connotes the purity of their tradition and the artistry of the specialization. More characteristically, they are referred to as dhrupadiyas; their social organization will be considered separately.

Although *Kalawant* is now used in a categorical sense to refer to hereditary musician families specializing in vocal music, it is not a term by which they typically identify themselves. Their own identity is established by their descent in a particular family. All Kalawant families are connected to each other through potential or actual marriage relationships, and all the members of the Kalawants comprise a *birādarī* (in this context, "brotherhood") which is, however, not named. Kalawants are often considered the elite of the musical world because it is *their* families which are usually thought of as having carried on the artistic tradition of Indian classical music during the last few centuries.

Kalawants are always Muslims. They trace their descent from a founding ancestor or a sibling pair of ancestors. Descent is from father to son, and the lineage, as well as the descent group, is known as a *khāndān*. The genealogy given here illustrates the khandan of Ustad Wahid Hussein Khan.

Khandan of Ustad Wahid Hussein Khan (Khurja Khandan)

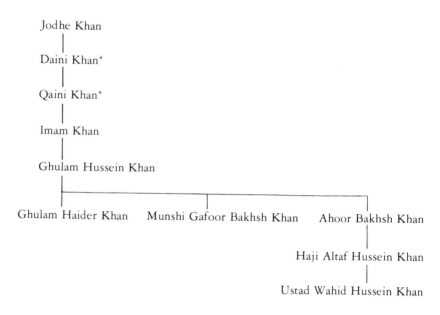

Jodhe Khan
|
Daini Khan*
|
Qaini Khan*
|
Imam Khan
|
Ghulam Hussein Khan

Ghulam Haider Khan   Munshi Gafoor Bakhsh Khan   Ahoor Bakhsh Khan
|
Haji Altaf Hussein Khan
|
Ustad Wahid Hussein Khan

This khandan is called Khurja khandan because Wahid Khan's ancestors originally came from Khurja, a small town in Uttar Pradesh, about fifty miles southeast of Delhi. If a khandan is named after a place, it usually corresponds to a recognized gharana, and the terms are sometimes used interchangeably, although they do not include the same range of connotations. Wahid Khan also used the term *Khurja gharana,* and his lineage is generally referred to in this way. Vilayat Hussein Khan's authoritative work on musicians and gharanas, *Sangitagyon ke Samsmaran* [In memorialization of musicians] devotes a section to the Khurja gharana, and gives the genealogy which corresponds to the one I collected, except for those ancestors (here marked by asterisk) whom he omits (1959:191–93).

Descent from father to son is significant only in certain prescribed conditions. The oldest direct patrilineal descendant of the khandan's founder(s) will be the *khalīfā*[8] of the khandan. His status is that of the head of the khandan, and of the gharana, regarding musical matters. His is the final authority, for example, if there is a dispute about how a rāg is to be performed in the style of that khandan. Other members of the khandan who are not direct patrilineal descendants are believed not to have received the total musical knowledge which is said to be passed on only from father to son. With respect to the stylistic inheritance of a particular khandan, only direct patrilineal descendants are considered fully authoritative.

A musician also traces his ancestry through his mother, and stresses its importance, especially if his mother has come from a distinguished khandan. Thus, although Wahid Khan states his sociomusical identity as the Khurja khandan, he also stresses the significance of his mother's ancestry, which goes directly back to Tanras Khan, founder of the original Delhi gharana. Wahid Khan is also, as illustrated in the genealogy, married to his first cousin, the daughter of his mother's brother (MBD).

Tanras Khan Khandan

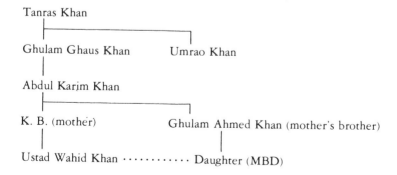

Marriage between close relations is preferred. Cousin marriages of all varieties are allowed in Islam, and all are practiced by Muslim musicians. Among Kalawants, the stated preference is to marry within the khandan, meaning in this context, all consanguineal relations.[9] Thus, for example, a man (ego) can marry a distant cousin even though he and his wife are related in this khandan only through their respective paternal grandmothers, and, if one considers patrilineal descent, they actually belong to different khandans (see accompanying illustration).

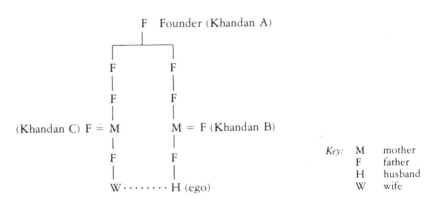

The situation is made more complex, however, by the fact of ancestral cousin marriage, so that individuals can be related in a number of ways. In the above example (which represents an actual situation), ego's wife is not only a parallel cousin of the fourth degree, but also his mother's brother's daughter (not illustrated). If she were not also descended, like her husband, from the founder of Khandan A, then she would be unrelated to him in terms of descent, which in certain situations—specifically the inheritance of musical knowledge—may be an important factor in decisions about whom to marry (see Chapter 5). For now, it is important to note only that the stated reason for marrying within the khandan is that it keeps the musical knowledge within the khandan.

No khandan is a closed system. Women are not always available, and at any given time each khandan exchanges women with other khandans. One can speak of exchanging women not only because the bride always goes to reside in the groom's household but also because, from any man's point of view, having his own daughters and sisters leave the khandan is less desirable than receiving women from other khandans. Since the male offspring belong to the father and carry on the musical tradition, sending daughters out to another khandan means the loss of her offspring to that khandan. Conversely, marrying a woman from another khandan has no negative effect, because she may bring in musical knowledge, and her children will belong to her husband's lineage. This is implicit in musicians' discussions when they use as an example not their sons or themselves, but their daughters. "My daughter can (or cannot) marry into that khandan."

According to Wahid Khan, there are four families of Kalawants who marry among themselves. In this context he uses the word *gharana,* for *gharana* is a more general and inclusive term than *khandan.* The four gharanas he names are Khurja, Delhi, Hapur, and Gwalior. However, Delhi has branched off (according to him) to form four derived but distinct gharanas: Delhi, Agra, Secundra, and Gwalior. If a woman is not available in the Khurja gharana, for example, a father looks to another gharana, the only stipulation being that the gharanas must be equal in rank. Or, as Wahid Khan put it, "If musicians do marry outside their gharana, they believe that after marriage the two gharanas become equal." The equality of rank must obtain between individuals as well (see Chapter 5).

Certain khandans systematically exchange women, with the result that the khandans join to form a larger khandan and a more inclusive gharana. Thus the Agra khandan has for several generations been exchanging women with the Atrauli khandan, and one now finds individuals who identify themselves sociomusically as Agra-Atrauli.

Kalawants say they never intermarry with musician families having sarangi or tabla players among their members, even if only as ancestors. A daughter of the Agra gharana, for example, is not even allowed to marry a famous sitarist because three or four generations back there were sarangiyas and tabliyas in his family.

Although Kalawants are now defined by the fact that they

are, as families, specialists in vocal music, they have instrumentalists in the family as well. In Wahid Khan's complete genealogy there are twenty-seven males listed, all of whom are musicians. Twenty-three of these are vocalists, two are sitarists, and two are both vocalist and sitarist. In Ustad Yunus Khan's genealogical chart there are thirty-seven vocalists and six sitarists, two of whom are also vocalists.

Aside from Kalawants, there is only one other kind of musician belonging to families specializing more or less exclusively in vocal music. These are women of the courtesan tradition. In the past, courtesans were sometimes kept as concubines of landowners or the nobility. Other courtesans of a less esteemed social position entertained in salons as singing and dancing girls. Not all courtesans are vocalists, but until the early part of this century virtually all female vocalists were courtesans.

Although there are now a growing number of women vocalists who do not come from hereditary families of musicians, most of the prominent women artists do. The latter have either been introduced to music by others or have inherited the specialty of vocal music from their mothers or other female relatives. The music itself, however, is formally acknowledged as having been learned from a guru or ustad; through this identity, female vocalists usually affiliate themselves with a gharana as well.

There are a number of terms to refer to a woman of this social category, but the most common around Delhi seems to be *tawaif*. She is addressed as *baijī* or *bai* is attached to the end of her name, so that a woman will be known, for example, as Mumtazbai. The connotations of *bai*, like those of English *dame*, depend on the locale where it is used. In Maharashtra, for example, *baijī* as a term of address is an honorific.

The male offspring of tawaifs are said to be acknowledged and cared for by their fathers. Some of these sons have risen to important positions. Their fathers, typically of the wealthy classes, were often influential in securing important positions for their offspring. Those who go on to become musicians are called *deredārs,* and although I was told such musicians exist, I never met one who identified himself as such. Tawaifs are also said to have a *panchāyat* (caste council), in Delhi currently headed by a male, according to my informants; but according to Crooke (1931:111), the leader of a tawaif panchayat is a woman. Other musicians, be they soloists or accompanists, say they will not take women from the tawaif community, nor allow their daughters to marry dere-dars. Occasionally, however, marriages are contracted between musicians and tawaifs.[10]

The daughters of these courtesan communities apparently inherit goods and even land from their mothers. They do not become instrumentalists of any sort, remaining exclusively within the vocal tradition.[11] They tend to specialize in the lighter varieties of Indian classical music such as thumri, dadra, and ghazal, although many also sing khayal, some only exclusively. They do not, however, sing in the dhrupad style. Although generally classed as courtesans, the eminent ones among them are highly respected by other musicians as well as by the larger musical circle. They are now said to marry with men of respectable families, although the exact status of these marriages is not always clear.[12]

A clear distinction is made between merely ordinary entertainers and professional singers. I interviewed one tawaif, a resident of G.B. Road (the now largely defunct red light district in Old Delhi), who is not recognized as a classical vocalist although she claims she can sing in the classical style. The primary distinction is her training, and the second is the context of her performances. If a tawaif has learned from a reputable ustad of an established gharana, then she can establish her own identity as being primarily a vocalist by profession. If she cannot claim to be a disciple, then her identity will be that of an entertainer, that is, a singer and/or dancer, which is subordinate to her primary identity as a courtesan, if not a common prostitute.

Although I have listed one woman as coming from a musician and particularly a vocalist family, strictly speaking this inheritance is not equivalent to that of Kalawant families. What is inherited is a specialty under the larger category of courtesan. Tawaifs will not ordinarily refer to their matrilineage in a musical context. Only exceptionally do they talk about female ancestors who were famous vocalists in a particular court, as other musicians speak of their great-grandfathers. Rather they go immediately to their gurus and ustads, identifying with that particular lineage. Nevertheless, I have classed them as members of families of musicians and vocalists because that specialty is indeed inherited. It is at any rate informally acknowledged that mothers do teach their daughters, although my informant stressed the fact that she had been formally initiated as a disciple and learned from both a guru and an ustad.[13]

The second type of vocalist, one who comes from a family of musicians which does not specialize in vocal music, is represented by three musicians in Table 1, all Muslims and all Mirasi by caste. In Delhi Mirasis are the predominant musician community in terms of having a distinctive caste identity. Musicians from this community are traditionally low in rank both socially and musically, in contrast to Kalawants, who are ranked much higher musically. Mirasi families specialize in the performance of sarangi and tabla, forming as a result a musician caste of accompanists. Historically, they are associated with the tawaif communities, serving as their accompanists in musical performance. This is the primary reason given for their low rank as a group.

Although Mirasi musicians have traditionally performed the role of accompanist, some of their members have gone on to become famous vocalists and instrumentalists. This transition has been especially true of sarangi players, who are knowledgeable about vocal performance styles since their function is to accompany vocalists.[14] They have also been the ustads of vocalists, particularly of their own sons who became vocalists and of female vocalists within the courtesan communities.

Perhaps the most important point about this transition is that it must be complete; one cannot have the status of both a sarangi player and a vocalist at the same time. V. H. Khan cites an interesting example.

There is one thing about the musical sittings which I still remember. Sarangi players were not allowed to take tanpura and sing. . . . in one such mehfil a sarangi player who sang very well started singing in the mehfil. The sabhāpati [musican event organizer or sponsor] asked him to stop singing and told him to stop playing the sarangi and then only would he be allowed to sing in all the mehfils. So he completely stopped playing sarangi and started singing. After that he was praised by good vocalists and became famous. By mentioning this I mean to say that in those days, music [sangīt] was the purest and highest form of education and it was very necessary to respect it. [1959:5]

Of the three Mirasi vocalists, only one is well known as such. The other two, although they are listed as vocalists and give occasional recitals over the radio, work primarily as tanpura players (see Chapter 6). The practicing vocalist is Ustad Chand Khan, the senior member of his khandan and a highly respected artist in India. The history of his family is worth repeating here, since it provides important perspectives on Mirasis.

Ustad Chand Khan is now in his eighties. He is the son of Ustad Mamman Khan (d. 1940), the founder of the current Delhi gharana, and a famous sarangi player of his own day. He is also the inventor of the *sursāgar,* a bass version of the sarangi, now very rare. No one in the immediate family plays the sarangi, although Chand Khan's brother's son, who is also his son-in-law, plays the violin. In contrast to most Mirasis, who usually do not want to be identified as such (one told me it was an insult to be called a Mirasi), Chand Khan has argued that the Mirasi identity is, or should be, a high and honorable one and that musicians are silly to try to hide it. The summary of his published pamphlet on the subject (the text of an address given at the urs of his father) is relevant here.[15]

Ustad Chand Khan's father traces his ancestry back to Amir Fakhar Quraishi, who came to India with Mohammad Bin Qasim, the conqueror of Sind in A.D. 712. He was awarded the title *Abdul Islah* and given the job of "divider of inheritance." "Inheritance" is *mīrās* (also *wīrāsāt*) in Arabic, so the ancestor and his descendants came to be known as Mirasi. They were also entitled to use the word *Amir* or *Mir* before their names. The use of both *Mir* and *Khan* with the names of eminent musicians of India˙ and Pakistan is evidence of the connection between them and the Quraishi clan of the Arabs. Chand Khan also traces his father's mother's ancestry back to Amir Fakhar Quraishi; hence both sides of the family are descended from the same ancestor at the beginning of the eighth century.[16]

As I have mentioned, families of musicians who have sarangi or tabla players among them, either in the past or in the present, will not be recognized as Kalawants. Ustad Chand Khan does not claim a Kalawant identity, but he insists that his family represents the oldest gharana in India and that others have tried to underrate the importance of this gharana because of its association with sarangi. He considers such scorn nonsense, because, according to him, the sarangi is the oldest instrument, and in the hands of a master is capable of the finest music. As evidence he offers his own father's mastery of the instrument, as well as that of his cousin, the great Bundu Khan, who was one of the musical giants of his day.[17] He also presents evidence that his family has a long tradition of vocal music as well as bīn and *rabāb*.

The Delhi gharana of Chand Khan is still in the process of establishing itself. Although members of Chand Khan's family call themselves members of the Delhi gharana, some other musicians and connoisseurs do not completely recognize this claim. It is not, however, because they are Mirasi, because there are certain other recognized gharanas whose leading members in recent times were Mirasis. There are, however, still other conditions for becoming a gharana, which this khandan, according to some, does not completely fulfill. These conditions will be examined in detail in the next chapter.

Six persons on the list of vocalists do not come from hereditary musician families. They are all Brahmans, and, as I have indicated, knowledge of music is a traditional mode for Brahman study. Three of them have pursued music scholarship as well as performance.

Before the coming of the Muslims, cultivated music was the prerogative of Brahmans, who performed in the context of the temple and only secondarily in the context of the court. Tansen was a Brahman who, when he entered the court, apparently became a Muslim. According to Ustad Zia M. Dagar, Gopal Das, founder of his khandan, was originally a Saraswat Brahman from Uttar Pradesh. He recounts the conditions leading to Gopal Das's conversion:

> In the Darbar of Rangile Shah, he went to sing. There he was presented with gold, pearls, and together with these things pān was kept. And it so happens that giving pān is a good custom, and is given when one is pleased by someone. So one cannot throw the pān

away, that is an insult to the King, so Gopal Das ate the pān. Now all
the disciples started saying, "Guruji, you have been polluted"
[*bhrisht, lit.,* "parched"]. Now you are converted. Then Gopal Das
said it is natural to eat pān, there is nothing in it. But they kept
saying, "No, no." In those days singing was taught in ashrams. So he,
Gopal Das, said, "If you say so, then I am a Muslim." So he changed
his name to Imam Bakhsh. He took it after some good pir, like
Imam Hussein. *Imam* means "Khalifa."

There is no evidence that music was a hereditary profession among Brahmans, in the pre- and early Islamic era, although
as a specialty it was inherited, at least in South India.[18] As I have
indicated, the professionalization of art music as a hereditary
occupation apparently began only with the coming of the Muslims. With two qualified exceptions, all gharanas have been
founded by Muslims. The only Hindu hereditary traditions are
the Banaras baj (style) of tabla playing and the Vishnupur gharana of dhrupad singers (and later) instrumentalists. In both these
cases, the Hindu founders learned their art from Muslim ustads
(Roach 1972:30; cf. Shepard 1976; Owens 1969).

The oldest, and in that sense the most prestigious, gharana
is the Gwalior gharana, which was founded by two brothers,
Haddu Khan and Hassu Khan, around the middle of the nineteenth century. Haddu Khan and Hassu Khan had a number of
Hindu disciples, most of them Brahmans, from Maharashtra
(Khan 1959:149). According to V. H. Khan, Balkrishna Bua
Ichalkaranjikar, a disciple of both brothers, made the Gwalior
gharana famous (ibid.:150). One of his students was Vishnu Digambar Paluskar, who along with Bhatkhande is credited with
the revitalization of Indian classical music in this century. Most
of the famous Hindu vocalists until the first half of this century
were identified with this gharana. From 1922, with the death of
Rehmat Khan (son of Haddu Khan), until the present time, the
Gwalior gharana—as represented by its noted vocalists—has
been almost entirely Hindu (see Misra 1955:114–22).

There are a very few, little-known cases where hereditary
Muslim musicians have converted back to Hinduism, or at least
they present themselves as Hindus by calling themselves pandit
and worshipping in temples. Their Muslim origins are known

only to their brother musicians, whose community they have left. This appears to be an entirely post-Partition (after 1947) phenomenon.[19]

To sum up, then, vocalists come from three major kinds of social backgrounds. The first two comprise social groups: families specializing in vocal music, including Kalawants and tawaifs, and Mirasi families specializing in sarangi and tabla performance. The third derives largely from various Brahman groups.

Some vocalists with a tradition of scholarship, others with a wide reputation, and still others with both, will be found teaching in institutions or in administrative positions, especially at All India Radio. Those who have little or no educational background are occupied either teaching privately or as staff artists at A.I.R. in the role of tanpura players.

Vocalists in India are in a position somewhat similar to that of pianists in the West. There are many of them, and they are so highly specialized musically that there is a greater supply than demand. Whereas accompanists are much in demand, and solo instrumentalists are more able to adapt—by working in orchestras at A.I.R. or in the entertainment industry—vocalists are limited to solo concert performance so that there is great competition for an overcrowded niche. This situation, coupled with the fact that nowadays instrumental soloists are the stars of the musical world, makes it particularly difficult for vocalists who are not stars to succeed.

Instrumentalists

The instrumentalists discussed here are mainly sitar players (sitariyas) and sarod players (sarodiyas). The reason for this focus is that only sitariyas and sarodiyas have social and cultural traditions as instrumentalists which predate the present century. Bīn players (binkars) also have a long social and cultural history, but they are closely tied to the dhrupad vocal tradition and therefore will be treated separately.

Sitariyas and Sarodiyas. The sitar and sarod are the primary instruments for the performance of instrumental classical music.

Indeed, with the exception of Bismillah Khan, the Shahnai artist, virtually all the luminaries among instrumental soloists are either sitariyas or sarodiyas. The musicians who perform on these instruments are considered together here since culturally they constitute essentially one category—performers of plucked instruments—much as vocalists constitute another category.

Culturally, they share many characteristics, the most important being a similar instrumental style. Although the historical development of each instrument occurred independently, the instrumental performance style for each derives from a common source, that of the bīn style. They share other musical traditions as well. Sitarists can learn and have learned from sarod masters, sarodists have learned from sitarists, and both have learned from binkars. As with vocalists, family traditions and related stylistic schools exist. Sometimes these correspond with one or another of the instruments being considered, but in all cases they are connected in time to common sources.

In contrast to the three subsets of vocalists enumerated above, instrumentalists comprise only two which are socially significant. First are the instrumentalists who have been born into a family of instrumentalists and who are said to inherit the traditional repertoire and style of their ancestors. Like Kalawants, they are referred to as khandani musicians, with the compositions or style characteristic of the khandan, termed *khas khandani.*

Second are non-hereditary instrumentalists who are "adopted" by becoming disciples to ustads who are khandani musicians. Such an individual will have the distinguishing stylistic features of his or her ustad's family tradition. This kind of musician is then able to present a musical selection which is considered khas khandani, even though he is not a khandani musician himself.

The most important difference between the sociomusical identity of the vocalist and that of the instrumentalist is that whereas the former may derive from any one of more than a dozen gharanas, the latter is limited to one. Virtually all instrumentalists belong in one sense or another to the Seniya gharana, which is named after the revered Tansen.

Strictly speaking, gharanas were limited originally to vocal lineages and their associated styles, and Deshpande still considers only vocal traditions in his book on gharanas (Deshpande 1973; see also Powers 1979). The reason is that vocal music has always been considered the highest form of music, with instrumental forms subordinate to it. In practice, however, instrumental music in the north seems currently the predominant form, as gauged by the popularity of outstanding musicians like Ali Akbar Khan, Vilayat Khan, and Ravi Shankar.

Although no musician alive today can claim a direct genea-logical connection to Tansen, indirect connections are traced via the guru-disciple tradition by most musicians.[20] Perhaps because there is a common claim to Seniya status by virtually all instru-mentalists, it serves as a meaningful sociomusical identity only to a limited degree. To the extent that association with the Seniya tradition is used, it is in the sense that some musicians are more Seniya than others. If, for example, a musician studied with an authentic Seniya, his status and musical authority carry more weight than one who has studied with the disciple of an authentic Seniya.

The more relevant sociomusical identity of an instrumental-ist is his or her ustad's immediate and incontrovertible ancestry—the khandan. Some khandans are more famous and prestigious than others. The reasons vary, but the major criterion is the repu-tation of the leading representative(s). For a khandan to be estab-lished and continued as a distinct and recognized tradition, it must, as with vocal gharanas, have a continual line of charismatic representatives; musicians who have what Max Weber describes as "an extraordinary, at least not generally available, quality [which] adheres to the person." Weber continues: " 'Clan charisma' [for "clan" read "khandan"] means that this extraordinary quality ad-heres to sib members per se and not, as originally to a single person" (Weber 1958:49).

Instrumentalists coming from musical families detail their pedigrees, stress their genealogical depth, their famous ancestors, and in some cases accentuate the fact that either the sitar or the sarod—one to the exclusion of the other—has been a family specialty for a given number of generations. Nevertheless, one finds now, as in the past, khandani musicians going outside their khandans for ustads and gurus, and in some cases acknowledging them as their primary teachers. A good example of this in the recent past is Hafeez Ali Khan (d. 1972), whose sarod style is one of the two major kinds performed in India now. He was descended from a line of sarodists and rabab players going back three generations. His great-grandfather, Ghulam Bandagi Khan Bangash, was a rabab player who came to India from Afghanistan. Hafeez Ali Khan's father and uncles were also instrumentalists, but Hafeez Ali Khan received much of his instrumental training from Ustad Wazir Khan, the great binkar and chief musician at the Court of Rampur. Because of this discipleship, Hafeez Ali Khan, his disciples, and indeed his own particular style of sarod playing are all associated with both Wazir Khan and the Tansen gharana, as Wazir Khan was a direct descendant of Tansen's daughter.

Musicians outside the khandan will also trace connections to the charismatic gravity points of outstanding musical personalities. Radika Mohan Moitra, for example, studied sarod with a renowned disciple of Hafeez Ali Khan's father's brother, Murad Ali Khan. But his sociomusical identity is with Hafeez Ali Khan, although he always acknowledges his own discipleship to his own guru.

What we find, then, are musicians who, in the absence of discrete gharanas characteristic of vocalists, identify with and claim representation of stylistic schools which are identified with, but not named after, their originators. There is no Hafeez Ali Khan gharana, or Allaudin Khan gharana as such, but one often hears association with the gharana of so-and-so, whoever it might be. In this way *gharana* covers a multiplicity of meanings, enveloping ever larger sociomusical identity categories. When Radika Mohan Moitra says he belongs to the gharana of Hafeez Ali Khan, *gharana* can have several connotations. The first is the particular style of sarod playing characteristic of Hafeez Ali Khan's khandan. This includes, among other features, the particular technique of playing the sarod. The second includes association with Hafeez Ali Khan's ustad, the great Ustad Wazir Khan. Purnima Sinha has characterized one of the two major instrumental styles as "Uzir Khani," named after Ustad Wazir Khan (1970:45). Although this is not a generally accepted or

Ustad Ali Akbar Khan announcing the rāg he is about to perform at the Hardballabh Music Conference. He is accompanied on the tabla by Shankar Ghosh.

named style, association with Wazir Khan because of his prominence, as well as his Seniya heritage, makes the identification significant. The third and final link reverts to Tansen through Wazir Khan, who, as noted, was considered a direct descendant through his daughter Saraswati (see Table 24).

These different levels of identity are utilized by instrumentalists in different contexts. Because of the diversity of instrumental khandans, more general categories are utilized for public announcements. Depending on the particular context as well as the individual musician, the ustad will be named, with perhaps a genealogical synopsis of his connection to Tansen, and, on some occasions, with a detailed pedigree.

Ustad Hafeez Ali Khan as a young man. He and Ustad Allaudin Khan
were the outstanding sarod players of their day, and their sons, Amjad
Ali Khan and Ali Akbar Khan, respectively, are considered the major
sarodists today.

Ustad Amjad Ali Khan performing on the sarod at the Hardballabh
Music Conference. He is accompanied by Ustad Latif Ahmed Khan on
the tabla. Both artists live in Delhi. The tanpura player in the background is a disciple of Amjad Ali Khan.

Among instrumentalists one does not find neat, homogeneous ethnic categories corresponding to particular gharanas or khandans. Musicians from hereditary families are almost always Muslims, particularly if they come from families of instrumental specialists. Distinctions between instrumentalists coming from vocal and accompanist backgrounds are, in certain cases, virtually irrelevant. One outstanding sitarist, for example, has sarangiyas and tabliyas in his family; but his own personal prestige is very high—he is one of the most respected instrumentalists in India—in part, because he can trace a rather direct, recent, and publicly known discipleship connection to the Seniya tradition.

The social background of other Muslim instrumentalists is usually obscure. In some cases connections are traced outside India, a practice that seems to be characteristic of certain sarod khandans, who sometimes trace their origins to rabab players from Afghanistan (Sen 1972:274–82). Sitarists tend to begin their family line with binkars who were disciples of established ustads. Sometimes social backgrounds can be roughly inferred. For example, one musician belongs to a family of sitarists and binkars, although it is not recognized as a Kalawant lineage. His great-grandfather, with whom the line starts, studied with Bande Ali Khan, the famous binkar, who also taught sarangi. This fact and certain other evidence suggests that this family has a Mirasi, or at least an equivalently modest, musical background.

Non-hereditary musicians are usually Hindus and often Brahmans, although there are also two Kayasths (the traditional caste of scribes) on the list—one a sitarist and the other a sarodist (see Tables 2 and 3). Two of the persons listed come from *zamīndār* (landlord) families and learned music from musicians in their household employ.[21] Of the Brahman instrumentalists listed, one is professional only in a qualified sense. He gives public performances and is an occasional artist at A.I.R. However, his main source of income is a poultry business, although he would like eventually to become a full-fledged performer. Other instrumentalists, not from hereditary families, teach either in music departments in a university or in music colleges. Two sitarists and two sarodists are not institutionally related on a regular basis, relying solely on concert engagements and students. One sarodist was a music producer at A.I.R. but recently retired to an ascetic life, and two sitarists are staff artists at A.I.R. Others are only marginally employed. One sitarist has just started playing in a hotel orchestra, while another claimed to give private lessons. Another sarodist performs occasionally over A.I.R. These last three come from families of sarangiyas and tabliyas, and at least in the case of the sarodist, it was the explicit intention of the father to have the son move out of the sarangi class into the solo instrumental class.

What we find with instrumental soloists, especially the younger generation, is a primary sociomusical identity with each one's particular ustad or ustads. The outstanding personalities in the musical world are sitarists and sarodists, several having become stars for the public at large. Instrumentalists will not overstress their genealogical music inheritance, if they can advertise the prestige of having studied with an especially famous ustad. Since sitar and sarod performers are usually the drawing cards at musical festivals, part of the strategy of making a name is to align oneself with a famous performer. For example, those who come from accompanist family backgrounds often claim as ustad, not, as they could, their father but someone famous from whom they have learned.

A young, rising sitarist, coming from a family of instrumentalists (although not a famous one), acknowledges his learning from Ravi Shankar. He describes the court life of his grandfather's days "when musicians had a very simple way of living . . . and they mainly used to sing the praise of their patrons." He feels now that musicians are "in the public eye," they must behave accordingly:

> Now it is different. The personality of the musician is more important. If you like me and respect me, then you would come to me. I met you for the first time a few days back. I can't say about your feelings of what you thought of me, but I feel you must have thought that this man is wearing nice clothes and has a good personality. That is why you have come to me. This is entirely due to Pandit Ravi Shankar and Ustad Vilayat Khan.

Other Instrumentalists. Quite a few other instruments (see Table 6) are now utilized for the performance of classical music. The shahnai is commonly heard, but its rise to the status of classical instrument is very recent, being due almost entirely to the successful efforts of Ustad Bismillah Khan. Earlier the shahnai was not taken seriously as a concert instrument. One of my informants recalls that a famous tabla player was asked to accompany a shahnai player at a music conference in Lucknow many years ago. At first he refused, insulted that he should be asked to accompany a shahnai player whose job, after all, was to play at weddings. He finally relented, but agreed to play only on the bayan (the left-hand drum), not on the (right-hand) tabla.[22]

The violin, although part of the South Indian (Karnatak) music tradition at least since 1784 (Sambamoorthy 1971:III, 99) and now a major solo and accompanying concert instrument there, has never assumed a very important role in the Hindustani music tradition. Perhaps it is because the sarangi, already present, left little room for the violin. In South India, there is no bowed instrument in the classical tradition aside from the violin.[23] Whatever the reason, the violin in the North is almost always used as a solo instrument, sometimes in duet, but rarely as accompaniment.

The three violinists I interviewed come from a diversity of backgrounds. Zahoor Khan is the son-in-law (and nephew) of Chand Khan. Another violinist, Mr. Gulati, was actually first trained in Western music, having studied the violin in Europe before returning. He then studied classical Indian music with a vocalist, and has just retired as leader and composer/arranger for an orchestra playing Indian style music in the Asoka Hotel in Delhi. Another violinist, Satyadev Pawar, a disciple of Ravi Shankar and a staff artist at A.I.R., gives recitals in public in addition to being a member of the All India Radio Orchestra. Only Zahoor Khan comes from a hereditary musician family.

The *bānsrī* (flute) is another increasingly popular instrument heard in the performance of art music. Again its "classical" status, like that of the shahnai, is due principally to one man, the late Pannalal Ghosh. Largely self-taught, he started studying with Ustad Allauddin Khan at the age of thirty-seven, and was the teacher of several flutists performing today. Although there are none on my list, one renowned performer, Prakash Wadera, is a noted music critic.

Other instruments occasionally heard today, mainly over A.I.R., are the *dilrubā* and *esrāj*—fretted, bowed instruments from the Panjab and Bengal respectively. There are two dilruba players on my list, both from Panjab and both working at A.I.R. Delhi. Neither comes from a musician family. One is a Brahman who studied music first with his father, an amateur vocalist who was a printing press operator, and then the vocal and dilruba techniques from a professional vocalist also from Panjab.

The one esraj player on the list is the son of a sarangi player. In 1969, he was still at the learning stage, but now he has concertized outside of India and performs as a freelance artist. He was taught the esraj by his father, but has developed his own technique on the instrument based, he says, on the sarangi style of playing.

The *vichitr vīnā* (unfretted stick zither stopped with a smooth, egg-shaped piece of glass) was developed at the beginning of this century. It is said to have had a predecessor called *mahanātakām vīnā*. To this instrument, two gourds were added by a musical instrument dealer in Delhi. He presented it to a famous sarangi player, Ustad Abdul Aziz Khan of Patiala, who named it vichitr vina (Sen 1972:160–64). Ustad Ahmed Reza Khan, a disciple of Abdul Aziz Khan and probably the foremost performer on this instrument today, is one of the vichitr vina players listed in Table 6. From Moradabad and related to Ustad Sabri Khan, he also plays the sarangi and is a staff artist at A.I.R. Ramesh Prem, the other vichitr vina player, lives in Bombay. His is not a hereditary musician background, but in his training from a disciple of Abdul Aziz Khan he learned the technique of vichitr vina. He also studied with Jivan Lal Mattoo, from whom he learned music theory. He gives public performances, but his livelihood comes from composing and recording advertising music over the radio.

There is also one guitarist on my list. He performs classical music on the electric guitar with a slide, "Hawaiian" style. He is a fourth generation Christian whose family were originally Muslims. A staff artist at A.I.R., he also leads a band in the performance of popular music for engagements which he books. He has a few students and was himself a student of Ahmed Reza, the vichitr vina player.

Ramesh Prem of Bombay performing on the vichitr vina.

Ustad Asad Ali Khan performing on his bīn.

Ustad Zia Mohiuddin Dagar in concert at the University of Washington, Seattle, in 1979.

Ustad Sabri Khan with his sarangi. The instrument has three main playing strings, which are bowed, and thirty-five to forty sympathetic strings located beneath and to the side of the main strings. The resonance of the sympathetic strings gives the sound of the sarangi its shimmering quality.

This completes the list of instrumentalists performing Hindustani classical music. One other instrumental specialty, the bīn, requires special attention.

Binkars. Certain families have specialized for several generations in the performance of the dhrupad style, which is characterized as being very old, very serious, and eminently traditional. The texts of dhrupads are typically spiritual in theme and Hindu in subject. Along with singers of dhrupad (dhrupadiyas) there have also been binkars coming from the same family traditions and performing in the same style. The dhrupad style, whether sung or played, is invariably accompanied by the pakhawaj, as the *bols* (*lit.,* "words") of this barrel drum are compatible with dhrupad bols, whereas the tabla bols are not.[24]

Most musicians, particularly soloists, trace their descent via the guru-disciple tradition or genealogically from some ancestor who was either a dhrupadiya or binkar or both, claiming as their own a style which has developed directly from this tradition. As in sitar and sarod technique, many elements are said to have been borrowed from the performance practices of binkars.

In terms of a traditional perspective, dhrupad specialists enjoy great prestige as artists. The dhrupad has its origins in the music of the temple, is cultivated by Brahmans and maintained, it is believed, close to its original forms. Those who perform it today see themselves as the last of their kind. Actually, there is only one family, called Dagar, whose members are dhrupad specialists. It is also a khandan, which claims its own heritage and pedigree separate from that of Tansen. At least one of its members makes a distinction between khandani musicians who can trace their ancestry far back, and relative newcomers who are known as *shāgirdī,* that is, disciples of a khandani tradition.

Although there are no dhrupad vocalists on my lists, there are four binkars, two of whom, Ustad Zia M. Dagar and Ustad Asad Ali Khan, come from a long and distinguished family of musicians. Shamsuddin Farriddi performs on sitar and bīn. The late Birendra Kishore Roychoudhury, a former zamindar and a renowned scholar who published widely on Indian music, was highly respected for his knowledge of the older traditions of music. Aside from the bīn, he played the sursringār (a bass version of the sarod) and the rabab.

Dhrupadiyas and binkars are identified with one of four traditional dhrupad styles (*bānī*), known as *dāgārbānī, khāndārbānī, nauhārbānī,* and *gaudhārbānī.* They are thought to be the precursors of gharana styles, and the ancestors of today's khandani musicians are said to have been specialists in at least one of them.

Asad Ali Khan is the only bīn performer in the Khandarbani style. Originally from Rajasthan, his ancestors were court musicians in Alwar and Jaipur, and his father was one of the outstanding artists at Rampur. At the time of my initial fieldwork, Asad Ali Khan was a highly respected artist but known only to relatively few connoisseurs. Since that time he has concertized more widely, going abroad as well. In 1977 he was awarded the prestigious Sangeet Natak award, which formally established his position as a top-ranked musician in India.

Zia Mohiuddin Dagar lives in Bombay, but has spent part of the last several years teaching in the United States. He is a member of the famous Dagar family, which takes its name from the dagarbani, the style of dhrupad in which the members perform. Zia M. Dagar is the only bīn player in the family today, all others being vocalists.

If there is a resurgence of interest in the bīn, it is due primarily to Zia M. Dagar and Asad Ali Khan. They are now the only regularly concertizing bīn players in India, and both have had very enthusiastic receptions to their performances abroad. Dhrupad in general, and the bīn in particular, are considered esoteric in India; somewhat paradoxically, there has been much interest in this tradition in the West.

Accompanists

From a sociological perspective, accompanists comprise perhaps the most interesting type of musician. Of the numerous reasons for this, the most important is that their caste identity corresponds in most instances to their actual occupation. Whereas soloists come from a fairly wide variety of ethnic, caste, regional, and religious backgrounds, accompanists tend much more to be members of specific occupational groups.

Recognized and named gharanas are specific sociomusical identities which are properly those of soloists. Some accompanists, notably tabla players, will be said to perform in a given baj. A baj is distinguished from a gharana in that the former does not require a genealogical history although it may have one. *Baj* is derived from the verb *bajnā,* "to hit or beat," and is used by sitarists and sarodists as well. Perhaps the most precise translation of *baj* is "technical style," meaning a style of performance that is a result of the particular manner in which the instrument is hit or struck. Sarangiyas may claim a gharana identity, but other musicians typically do not recognize this claim. Put another way, the soloist as artist inherits an artistic tradition which includes not only the style of that tradition, but also its heritage. The accompanist is an artisan who inherits an occupation (that of accompanist), and although he may execute his work in a number of styles, his heritage is largely seen by others more in the nature of the work itself, and less in what is actually produced.

Although accompanists are as a social category the same kind of person, musically they perform two distinct roles: that of the rhythmic accompanist, almost always a tabla player and that of melodic accompanist, traditionally a sarangi player.

Sarangiyas. The sarangi, although ubiquitous in Hindustani vocal performances, is an instrument little known outside the circle of those who perform on it.[25] It is also a folk instrument in India, although the folk varieties are somewhat smaller than those used in classical music and do not always have sympathetic strings. It is not known for certain when the sarangi first appeared in the performance of classical music. There is no mention of sarangi players in Akbar's court, although the instrument is mentioned in the *Ain-i-Akbari* (cf. Fazl 1948). In Francis Gladwin's translation of the same work, the "Saringee" is said to also be called *Soorbotan.* The subsequent description of the instrument, however, leaves no doubt that it was very different from the modern sarangi, for it "is the shape of a bow, with two hollow cups inverted at each end. It has one string of gut, resembling a bow-string.

They hold under the string a small gourd, and play with a plectrum" (Gladwin 1965:206). Augustus Willard's work, first published in 1834, describes the sarangi as the "Hindustanee fiddle, a modern invention" (Tagore 1965:viii). He includes the sarangi as part of the royal ensemble (*naubut*) and gives a more detailed description of its construction, tuning, and playing style (ibid.:92, 94, 96–97). Sarangi players are mentioned in large numbers by the middle of the nineteenth century (Imam 1959a:22,24).

The sarangi is now used primarily to accompany vocal performances of khayal, thumri, ghazal and other idioms, but almost never to accompany a dhrupad performance. From all available evidence, the use of the sarangi in the art music tradition accompanies the rise of the khayal form of vocal music (Mattoo 1969). The ascendancy of khayal apparently begins in the court of Mohammed Shah Rangile (1719–1748), and regular sarangi accompaniment probably does not antedate his time. This is corroborated by the recent publication of Sharar, who wrote that the sarangi was invented by Mian Sarang, a musician in Mohammed Shah Rangile's court (1975:140).

The role of the sarangiya is principally to echo the melodic line of the vocalist, resulting in a heterophonic display. A good sarangi accompaniment is measured by how quickly and accurately the sarangiya can copy what the vocalist produces. Many vocalists do not utilize sarangi accompaniment, saying that the sarangi is too loud and that sarangiyas cannot play in tune, this in spite of the fact that the sarangi is said to have been introduced to help keep singers in tune (Sharar 1975:140).[26] Vocalists also complain that sarangiyas try to play their own music rather than just provide the accompaniment (Keshkar 1967:22).

Vocalists who utilize sarangi accompaniment (and/or harmonium) often have their favorite accompanists. Thus, when vocalists come to Delhi to give a concert, some are regularly seen with the same accompanist. A particular accompanist may be known as an expert thumri accompanist, and vocalists who specialize in or are known primarily for their thumri singing will ask specifically for him as accompanist.

There are, however, no named or generally recognized sarangi styles. That is, those who are not sarangi players have no specific sense of sarangi styles and traditions, only the concept of a good accompanist or a merely mediocre one. Sarangi players do employ several different kinds of techniques in their performance practices, but these are not generalized as a style, remaining essentially idiosyncratic.

Sarangi players are not usually recognized by others as being authorities on musical theory, although they themselves claim to be so. This does not mean that some of them are not considered great musicians. Ustad Bade Ghulam Sabir was famous as a sarangi player not only because he performed beautiful music, both solo and accompaniment, but also because he would sometimes not know the name of the rāg he was performing. This would be equivalent to Yehudi Menuhin performing the Beethoven violin concerto without knowing which key it is in. The story is perhaps exaggerated, but it does point out the way in which sarangiyas' theoretical knowledge is regarded. If they are known to have theoretical expertise, it is usually because they have been disciples of soloists, who may or may not be members of their own community.

Some sarangiyas are said to be knowledgeable because they have had considerable experience providing accompaniment to vocalists. They say that since they accompany so many different vocalists, they acquire experience in a variety of styles and can thus perform solo recitals in any style, that is, of any gharana. Knowing the style, the rāg, and the compositions in a performance sense (rather than a theoretical one) is important, since the skill of sarangi accompaniment depends on the degree to which the sarangiya can anticipate and immediately duplicate what the vocalist does.

Accompanist knowledge, therefore, is different from soloist knowledge. The sarangiya must, in essence, know the formulas well enough to duplicate them without taking time to think about them. Yet he does not have to know the music in a creative sense. He is not required to develop a rāg, or a series of tans in a particular manner—although sarangiyas can do this—but he must be able to follow the vocalist, which involves having a "theory" of what the vocalist will do. As a craftsman he must be skilled technically, minimally as much as the vocalist, and according to sarangiyas more so, since the replication must be immediate. Indeed, sarangiyas claim that accompaniment requires much more expertise than performing solo on the sarangi.

Tabliyas. The rhythmic dimension in Indian music is its own universe, even though all musicians ideally are expected to study some tabla and be able minimally to play the *ṭhekās* of the major tals. In the same way, tabla players are said to have some vocal training, although their knowledge of rāgs is not expected to be profound. My own observations bear this out. During concerts when I have inquired about the rāg, the tabla players sometimes are not sure which rāg is being performed or must think a moment before answering.

It seems appropriate first to summarize what is generally known regarding the musical role of the tabla. Essentially, the tabla player provides the theka, the skeletal framework of a particular rhythmic cycle. He accompanies only those musical sections which include composed pieces, such as a gat. Thus, during a long alap, the tabla player sits next to the soloist and waits until it is finished before he is able to execute his role. However, in actual performance practice, the tabla player does much more than just provide the theka. If given the opportunity, he performs his own improvisations, while the soloist plays the composed piece set to that particular cycle.

Tabla accompaniment is indispensable; and in contrast to the sarangi, no other rhythmic instrument can be substituted for it. Tabla is mandatory as the drum accompaniment for all Hindustani musical performances (as well as for dance, i.e., Katthak) except dhrupad and shahnai performances.

Again, in contrast to sarangi performance, there is a well-developed solo repertoire, with solo performances on the tabla sometimes being presented as separate features in a music program. A good tabla player is in part defined by his knowledge of improvisational techniques, and most soloists desire a tabla player who can provide a virtuoso display during the tabla solo interludes.[27]

Tabla performance implies—when it is more than just providing the theka—extensive knowledge. Veterans are known to have an extensive repertoire in a variety of forms such as *qāydā, peshkār,* and gat. There are stories of tabla players who have given performances for hours without ever repeating an identical phrase (e.g., see Roach 1972). As we shall see, the role of the tabla player is becoming increasingly important and seems to be undergoing a distinct change from his past role as primarily an accompanist.

The Social Organization of Accompanists

Sarangiyas and tabliyas are associated by outsiders with dancing girls, tawaifs and brothels, and because of this association there is a stigma attached to being a sarangi or tabla player. These two kinds of accompanists are found in association not only with the dancing and singing girl tradition, but almost always with each other. That is, they usually are members of a particular social group whose primary identity is defined by the occupations of sarangi and tabla performance. One is not found without the other.

In North India there are two communities, one of them Muslim (the aforementioned Mirasi) and the other Hindu (known as Katthak), who together have contributed the vast majority of Hindustani accompanists. The Mirasi are found in the North around Delhi and the Katthak are in Eastern Uttar Pradesh, with a large concentration in Banaras. My concern is primarily the Mirasi for the main reason that they are represented in Delhi.

The Ethnography of Mirasi Musicians in Delhi. The term *Mirasi* is used today in several different ways, but like *Kalawants,* it is rarely used by those to whom it is applied. Rather, if asked what his *jāti* (caste) is, a Mirasi will often reply by giving his religion, i.e., *Musalmān,* the caste category, *Shaikh,* or the subcategory *Shaikh Qurāishī.*[28] Claiming Shaikh identity implies that one's origins are outside India, and, by extension, that one is not descended from converted groups. Quraishi is said by some Mirasis to be a "family" from Arabia from which they are descended. Others know that this is the tribe to which Muhammad belonged. In fact, since *Shaikh* has this extraterritorial implication, many indigenous Muslim converts used that title in the past.

Because this strategy is also commonly known, the interpretation of that title is often the opposite of what is intended, a point already reported by H. A. Rose at the end of the last century (1970:III, 399).

Others who are not Mirasis do not take these claims seriously. One Kalawant, in the presence of a Mirasi friend, said that the name Quraishi "was adopted by them thirty or forty years back." Mirasis themselves sometimes admit to having a Hindu ancestry, even after reciting their ancestry from non-Indian Muslims. Indeed, one musician related his Quraishi origins on one occasion, only to describe his ancestors as Hindu on another:

> There weren't any Muslims in Hindustan before, and our ancestors, perhaps, were Hindus. Some people from Arabia came and converted the Hindus to Muslims. So, in reality the effect in our blood was Hindu. Our great-grandfathers—two to four generations before—were Hindus, and they were great musicians. He taught his son, but the son converted to Islam. He learned music from his father and after learning became a Muslim. . . . When he converted to Islam he had music in his house because he got it from his father. Now he taught music to his sons.

To the extent that caste is defined by endogamy and occupational specialization, Mirasis are a caste.[29] Yet in those instances where a musician who is a soloist comes from an immediate ancestry known to be a soloist family, yet having more distantly a Mirasi background, he is never referred to as a Mirasi, unless a slur is intended. Kalawants claim that they will not marry into even a renowned soloist khandan if there are any sarangiyas or tabliyas in their ancestry, because for marriage purposes even a respected khandan is still Mirasi. By entering into such a relationship, a Kalawant family would be connected by marriage with sarangiyas and tabliyas, thus making their descendants non-Kalawant by definition.

Mirasi, considered as a social category, has then at least two loci. One is as an *occupational* term for Muslim musicians playing either tabla or sarangi, but not usually applied if one of them becomes a soloist. The other is as a *caste category* where marriage is concerned. Among Mirasis, several smaller endogamous units must be considered.

Mirasis, like Kalawants, state that their first preference for marriage is within the khandan. In this context the khandan includes close relations on the mother's side as well as the father's side. Cousin marriages of all kinds occur, the most prevalent being father's brother's daughter and mother's brother's daughter marriages. This it should be emphasized, is stated as a preference and not a rule. The reason given for khandani (i.e., within the khandan) marriages is again that they maintain the integrity of the khandan's particular musical style.[30]

From a non-Mirasi musician, this explanation elicits an amused smile. With the exception of Mirasi khandans which have established recognized gharanas, Mirasi khandans are not considered to have distinctive musical styles; hence there is nothing stylistic to be preserved and limited. Mirasis themselves say that this exclusiveness was the rationale of their elders and that nowadays musical knowledge is more freely shared. If a woman is not available from among the group of close relations, they will look to another khandan for a wife.

As with Kalawants, certain Mirasi khandans enter into regular relationships with each other by intermarrying. Any one khandan involved in such a relationship with another acknowledges thereby an equivalence in rank. After a generation, another khandan, in the extended family sense, is established. Thus, over a period of minimally two generations, such a marriage circle itself can constitute a khandan of consanguineally related individuals, in which cousin marriages again become a characteristic relationship.[31]

The next larger endogamous group is the biradari. Members of the biradari refer to each other as bhai ("brothers"), although if there are no known connections by blood or by marriage, they are not considered relatives (*rishtedār*).

The Mirasi biradari is a territorially defined group. All Mirasis having their ancestral home in a given locality are "brothers" of that biradari. Thus all Mirasis tracing their ancestral descent from Moradabad belong to the Moradabad biradari, and similarly all Mirasis tracing their descent from Delhi belong to the Delhi biradari.

The biradari as such is not named except as it is identified as originating in one or another place. If some members of the biradari develop a distinctive musical style and as a result become famous, or if they claim a distinctive style—whether or not it is so recognized—then the place name of the biradari will become the name of the gharana. The biradari as a whole is in fact often referred to as a gharana, with musicians stating, for example, that "we prefer to marry within our gharana" or "my wife is from outside my gharana."

Several differences between the Mirasi khandan, biradari, and gharana should be clarified. The khandan includes all those individuals who are consanguineally related through *known* ancestral links. The biradari includes all those individuals who share a common ancestral place of origin and between whom there are potential or existing marriage links. Both *khandan* and *biradari* imply a social group. *Gharana* implies a social category which includes the biradari as its social component, and its place of origin (and in some cases a musical style) as a social identity.

Disputes within the biradari are heard by members of the biradari. In any given locality where members live, some are chosen to constitute the panchayat, which is led by the *chaudharī,* the head of the whole biradari. If the chaudhari lives in another locality, he need not be present at a hearing. The membership in any given panchayat is not fixed and can be changed if, for example, one member has moved to another city or is too ill to attend. The chaudhari, on the other hand, serves for life, the office being in principle hereditary.[32]

If there is the threat of divorce, or a divorce has taken place, the biradari as a whole is involved. In Islam, marriage is explicitly contractual (Levy 1957:100). A sum of money (*mēhar*) written into the marriage contract is stipulated as an obligation on the part of the husband to his wife. In the event of divorce or death, this sum is considered the property of the wife (cf. Vreede-Desteuers 1968:13–17). In recent times the size of the mehar has often been inflated as a sign of prestige for the families involved. Alternatively, the mehar is sometimes made very small as a sign of confidence in the man. In either event, the panchayat must fix the amount due to a wife or direct that the mehar agreed upon be paid. If there is a separation but no divorce, then the panchayat decides how much is to be paid to the woman for her maintenance.

Ideally, the panchayat does not come to an agreement by itself, but listens to the arguments of all the members present. Although members of the panchayat are chosen because they are respected and thought to be impartial, accusations of impartiality are not uncommon. If a member refuses to abide by the decision of the panchayat, or if he offends the biradari in some manner, he is ostracized for a certain period of time (*huqqā pānī band,* "no smoking or eating with him by other members") or fined a sum of money.

The whole biradari is rarely, if ever, completely assembled simply because members are spread throughout North India. Yet within a locality where members of the biradari are grouped together, they gather for important life ceremonies. At the initiation of a disciple (*ganda bandhan,* "tying of the thread"), all members of the biradari are invited to attend, as they are at weddings and funerals. During certain religious festivals such as *Bakra Id,* members of the biradari come together and eat, while at Muharram, food purchased with the fines collected by the panchayat is distributed to the whole biradari.

There is a sense among members of being related in significant ways which separate them from other biradari. They can drop in unannounced to visit one another; and if, as often happens, a famous member of the biradari comes to town, other members come by and pay their respects. They are always welcome no matter how insignificant they may be as members. In other ways, however, there seems to be little fraternal recognition. For example, at All India Radio, friendships do not appear to follow biradari lines (see Chapter 6).

Marriage occasionally occurs outside the biradari. No expressed sanction exists against it, the only important consideration being that the other khandan be equivalent in rank. The biradari themselves are not ranked with respect to one another. No musician says that he cannot marry a woman from another gharana, nor does one Mirasi biradari ever claim social superiority over another. When looking for a wife, then, one "looks at the khandan." If the khandan is respectable and is given consent, the match is made.

As far as occupation is concerned, there is only a slight tendency for a son to follow the speciality of his father. Of the twenty-three Mirasi accompanists for whom I have data, fourteen perform on the same instrument as their fathers did, while nine do not (see accompanying table).

Inheritance of Specialties

Father: Son:	sarangi sarangi	sarangi tabla	tabla sarangi	tabla tabla	vocal sarangi
	10	5	2	4	2*

*One is the only son of a very famous vocalist, who died when the child was very young so that he was trained by his mother's brother. The other case is uncertain. The father actually worked as a tanpura player at A.I.R., so that, perhaps in only a technical sense was he a vocalist.

No particular stigma is attached to learning an instrument different from that of one's father, since uncles in the khandan on both sides typically play either one or the other of the accompanying instruments.

The only other major communities of accompanists are members of the Katthak caste. Dancers, as well as tabla and sarangi players, they are now concentrated in Banaras, although other communities of Katthaks are found in Eastern Uttar Pradesh. They are an endogamous group, who claim not to intermarry with the female vocalists of Banaras, although they serve as their accompanists and often as their gurus.[33]

A Historical Interpretation

If we compare the classification of musicians in earlier times outlined at the beginning of this chapter with the typology just presented, what appears common to them is the hierarchical ranking of musical specialists. If we recall Imam's discussion of musicians, however, one important difference emerges: Dharis appear to be supplanted by Mirasis, and this within a very short space of time.

Imam was writing in 1856–57, a crucial period in Indian

history. In 1856 the province of Oudh was annexed by the British, and the then Nawab, Wajid Ali Shah had to move to Calcutta followed by his court entourage, including many musicians. The year 1857 is, of course, the watershed of British relations with India. What was known as the Sepoy Mutiny turned out to be the first major rebellion against the British in India.

There were other important developments during this period as well. The telegraph and railways were first introduced in 1851 and 1853 respectively. By 1855 the major cities of India were connected by telegraph, and by 1875 Delhi was connected by rail with Bombay and Calcutta.

The fact that Imam makes no mention of Mirasis in 1856, but that in little more than a decade they make their appearance in the literature (in Khan 1871? and Sherring 1872:275) suggests that as with all sectors of political and social life in India, rapid changes were taking place.[34] Somehow, within a short period of time, Mirasis begin to take the place of Dharis, or at least the terminology changes. The simplest explanation for this change is that Imam is discussing Lucknow, and Sherring is dealing with Banaras three hundred miles away, suggesting that the terminological difference is one of space rather than time. Yet Khan's publication in 1871 comes from Lucknow, and soon after this date numerous other references to Mirasis appear in the literature.

From this literature, essentially that of caste ethnographers and census data, it is clear that Mirasi is a social category which includes a wide range of musical specialists from wandering minstrels in rural areas to classical musicians in urban ones. At times Mirasis are characterized as the women of the community who sing and dance, leaving the men to act as accompanists and as procurers. In Banaras they are described as the teachers of singing and dancing girls, and are highly respected (Sherring 1872:93). Sometimes Mirasis are the subcategory of other castes, and still other descriptions make them the major category, with other castes attached to them. Dharis are enumerated in the 1883 Panjab census as a subgroup of Mirasis, but Ibbetson, the census commissioner, suggests this is mistaken because the two groups do not intermarry (1916:234–35).[35] The most vivid description of Mirasis in their rural milieu around the turn of the century is provided by Prakash Tandon in his autobiographical *Punjabi Century:*

> Another Muslim caste in the Jajmani system was that of the Mirasis. The Mirasis beat drums and played the shehnai, a flute [sic] with a trumpet end, at weddings and other auspicious occasions, but their specialty was wit and repartee, which they could exercise with traditional immunity on the highest and lowest in the society. The victim could not take umbrage at the Mirasi's wit. They would come to weddings and other gatherings, invited or uninvited, and begin to poke fun at guests and hosts alike. Their wit was inherited down the generations and practiced from childhood; it was sharp and very quick, and at times brilliant. Woe betide a man who tried to retaliate and get the better of them, for they could reduce him to rags before a company. A problem with the Mirasis was how to send them away satisfied; anything short of that would lead to a special session against the poor host; and it was the respected custom to let the Mirasi say whatever he liked without showing anger or rancour. In any case, retaliation could only lead to an admission of lack of humour; the Mirasi had nothing to lose. The Mirasi women also worked, playing small drums and singing, but they never excelled in wit, only in vulgarity. Men and women sang praises of the family and recited its genealogy at weddings. They were also the vehicle of old ballads and songs. The word Mirasi in the Punjabi language has come to mean witty and funny in an overdone, vulgar manner. They live as a close community in their own mohallas. Although Muslims, other Muslims never inter-married with them. Their women were slim and attractive in a brazen way, and of easy virtue. [1961:79–80]

The genealogical function Tandon ascribes to the Mirasis recalls their function as "dividers of inheritance" that Ustad Chand Khan ascribes to Mirasis discussed earlier. Rural Mirasis in contemporary Haryana (a state formed out of the southern part of Panjab in 1967), who still specialize in music, no longer allow their women to perform in public, and the more affluent of them have nothing but disdain for the hereditary patron-client relationship (*jajmani*) Tandon mentions.

Mirasis who are classical musicians are, virtually without exception, urban dwellers. Although they often claim village origins, places and names have usually been forgotten. Rather, these classical musicians have their more immediate origins in towns and cities, and in these urban areas they are usually concentrated in certain wards (*muhallās*), a practice which for musicians in Delhi can be traced back to the fourteenth century.[36]

These urban Mirasis trace their classical music connections to Kalawants, usually two or three generations back. Their recollections of occupations, origins, and religion before that time are indistinct and hazy. When asked about Dharis they appear as ill-informed as anyone else.

Part of the solution to the mystery of the eclipse of Dharis by Mirasis is suggested by changes in the social organization of musical specialists between Imam's time and today. One can infer from Imam's statements that the sociological distinctions and endogamous rules concerning musical specialists were very different from practices now. For example, Imam refers to sarangi players who were Kalawants (1959a:24). He lists Naqqarchis as a separate musician community (as Mirasis still today consider them) but indicates intermarriage between Dharis and Naqqarchis. He also indirectly makes known intermarriage between Kalawants and Dharis:

> The sons of Umrao Khan play bīn while Hassan Khan (Dhari) plays the sitar baj on the bīn. The trouble is, the rules of bīn are taught by the ustads to their sons only and not even to their daughters' children, therefore Hassan Khan did not have the privilege of learning it. [1959a:23]

The inference from this quotation is not only that there was intermarriage between Kalawant and Dhari families (and possibly that only Kalawant women married Dhari men and not the other way around) but also that among binkars, the inheritance of musical knowledge was strictly patrilineal.

Common to both contemporary attitudes and Imam's descriptions is the low esteem in which tawaif accompanists were held. Imam himself distinguished Dharis of two kinds: those who degraded themselves by accompanying dancing girls, and those others, whom he lists by name, as notable musicians at the court of Wajid Ali Shah.

From these bits of evidence, the following hypothetical historical reconstruction is suggested.

Dharis intermarrying with Kalawants became soloists and separated themselves from those Dharis who accompanied tawaifs and who probably intermarried with Mirasis practicing the same occupation. For their part, Mirasis entered the classical tradition from a rural folk musician background through urban migration. (This is the significance of Mirasi brotherhoods being organized and identified on the basis of urban origins.) Once in the city, the stepping-stone from the folk to the classical tradition was through the medium of the courtesan salons (Neuman 1979). The courtesan tradition, we recall, tends towards the lighter varieties of the art tradition such as thumri, which has always been less formal in performance practice and undoubtably more amenable to outside influences such as folk music. In the cities, Mirasis brought their rural talents to bear, becoming the entrepreneurs of the entertainment districts, ranging the spectrum from being procurers (as the British politely put it) to ustads. It is still unclear why Dharis were subsumed socially and terminologically in the Mirasi fold, but I think it was due to the ambiguity of the social tag "Dhari" with a now double social identity split between Kalawant and Mirasi. Substituting "Mirasi" as the general social tag resolved any ambiguity in meaning about who was what, a concern of no small importance in Indian society.

A somewhat similar set of circumstances a century earlier lends a certain credence to this reconstruction. In 1739, Nadir Shah, the Persian emperor, invaded India and completely sacked Delhi. This was the first of a series of invasions that lasted for several decades and brought Delhi down from being one of the greatest cities in the world to the level of a provincial town. The Mughal empire was in its death throes, and the British, Marathas, and Afghans were in active contention to inherit the mantle. This period in Delhi was known as the "time of troubles," and musicians and poets left the city, emigrating to provincial capitals like Lucknow. During or immediately preceeding this period, however, important innovations in Hindustani music were taking place during the reign of Muhammad Shah Rangile (1719–1748). If the story given to Sharmistha Sen is correct (1972:156–57), virtually all instrumentalists used to be accompanists, the practice of performing as soloists only beginning at the court of Muhammad Shah Rangile, where, as we have seen earlier, khayal in its modern form is also generally thought to have developed:

> It appears that Sadarang being a creative artist, was keen on proving his mettle as a solo player, as this would give him scope for displaying his virtuosity. He also felt that instrumentalists did not get the same recognition like the vocalists. During Muhammad Shah's time dhrupad had already reached its peak and people were now looking eagerly for something new, something more emotional and imaginative. Being a musician of ideas, Sadarang seized upon this opportunity and composed a number of songs within the framework of dhrupad, yet less circumscribed and more imaginative. He taught these compositions to two young boys, Ghulam Rasool and Jani Rasool who sang these to the public. The songs at once became popular having caught the people's fancy. This musical form has come to be known as Khayal. Muhammad Shah was so pleased now with Sadarang that he permitted him to give solo performances on the veena [i.e., bīn] at his court. It is said that from that time onwards the veena became a solo instrument.

Presumably, the bīn was occasionally played as a solo instrument before this time, although other musicians did not look favorably on such music. Sen (1972:150) implies that the term for solo instrumental music, *Shuska-Vadya* (dry instrumental music) was used at the time of Akbar.

The story of Sadarang is revealing in other ways and suggests the history of social separation between accompanists and soloists. Implicit in the first two sentences is a hierarchical distinction between instrumentalists and vocalists, the former being subordinate to the latter. Even now, in terms of conscious ideology—though not always in practice—a higher value is placed on vocal music than on instrumental music. In addition, the introduction of musical innovation was indirect in two respects: through the use of other (minor) musicians (the two young boys) and through the medium of vocal music, perhaps because of its power as a legitimizing vehicle.

The beginnings of khayal, closely associated with the rise of sarangi and tabla accompaniment, coincides with acceptance of the bīn as a solo instrument. As noted before, the introduction of the sarangi into the classical tradition most likely occurred during this same period in the first half of the eighteenth century. The bīn ceased to be used primarily as an accompanying instrument, just as the sarangi began to be used in this way. The sarangi filled the musical niche vacated by the bīn.

The sarangi is almost certainly an indigenous folk instrument of India, and it probably entered the classical tradition in the hands of rural musicians. The only other possibility, that art musicians took up the sarangi, is inherently implausible since the sarangi was a folk instrument and adoption of it would have been demeaning. The folk musicians who introduced the sarangi were probably Dharis, who like the Mirasis after them continued to have "cousins" in the countryside as wandering minstrels.

The importance of the change from bīn to sarangi accompaniment was not only a matter of instruments: it was also a change in the mode of recruitment. Binkar accompanists were recruited from the same families as the vocalists they accompanied, but sarangi accompanists almost certainly were not. (It is only by Imam's time that intermarriage is evident). Binkars, by changing their musical role from accompanist to soloist, succeeded thereby in establishing an equivalence in musical rank which accorded with the actual equivalence in social rank between vocalists and themselves. Sarangi and tabla players then occupied the status of accompanist in the art tradition, accepting at the same time its subordinate musical role and concomitant social rank. From their point of view, to occupy the status of accompanist in this tradition was to move upward to a position superior to their former rank as minstrels. It is in this manner, I believe, that accompanists came to be recruited from social groups different from that of soloists, establishing a pattern that anticipated a similar strategy by Mirasis a century or so later and largely persisted until today. I also think that the most important social change in Hindustani music culture in the second half of this century is the attempt by accompanists to break away from the pattern and define themselves as soloists, replicating the strategy of binkar accompanists two centuries earlier. This is a point to which I shall return in Chapter 6.

From Social Structure to Music Structure

I would like to suggest that the separation of the soloist and accompanist *socially* in the eighteenth century solved two musical problems. Before the separation, the musical hierarchy of solo and accompaniment had no social correlate. The problem of who was to lead and who to follow had to be either a family or personal decision. Within the context of family life in India this situation ordinarily would present no real problem since there was an authority pattern already available in the age grading of brothers. Yet there must also have been a certain amount of tension and frustration if years of training resulted only in years of accompanying. Certainly Sadarang wanted to become a soloist. By relegating the subordinate musical function to separate and socially inferior musical specialists, the problem of leading and following was resolved through Indian civilization's classic strategy, occupational caste specialization.

The other solution provided, and historically perhaps the more important, was that lower-ranked musicians could make the breaks with tradition and provide the kind of "lighter" music Indian society seemed to require at the time, particularly since these musicians, coming from the countryside and introducing the sarangi and tabla, were by their very presence a breaking of the classicial tradition. We recall Sadarang's strategy of introducing "less circumscribed and more imaginative" music through the two young boys who were also outside the classical tradition: he certainly could not do it himself simply for reasons of family honor and personal prestige. In later chapters we shall witness similar strategies for introducing musical innovations. The important point here is that new musics in India have required new kinds of social beings.

What were the musical results of this social differentiation of soloist and accompanist? It allowed a strict division of musical labor and a hierarchical organization of performance which only in the last few decades has begun to be questioned.

From the first moments of performance we observe that the soloist begins alone and only afterwards do the accompanists join in. Although there is room for elaboration, the basic musical function of accompanists is really quite elementary. The tabla player has only to provide the basic rhythmic cycle (theka) repeatedly. Although in common practice tabliyas are expected to do much more than this, particularly when accompanying instrumentalists, there are soloists who indeed require and desire nothing more than the theka.

The function of the melodic accompanying instrument, whether sarangi or harmonium, is more difficult to describe since it does not add a new dimension to the musical performance, as rhythm clearly does with respect to melody. The melodic accompaniment fills out the spaces and hollows in the total musical performance, manifesting itself primarily as an echo effect—repeating as faithfully as possible the vocalist's sounds. Musician, composer, musicologist, and teacher D. T. Joshi states: "The accompanying melodic instruments are meant for accompanying the singer because without some melodic accompaniment the music will not be—shall I say—very full and it needs some sort of support. . . . without any instrumental support, any melodic support, the vocalist will sound rather hollow." From the vocalist's perspective, the function of the accompaniment seems primarily that of giving him some breathing space and some time to think. As Wahid Khan put it. "While singing with the sarangi I feel I have a companion with me. After I sing a tan the sarangi repeats the same notes which gives me time to regain my breath and to think over a different arrangement of notes." Sarangiyas are not always as articulate as he in describing their own part, as shown by the following excerpt from an interview with a sarangi player at All India Radio:

Q. What do you do when you accompany?
A. My job is to ask what rāg you are going to play, which rāg you will sing. The rāg which he will ask me to play, I'll play. I will tune in the same *thāt* (scale) on the sarangi.
Q. While you play what are your duties?
A. I will play as he sings.
Q. Do you play something new?
A. My job is that whatever the vocalist sings, I'll only play that. I don't go in for "sawal-jawab."

This is indeed the basic function of the melodic accompaniment. Whatever the duties or desires of the accompanist, the rights of the soloist in performance are paramount with respect to all musical decisions.[37] They may be summed up as follows:

1. *The soloist regulates the tuning of the accompanist.* Backstage before the concert, the accompanying instrument—the tanpura, the tabla, or the sarangi—and the solo instrument are tuned. If the soloist is a vocalist, the harmonium is often employed for the ground note, *sa*. The vocalist says, for example, "Ek safed," which means "one white" and refers to the white key, note C on the harmonium (cf. Kaufmann 1968). The tanpura player, either a disciple in fact or an admirer, rough-tunes the tanpura, after which the soloist makes the final adjustments, for the fine tuning. The tabla player also tunes with or without help of the soloist, as does the sarangiya regarding his main playing strings, not his sympathetic strings (*tarab*). Once onstage, the tanpura is usually retuned by the soloist. In the case of vocal music, where the alap will be short, the tabla is tuned before the performance begins; the tabla player tunes around the head of the tabla with a little hammer (*hathaurī*) and the soloist, with a nod of the head, indicates whether at a particular spot the tone should be changed or not. If the tone is too sharp, he nods down, and the tabla player hammers up, to loosen the head and flatten the pitch. If the tone is flat, the opposite happens. Once the right tone is reached a "glissando" nod indicates assent. If the alap is a long one, and if, as often happens at outdoor concerts, the tabla has gone out of tune, then it is retuned. Again the soloist is the final judge of when the tabla is in tune.

2. *The soloist decides the tal.* Before and sometimes during a performance, the soloist tells the tabla player, if he doesn't know, which tal the composition is to be set to. Sometimes the soloist changes the tal during the performance when, for example, going from the slow (*vilambit*) movement to the fast (*drut*) movement. Usually the tabla player will know which tal is required, although he may need to listen to the composition through more than one cycle. Because compositions are framed within the boundaries of a given cycle—within sixteen beats (*mātrā*) if the composition is in *tintal*—the soloist, by deciding

on the composition he will play, automatically regulates the tal which the tabla player will provide.[38]

3. *The soloist regulates the tempo.* In Indian classical music there is a gradual increase in tempo as the performance proceeds. The rate of this increase is, in principle, under the control of the soloist, although at times a tabla player, "to be mischievous," will change the tempo. A solo instrumentalist indicates the tempo by the right-hand strokes, and if he desires to increase the tempo, he usually initiates the movement, indicating the increase with his head.

4. *The soloist allocates the time for the accompanist's solo sections.* In the case of the tabla, this solo is always within minimally a rhythmic cycle of one or a multiple thereof, but the soloist regulates the number of cycles. This regulatory condition is not as clear-cut as it may seem, however, because the tabliya may initiate a pattern that spreads over several cycles. The soloist will not interrupt, but he can prevent the tabla player from having many, or any, opportunities. Sarangiyas also have little snatches of solo playing, but the vocalist can, and often does, interrupt the sarangiya. This apparently irritates the sarangiyas, since it is their only opportunity for a solo. The sarangiya is not supposed to play a note that has not yet been elaborated by the vocalist, and is also not supposed to introduce a new melodic idea, except perhaps when the vocalist is a novice.

5. *The soloist determines the beginning and end.* A soloist can play a very long alap, and is in no sense obligated to hurry so as to let the tabla player begin. (Although the tabla player is usually expected to sit throughout the alap, in informal contexts he sometimes can wait to enter the stage until his own participation is to begin.) With rare exceptions soloists also determine the end of the performance. Once, in the United States, I saw a tabla player extend the performance beyond the end point which the soloist had indicated. The reason he gave to the soloist for the extension was that he wanted to show "what I can do" to another tabla player sitting in the audience.

The rights of the soloist in part define his status. Only in the second right listed—the right to decide the tal—is the explicit rule a function of the musical requisite. The other four contain possibilities for exceptions and are subject to differing interpretations.

Onstage the observer would discover little that is incongruous in the manifest behavior, which is indeed largely ritualized. The soloist comes onstage first (after his instrument if he has one has been delivered to the platform, usually by one of his students). If he has a flair for the dramatic he enters with a graceful flourish of *salāms* to the audience, or he may just sit down quickly and *namaste* the audience.[39] Following immediately, or in a moment, is the accompanist or accompanists. If there are both a tabliya and a sarangiya (and/or a harmonium player) they usually all come out together after the soloist.

The soloist sits at the center of the stage, the tabla player to his right and the melodic accompanist to the left.[40] If there is a harmonium in addition to a sarangi, the harmonium player sits behind and to the right of the sarangiya, or behind and to the right of the soloist. The one or two (rarely more) tanpura players sit behind and to either side of the soloist.

Offstage the relationship between the soloist and the accompanist corresponds with their relationship onstage. The soloist can request little favors of the accompanist, as he would of a disciple—getting him some cigarettes, a glass of water, ice for his drink, and a light for his smoke. The accompanist never asks the soloist.

The soloist often chooses who is to accompany him; and if a selection has otherwise been made, the soloist may veto the choice. Once I observed a famous vocalist arriving at his hotel at a music conference outside of Delhi to learn that a tabla player (who had a good reputation in his home town) was to accompany him. The vocalist had never heard of the man; and in spite of numerous entreaties by the conference organizers and other musicians, he refused to accept him as an accompanist. The accompanist in this sense owes his performance opportunity to the soloist. Also, the prestige of the soloist redounds to the accompanist. In program notes one sometimes finds the names of soloists with whom a given accompanist has performed.

As it happens, there is no systematic interaction between soloists and accompanists in extramusical contexts. Where musi-

cians are gathered together at a music conference, at All India
Radio, or at a mehfil, interaction occurs between known persons.
A soloist does not ask just any accompanist for favors, but one
whom he knows and has performed with before. If a disciple is
available, he tends to be the first to whom the soloist turns for
requests. Usually the only situation in which there is a continued
interrelationship between a soloist and accompanist is on tour
abroad.[41] There the accompanist is directly dependent on the
soloist because only the soloist is paid a fee by music organizers;
the accompanist then receives a percentage from the soloist.

The exceptions to the hierarchical structure of relationships between soloist and accompanist occur in the case of multiple, ambiguous, or contradictory statuses. These can be summarized under the following rubrics:

1. *A soloist recently come from a non-soloist social background.*
We have already presented the case of the tabla player who
refused to accompany a shahnai player. Another type of situation
occurs when two brothers perform together, the older one accompanying with the younger playing solo. In this case, there
may be no real authority on the part of the soloist to regulate
tuning, for example, although there may be a ritual demonstra-
tion of this authority.

2. *Relative personal prestige difference.* A famous accompanist
and "novice" soloist performing together will normally exhibit the
structured status relationship, although the potential for conflict is
easily manifest. A famous sarangiya accompanying someone
whom he considers his subordinate for any number of reasons ex-
ercises more freedom in taking the lead than is customary. Sometimes this is considered helpful. If the vocalist is inexperienced,
the sarangiya might suggest a musical idea to him. Most vocalists,
however, do not accept this "musical" advice, and it is not uncommon to hear a vocalist complain that the sarangiya attempted to
anticipate him, and thus to mislead his own melodic development.

3. *Reinterpretation of traditional status relationships.* Recently there have been a few examples of accompanists who,
because of changed circumstances, are reluctant to take an explicitly subordinate role. The changed circumstances seem to result from two major causes. In a few instances, accompanists

have toured abroad and returned with an enhanced sense of prestige. This is partially due to the reaction of Western audiences, who interpret the relationship indiscriminately, seeing the soloist and the rhythmic accompanist as equals in a duet.

The other phenomenon is an increased demand for accompanists, particularly good tabla players. Music has, as any connoisseur knows, become increasingly *layakārī*—rhythm-oriented—and it is important for soloists, particularly instrumentalists, to have a good tabla player as accompanist. Most observers attribute this demand to Allaudin Khan and his two major disciples, Ali Akbar Khan and Ravi Shankar. The latter is especially noted for the intricate rhythmic patterns of his performances, and the importance he gives to tabla players and their solo interludes.

Tabla players are also in demand (in Delhi, at least) because of the absolute increase in the annual number of music performances since India gained independence. The middle-class young have increasingly taken to learning music, which requires tabla accompanists as well. Thus, tabla players now have a wider diversity of possibilities and are less dependent for their reputations on a few major soloists.

Simultaneously, the number of accompanists has probably decreased. Although there are no statistics available, it is known that many musicians from the hereditary families left Delhi for Pakistan during Partition. Wahid Hussein, who migrated to Pakistan after I interviewed him, claimed that before Partition, between six and seven thousand hereditary musicians lived in Delhi. In 1969 he estimated only between 350 and 400 in residence. The first set of figures seems too high, but it does indicate the extent of the exodus. (Most Muslim families of musicians have some relatives in Pakistan). This has had other ramifications too; for example, by creating a vacuum, which was filled by many Hindu musicians, as Mattoo has informed me (personal communication, 1969).

Artists and Artisans

Both the social structure and performance relationships of soloists and accompanists suggest an analytical distinction comparable to

Western notions of artists and artisans. This is not to say that there are no accompanists who are considered artists. A sarangi player like Ustad Bundu Khan or a tabla player like Ustad Ahmed Jan Thirakwa was certainly considered an artist: but, in terms of a more general cultural classification, accompanists as a group were considered artisans and soloists as a group were considered artists.

This is evident not only in the elementary musical functions of accompanists but also in their group organization. If one compares the social organization of Kalawants with that of Mirasis, it is clear that two fundamentally different types of social organization have been formed to produce the two different types of performers. The Kalawant group is actually a set of relatives: the different lineages having actual or potential marriage ties form a single category of persons who are allowed to intermarry. But this same set does not form a group. There is no political organization binding the members of the set together, and there is no communal social interaction by which all members celebrate their collectivity. The Kalawant biradari is a brotherhood only in a classificatory sense, classifying the set of persons who can enter into marriage relationships with one another.[42] The Mirasi brotherhood, like the Kalawant, extends beyond actual kin to include potential kin as well. What makes it different is that all members belong to a group, not only to a category. There is a political structure, the panchayat, which regulates communal affairs, and there are ritual occasions when all members are invited to participate as a collectivity.

These differences in the social organization between soloists and accompanists are, I would argue, appropriately adaptive to the requirements of Hindustani music culture. The social need for soloists has always been more limited and more *discriminating* than for accompanists. Their organization into small groups along family lines was the effective response to the limited opportunities soloists themselves perceived. Accompanists, in addition to being needed in concert situations, were also required, probably in fairly large numbers, in the salon context as well. Even today, when the salons have been severely restricted, one can still observe several performances by parties of tawaifs and their accompanists going on at the same time in different rooms of a building. The Mirasi biradaris, born as they were in the cities, fulfilled a social need for music which was much more extensive than that of Kalawant soloists. The extended network of actual and potential kin thus provided the larger group organization to meet this need.

The distinction between artist and artisan that I suggest is further corroborated by the differences between the two kinds of leaders of soloist and accompanist groups. The khalifa of the Kalawants has no political authority even within his own family except by virtue of being the eldest male. It is over musical matters that his authority is exercised, a domain of obvious relevance to an artistic tradition. The chaudhari of the Mirasi, in contrast, has no authority over musical matters. Indeed, the term *chaudhari* is common to many occupational castes in India and is even translated in one instance as "foreman" (Spear 1951:229). The chaudhari is the leader among equals in the caste council, an institution the Kalawant lack. The guild-like organization of the Mirasi biradari is suggested by Blunt, who reported that the caste council once had the power to boycott any tawaif if she dismissed her musicians during the marriage season (1931:244).

It appears that the musical role of the accompanist, at least as it was traditionally conceived, implied no necessary creative component or particular grading of talent and consequently was largely interchangeable between people. It was a role in which the "personality" of the accompanist could be treated as a constant and was not required to be expressed. One sarangi or tabla player performed essentially the same musical role as any other, and in this musical sense it was a largely non-competitive role. As with other artisan craft groups, internal competition for patronage was probably regulated by the caste council. The soloist, however, was always in competition with other soloists, often on the stage at the same time! The individuality of the soloist was crucial to his self-definition as creative artist. For this role, the resources of small family units were brought to bear, concentrating on a few individuals for long-term teaching. As finely tuned organizations of specialized knowledge, these families came to be distinguished by their pedigrees and recognized as gharanas.

5. Gharanas:
The Politics of Pedigree

The survival of music as an art practiced by Indian Muslims
depends entirely on the few *gharanas* that still exist.
M. Mujeeb, *The Indian Muslims*

Another thing plagues Hindustani music. This is what is known as
the '*gharana*' system.
B. V. Keshkar, *Indian Music*

 The difference in attitude exhibited by the two epigraphs to this chapter reflects a fundamental ambivalence prevalent in North India about the relevance of
gharanas for contemporary Hindustani music. Discussions about and between gharanas center ultimately on one issue,
authority: the authority of gharanas as institutions determining
stylistic appropriateness, and the relative authority of different
gharanas as legislators of stylistic authenticity. Seen in a more
general light, the question of authority is wedded to the definition and salience of tradition and the role of pedigrees as the
embodiment of tradition. This is a problem which one readily
recognizes as not limited to music culture alone; it speaks to the
whole question of the place of tradition in any contemporary
society.

145

Although gharanas connote many things to many people, the concept may be said to include, minimally, a lineage of hereditary musicians, their disciples, and the particular musical style they represent. It is thus a compound of social feature (the membership) and cultural feature (musical style). One has constantly to keep in mind that gharanas are essentially abstract categories: a musician may be said to "belong to" one or another gharana, but the membership as a whole hardly constitutes a collectivity. There are no gharana celebrations, virtually no political organization, no campus or central headquarters, and no administrative structure. The closest analogues I can think of in the West are the loosely structured European intellectual circles such as the Prague school of linguists, or the Vienna circle of logical positivists. They differ from gharanas in that their structural cores are non-familial institutions, whereas the structural core of a gharana is a lineage of hereditary musicians. What binds all such groups is style—formulated, shared, and represented by the membership. Style, be it intellectual, artistic, or more commonly some combination of both is the central reason for group being. In the sense I use the term, style is a solution formulated in response to a problem. It is not a solution to the problem itself, but rather a mode of approach to the problem (which also necessitates a formulation of the problem itself). Gharanas have answered the question of how to approach musical problems by providing a repertoire of stylistic elements—compositions, ornamentations, techniques, and structural organization—which come to be recognized as theirs. By what they include gharanas discriminate what is excluded. In this manner they have provided the rules of appropriateness for performance practices in Hindustani music.

The Origin and Kinship of Gharanas

Gharanas were conceived in the mid-nineteenth century and born in the twentieth.[1] Yet once having been born, they assumed an appearance of being ages old. In discussions today, the idea of a gharana is that it is if nothing else, hoary. This is not due to any artifice on the part of musicians but rather to their own sense of historical time by which cultural salience creates chronological depth. And this depth does not arise so much out of mythic reconstructions as from genealogical and discipleship connections to earlier times and people, linking the gharana phylogenetically to earlier lineages and styles. One could perhaps say that gharanas were born out of a union of earlier lineages and earlier styles, and integrated them as a unified expression of social and cultural features.

The pre-existent styles, the "mother" of gharanas, were the already mentioned banis (or vanis) which Imam had traced back to four major musicians in the court of Akbar. Although banis were originally said to be derived from these four musicians, and particular families were known to specialize in one bani or another, the styles themselves were not integrally linked with particular lineages. Banis could be described entirely in musical terms as pure style, without reference to individuals or lineages. Drawing upon an interview with the respected scholar and musician, the late Birendra Kishore Roy Chaudhury, Sharmistha Sen summarizes the stylistic features of each of the four:

[1] The *Gaudhari Vani,* also known as Govarhari . . . is characterized by smooth glides almost linear in character. Its gait is slow and elephantine and has the feeling of repose and peace.

[2] The *Khandari Vani* is rich in variety. . . . Its gait is majestic and it uses heavy and vigorous Gamakas, expressive of valour. . . . In marked contrast to *Gaudi* [Gaudhari] *Vani,* it is never sung in slow rhythm.

[3] The *Nauhari Vani* . . . is characterized by quick, jerky passages employing a variety of Gamakas. It usually moves in quick succession, moving as it were in slow curved lines accompanied by the judicious use of soft Gamakas from the first to its third or fourth notes. Thus the Nauhar Vani with its jumpy *Chuts* [short, quick musical runs] surprises us at each of its movements.

[4] The *Dagur Vani* or *Dangari Vani* . . . specializes in delicately executed meends (glides) with *Gamakas.* . . . It is marked by correct intonation, purity of design, simplicity of execution and massiveness of structure. It is mainly sung at medium speed with a judicious blending of Khandahar style to add colour to the performance. [1972:91–94]

Representatives of today's gharanas are said still to manifest stylistic elements traceable to one of these four banis. The style of the Agra gharana, for example, is derived from the otherwise extinct Nauhari bani, and the family of dhrupad singers and binkars known as Dagar takes its name from the Dagar bani. In most cases, however, the details of possible connections to particular banis are less important than the fact that banis at one time existed and thereby provide a conceptual link to verify the *idea* of stylistic ancestry, in other words a tradition.

As I have mentioned, the central structural feature of a gharana is a "core" lineage founded by an individual or sometimes two brothers. Founders are distinguished from their own ancestors (who are also often known) by virtue of having made to Hindustani music a significant stylistic contribution which then comes to be regarded as the central distinctive feature by their descendants and disciples. We do not know if these founders were, to borrow an idea from George Kubler, artistic precursors (shaping a new civilization) or rebels (defining the edges of a disintegrating one) or both (1962:91). In India they would not now be interpreted as either, but in their day they were probably considered rebels of a sort. The origin of the earliest gharana, Gwalior, and the relationships it spawned with the founders of others will serve as an illustration.

The Gwalior gharana is usually identified as the first.[2] The city of Gwalior itself remains historically important for all musicians because it is where Tansen matured into the great musician he came to be, and where he is now buried. The Rajas of Gwalior had a long tradition of generously patronizing musicians, and one Raja (Man Singh Tomwar, 1486–1516) is believed to have revived the dhrupad form of music. The founders of the gharana were two brothers, Haddu Khan and Hassu Khan, along with their brother or parallel cousin Nathu Khan. They started learning music from their father (the pattern for all founders) but then later learned from Bade Muhammad Khan. At first they hid behind a curtain to hear him practice (Khan 1959:70). After several years of learning in secret, they were called by the Maharaja (who had arranged for their "private" lessons) to perform before Muhammad Khan, who became upset when he heard his own music, obviously stolen, performed back to him. Neverthe-less, the Maharaja (Daulat Rao Scindia) persuaded Muhammad Khan to take Haddu and Hassu Khan as his disciples to complete their training.

Bade Muhammad Khan was himself one of the Qawwal Bachchhe, a group who traced their descent back to the time of Amir Khusrau. (Indeed, Amir Khusrau could be considered the inventor of learning by stealth, because a well-known tradition represents him as listening behind or under a throne to Gopal Nayak and then performing the same music back to the artist [Willard 1965:121].[3]) Bade Muhammad Khan was the son of Shakkar Khan (or Mian Shukar); he is mentioned by Imam sev-eral times, as are Haddu Khan and his brothers (1959a:18–20). However, Imam makes no mention of a relationship between Bade Muhammad Khan and Haddu Khan or his brothers, nor for that matter does he mention a Gwalior gharana, because the whole conception of gharana had not yet emerged. It is only from a later period that Haddu Khan and his brothers are seen as having established a new music tradition, the Gwalior gharana.

The belief that the Gwalior founders learned from a Qawwal Bachchhe is significant because in this way the Gwalior gharana is connected to a much older tradition, this lineage being so to speak the "father" of gharanas. The origin of the Qawwal Bachchhe is itself important because it provides a "birth" for hered-itary lineages and a beginning for such a social organization of musical specialists. The tale of how this lineage was born must be the strangest origin myth of any centuries-old line of musicians.

It is believed that during the reign of Sultan Iltutmish [1211–1236], there were two brothers in Delhi called Sawant and Bula. Amongst them, one was deaf and the other was dumb. The Badshah arranged a music program during a party. Someone told him of these two brothers [as a joke?] but poor things, what could they sing? When Hazrat Khwajja-i-Khwajjagan learned of their plight [by his own knowledge] he prayed to God to open their voice, and God did so. Then he [Hazrat] commanded the two brothers to sing. As soon as they received the command, they got their voice and started singing. These two brothers' khandan is known as the Qawwal Bachchhe khandan.[4] [Khan 1959:65]

149

Ustad Mushtaq Hussein Khan, a disciple of the Seheswan gharana's founder, Inayat Khan. He is pictured here with his tanpura. *Photograph courtesy of Naina Devi and Raag Rang Music Circle.*

Ustad Tanras Khan (d. 1890), vocalist at the court of the last Mughal king, Bahadur Shah Zafar. *Photograph from the collection of Yunus Hussein Khan.*

Ustad Fayyaz Khan, of the Agra gharana, one of the great virtuosi among vocalists until his death in 1950. *Photograph from the collection of Yunus Hussein Khan.*

Goura Jan, still remembered as an outstanding vocalist of the early 1900s, and one of the first musicians to be recorded. She is pictured here in a recording session (probably in 1902), accompanied by a harmonium player and a tabliya. To her right is a pān box and a small spittoon. To her left is a book probably containing solfège notations and texts of her songs. *Photograph by Arthur Clark from F. W. Gaisberg,* The Music Goes Round *(1942).*

The Gwalior gharana consequently has connections which are traced back to the thirteenth century. It also has connections to Tansen in the sixteenth century (Sinha 1970:32), but its most important connections are to those gharanas following Gwalior in time. These are illustrated in Table 7 as summarized here.

Genealogically, Gwalior is related to the founder of the Seheswan gharana, Inayat Khan, the Kirana gharana, Bande Ali Khan, and the Dagar family (which is conventionally not termed a gharana) through the brother founders, Bahram Khan and Haider Khan. One of the founders of the Agra gharana, Gagghe Khuda Baksh, although not genealogically related to Gwalior, left his family and went to study with Nathan Khan, the father of Haddu Khan and Hassu Khan.

There are other gharanas which are less directly connected and yet can still be considered within a more general network of relationships. The founders of the Patiala gharana, for instance, studied with Tanras Khan, founder of one of the Delhi gharanas. They also studied with the famous female vocalist Gokibai, who was herself a disciple of Bande Khan and thus connected to the Dagar tradition. Gwalior and the Khurja gharana, came close to being linked by marriage. Haddu Khan had apparently wanted to marry one of his daughters to Altaf Hussein Khan, the father of the aforementioned Wahid Khan of Khurja. But this match was not accepted because Altaf Hussein's father, the great poet-musician Zahoor Khan, did not feel his family worthy of it (Joshi 1959:15).

The Gwalior gharana was also important because the founders and their immediate relations taught a large number of Maharastrian Brahman vocalists. These earlier Brahman disciples are considered responsible for introducing Hindustani music to Maharastra and teaching their disciples, who continued to represent the Gwalior gharana after the lineage died out with Rehmat Khan in 1922. Currently, however, since there is no one of overriding fame, and no one from the original khandan, the Gwalior gharana is considered virtually extinct.

Since Delhi has been, off and on, the capital and the cultural center of the North Indian musical tradition, many families originally came from Delhi; hence V. H. Khan lists the khandans of Delhi and its environs rather than *a* Delhi gharana. One of the khandans listed is that of Tanras Khan, who was a famous vocalist at the court of Bahadur Shah Zafar, the last Mughal king. When the king was exiled to Rangoon, Tanras Khan went to Hyderabad, where he died around 1890. He is said to have first learned from his father Haider Bakhsh. According to Imam, he is descended from Sri Chand, one of the four Kalawant musicians at the Court of Akbar (1959a:14). Tanras Khan also learned from Mian Aachpal, a Qawwal Bachchhe. Tanras Khan's great-grandson is living in obscurity in Delhi today; but even in his father's time several decades earlier the tradition was considered finished (Chaubey 1945:78).

Perhaps the most viable of the vocal gharanas is that of Agra. The core khandan of the Agra gharana (the left side of Table 8) goes back four generations from Ustad Yunus Hussein Khan (No. 1 in Table 8), although members trace their ultimate origins to Sujjan Khan, a musician at the court of Akbar. The real founder of the Agra gharana is Ghagghe Khuda Baksh, although his brother, the great-great-grandfather of Yunus Khan, is also considered a co-founder.

This khandan has intermarried with a number of other Kalawant khandans, even though its principal exchanges have been with one of the Atrauli khandans. The following list of Kalawant khandans, given by Ustad Yunus Hussein Khan, represents all the khandans with which Agra members are connected by marriage. These khandans were given as "gharanas," in this sense used synonymously with "khandan."

1. Agra gharana of Sujjan Khan
2. Atrauli gharana of Mehboob Khan Daraspiya (No. 37 in Table 8)
3. Atrauli gharana of Alladiya Khan
4. Aligarh gharana of Bade Basheer Khan
5. Delhi gharana of Tanras Khan
6. Sikendra gharana of Ramzan Khan Rangile (known also as Rangile gharana)
7. Kurja gharana of Zahoor Khan Ramdass
8. Hapur gharana of Sajji Khan and Murad Khan
9. Mathura gharana of Kalle Khan Saraspiya

10. Bharatpur gharana
11. Fatehpur-Sikri gharana
12. Agra gharana of Reza Hussein Khan

The kinds of marriage links among these khandans are illustrated in Tables 9–11. Table 8 is a virtually complete genealogy of the Agra gharana and subsequent Tables 9–22 are abstracted from it.

The manner in which marriage relationships create a complex interlinking between two lineages is shown in Table 9. From the perspective of the present generation, kinship can be defined in a number of ways, so that many persons are considered kin both through marriage and descent relationships. Although technically the lineages of Agra and Atrauli can be said to maintain their autonomy, in fact they are now so closely related that they are largely considered as one khandan. Accordingly, on the basis of these multiple-linked genealogical relationships, the idea of Agra-Atrauli gharana can emerge. Men from each lineage have studied with their uncles from the other lineage; consequently, the musical requirements for a complete definition of gharana are fulfilled.

Musicians are sometimes identified with a particular gharana because the details of patrilineal descent are obscured or irrelevant in the public mind. Ustad Fayyaz Khan (Table 8, No. 49) was the outstanding representative of the Agra gharana until his death in 1950. However, he was related to the Agra khandan only through his mother (No. 15). His father (No. 48) belonged to the Sikendra (Rangile) gharana, and Fayyaz Khan is listed as such by Jairazbhoy (1971:24n.). But this fact is little known, and Fayyaz Khan is almost always identified as not only a member of the Agra gharana, but its leading exponent. This identification is musically authentic by virtue of Fayyaz Khan's discipleship under his maternal grandfather and granduncle, both sons of the founder, Gagghe Khuda Baksh (Nos. 19, 18, and 21, respectively). The Agra gharana has had many notable disciples outside the group of hereditary musicians including, ironically enough, B. V. Keshkar, whose pejorative remark concerning the institution of gharanas is one of the epigraphs to this chapter.

Requisites of a Gharana

Another gharana which, from some points of view, is in the process of establishing itself offers a contrast to the Agra gharana, which is established in every way.

In the discussion of Chand Khan's claim to be a member of the "Delhi gharana," I indicated some disagreement as to whether this gharana of his was in fact "authentic." Outsiders call it the Delhi gharana of Mamman Khan, to distinguish it from the Delhi gharana of Tanras Khan. Objections to recognizing this as an actual gharana come primarily from the more orthodox members of the music world. (Indeed, Deshpande does not even refer to a Delhi gharana in his book on vocal traditions [1973].)

Three main objections are advanced. First, it does not have three generations of distinguished vocalists. Kalawants claim that for a gharana to become established, it must have at least a three-generation depth of offspring or disciples who maintain a coherent and recognized style (Deshpande 1973:11). If the gharana begins with Mamman Khan, it is continued by his son, Chand Khan, and the third generation of Mamman Khan's descendants through the male line. There are several vocalists in this youngest generation—one a distinguished soloist. But purists maintain that only in the next generation will the gharana's credentials become established. Their objection is raised partly because there are not enough distinguished vocalists to give it weight. A second objection is, in a sense, a social one. In the past, members of the family were performers of tabla and sarangi; and other members outside the khandan, but in the biradari, still are. Gharanas as stylistic schools are represented only by soloists, not accompanists. Although Mamman Khan is recognized as a great musician, he was after all, a sarangiya. Thus, in terms of a soloist category, the gharana begins only with Chand Khan, who is a vocalist.

The third objection is that this gharana does not represent a truly unique and distinct style. A descendant of Tanras Khan told me that Chand Khan is a disciple of his gharana, and thus represents the Tanras Khan Delhi gharana. Chand Khan states somewhat the same thing but from a different perspective. He asserts that Umrao Khan (Tanras Khan's son) was the previous chief exponent of the Delhi gharana, and now he, Chand Khan, is the head of it. In other words, he does not claim to be its disciple, but its extension, as the Delhi gharana. He can assert this because members of this biradari claim descent from Mian Aachpal, an ustad of Tanras Khan.

Ustad Chand Khan's response to these objections is that, first, his ancestry goes back to the beginning of the eighth century, which gives him more than the necessary genealogical depth. Second, sarangi players are also great musicians, and furthermore, the family has always included vocalists and binkars in the past. In his pamphlet, from which I have previously quoted, he relates a story about a schism in his family because of the sarangi. It also implies that the sarangi is a recent addition to his patrilineage.

> According to a legend when, after the 1857 uprising in Delhi, some of the leading sarangi and bīn players of Delhi including Mamman Khan's maternal grandfather Ghulam Hussein Khan migrated to Ballabh Gahr, Mamman Khan's paternal grandfather treated these relatives rather shabbily because he disapproved of their association with a lowly instrument like the sarangi. This hurt the feelings of Mamman Khan's father Abdul Ghani Khan. As a protest against his father and uncle's behavior, Abdul Ghani Khan decided to take up the sarangi. This annoyed the elders who turned Abdul Ghani out of Ballabh Gahr. He then came back to live in Delhi with his father-in-law [Mamman Khan's maternal grandfather]. He turned his back on ancestral property and devoted his entire talent to the improvement of the sarangi. His devotion to the sarangi earned him the name Sarangi Khan which became Sangi Khan, by which name he is still known. Bundu Khan, one of his grandsons, took to sarangi after his grandfather, but the other grandson [Chand Khan, the narrator], in deference to the wishes of his great-grandfather (who was finally reconciled to his son's passion for sarangi) and with the approval of his grandfather, resumed the vocal tradition of his ancestors under the guidance of his grandfather and grand-uncles.

The legend explains not only that Chand Khan's tradition is a vocal one, through the male line, but also that the sarangi came in through the female line. In addition, it shows that although his great-grandfather and uncles had the same prejudices many musicians have today, they finally accepted their son and nephew, the sarangi player. Bundu Khan is a product of this tradition; in spite of being a sarangi player, he was universally recognized as one of India's foremost musicians.

In the same pamphlet, Chand Khan further establishes the unique identity of his gharana:

> Mamman Khan received his musical training from his paternal grand-father and grand-uncle and later from his father and maternal grand-father, Ghulam Hussein Khan. It is wrong to say that he got any training from Mian Kallu Khan of Patiala or Imdad Khan Sitariya or Chajju Khan Amar Shah. He had great respect for these masters, but he owes no debt of learning from them.

The assertion that Mamman Khan did not learn directly from the just-mentioned three musicians posed somewhat of a puzzle to me, since I had never heard otherwise. But in 1977 I received from a Kalawant artist a genealogy and some notes concerning the Mamman Khan Delhi Gharana, which made precisely these claims.

According to this information, Mamman Khan's ancestors five generations back came from Rajasthan, where they were folk musicians playing the folk sarangi, still found in the area. At the time of Mohammad Shah Rangile, Mamman Khan's great-grand-father abandoned the folk sarangi and adopted the "modern" sarangi. Mamman Khan and his older brother Samman Khan came to Delhi and became disciples of Sajji Khan and Murad Khan of Hapur, learning the style that came to be used in their gharana. Sometime later, Mamman Khan also became a disciple of Ali Baksh (one of the founders of the Patiala gharana) in the house of the vocalist Goura Jan in Calcutta. At still a later time, Mamman Khan became a disciple of Chajju Khan (originally of Moradabad, but later known as a founder of the Bindibazar gharana, which was named for the ward in Bombay where he and other members like Amanat Ali Khan lived. In this same account, Mamman Khan later became a disciple of Ashiq Ali Khan (son of the other founder of Patiala, Fateh Ali) and Imdad Khan, the grandfather of the contemporary sitar maestro Ustad Vilayat Khan.

Amanat Ali Khan, of the Bindibazar gharana, accompanied by tabla, two tanpuras, and harmonium. *Photograph courtesy of Naina Devi and Raag Rang Music Circle.*

Bade Ghulam Ali Khan, the doyen of the Patiala gharana and India's most popular classical vocalist until his death in 1964. *Photograph courtesy of Naina Devi and Raag Rang Music Circle.*

Ustad Mushtaq Ali Khan, considered by many to be the last exponent of the pure Seniya style of sitar playing.

It is obvious from the foregoing that Chand Khan denies these discipleship relations. The veracity of one or another version is less important than the fact of there being different versions. The politics of pedigrees is illustrated by these shifting claims, which can in fact go in either direction. If the intent is to demonstrate the autonomy of a gharana, and by extension the autonomy of the style, discipleship connections to other gharanas will be denied. On the other hand, if claims are being made about the great heritage of a gharana, connections to famous performers of the past will be insisted upon.[5]

Chand Khan says that the history of his khandan is far from unique regarding the presence of sarangi players; other families have also experienced schisms when one of their members decided to take up the sarangi. He adds that in the past families included all kinds of musicians and that there was no distinction between them. How much of this is actual history or rhetorical gesture is impossible to determine. However, this claim becomes particularly interesting in light of Mamman Khan's direct male descendants and the specialties they have adopted: none perform on the sarangi or tabla, all having become soloists (see Table 23). Outside Mamman Khan's lineage, most of the members of the biradari are still accompanists. Thus there exists a core lineage of soloists, and it seems only a matter of time before a new Delhi gharana will have become fully established.

Gharana: Style and Society

If one considers the two major components characterizing a gharana, as musical style and social system, the contrasting evaluations of gharanas by Mujeeb and Keshkar become more understandable. Mujeeb is concerned with the ongoing cultivation of Hindustani musical style, while Keshkar is denouncing what he later calls "castes," which he thinks gharanas have become. *Gharanadār* musicians (musicians born into a gharana) are sensitive to such criticisms, believing that their knowledge has a value which should not be sacrificed. For their part, disciples sometimes defend the system; at other times they ignore it. Musicologists, beginning with Bhatkhande, have interpreted gharanas as style dialects of a single musical system. To them the insularity and secretiveness of gharanadars have been a source of considerable frustration. To the extent that musicologists think of a gharana as a social system, they almost always regard it in a negative light. Among themselves, khandani musicians who form the core of the gharana consider it a social system within which flourish the three relationships of descent, learning, and marriage. From the first two flow the gharana's particular fund of knowledge, which appears as a distinctive musical style; the third produces the gharana's future core representatives. They will be the hereditary guardians of a tradition, enculturated to the significance of maintaining its purity.

In the concept of the gharana, the distinction between musical style and social system is fundamental, but not rigid. Indeed, the concept of gharana is still undergoing changes as it comes to be utilized as a source of identity by a much wider variety of musicians, presumably for an increasingly diverse audience. Controversy regarding what is and what is not a gharana, and who is and is not a member is still common and in many respects is political, as illustrated in the following discussion which summarizes the ways in which the concept is now used and the impression the user means to convey.

"Double Gharanas"

Certain gharanas are "double" in either of two ways. A gharana in the social sense may have two possible names because two different criteria for naming have been applied. Brian Silver found this to be true of the Indore gharana of sitariyas. Because members of this lineage have lived in Indore for a number of generations, they refer to their gharana after their residential locality. They also refer to themselves as belonging to the gharana of Bande Ali Khan, since members of the lineage studied with a disciple of Bande Ali Khan (Silver 1976:46–50).

There are two ways in which these appellations themselves are ambiguous. First, Bande Ali Khan is generally recognized as the founder of the Kirana gharana, a vocal gharana having no direct connection with the Indore sitariyas. Second, the late Ustad Amir Khan, who was raised in Indore, is often claimed as a representative of the Indore gharana, in this sense referring only to his vocal style and not to the sitariya family of Ustad Usman Khan and Ustad Ghulam Husain Khan mentioned by Silver. But what can make this sense of identity even more convoluted is the fact that Amir Khan was influenced by the Bindibazar and Kirana gharanas and, according to Deva, that the Indore gharana of Amir Khan was essentially derived from the other two (1975). Another locale which can refer to separate performing styles is Jaipur, where there are three possibilities. One Jaipur gharana is that of Alladiya Khan (see below). Another is a gharana of Katthak dancers. Still a third is made up of instrumentalists, descendants of Tansen's son (Suratsen or Tantarang Khan) who settled in Jaipur (Prajnanananda 1965:216–17; Sharma 1971:32–47). The *idea* of gharana encompasses other directions as well.

Biradari Identity as Gharana

Most gharanas are named after the ancestral locality of the khandan. Accompanists sometimes name their biradari after its town or city of origin and refer to it as a gharana. Sometimes the name corresponds with that of a known gharana such as the Delhi gharana of Mamman Khan or the Kirana gharana.

The Kirana gharana is traditionally said to have been founded by Ustad Bande Ali Khan, the great binkar; but as a vocal gharana it was actually founded by Abdul Karim Khan (1872–1937), who articulated its style in the first half of this century. Although Abdul Karim Khan lived most of his adult life in Miraj (Maharashtra), his gharana is named after Kirana, in Uttar Pradesh, where he was born (Deshpande 1972:30). Abdul Karim belonged to a biradari of Kirana accompanists, whose members now identify themselves as the Kirana gharana. For example, the late Shakur Khan, the only sarangiya recipient of the prestigious Sangeet Natak award, told me that his style of playing was in the Kirana style. His son is presently a young and upcoming vocalist, but virtually all of the other major contemporary vocalists of the Kirana gharana are non-hereditary disciples. Publicly, the Kirana gharana is known because of famous vocalists like Bhimsen Joshi and Hirabai Barodekar; but accompanists from Kirana, by virtue of their kinship to the founder and a presumed identity of musical style, also claim Kirana as gharana identity.

Sometimes, however, a named biradari corresponding with no established gharana is still used as an identity. Accompanists from Moradabad, for example, refer to the "Moradabad gharana" (rarely) or to "our gharana" (more commonly), which in this context is synonymous with "biradari."

Tabla Baj

Named tabla baj are conceptually distinct from gharanas, but in certain contexts "baj" and "gharana" are used interchangeably, as, for example, when the location of a biradari of which a tabla player is a member and a tabla style have the same name. As far as I know this is the case only for Delhi, where there is a distinct Delhi baj as well as the Delhi biradari. Members of this biradari call themselves the Delhi gharana, and the table players of this group are the primary representatives of this baj. In a program featuring younger artists, for example, a member of the Delhi biradari is described as a tabla player "belonging to the Delhi gharana." Another tabliya featured in the same program, "belongs to the Farukkabad gharana," although this "gharana" is the name only of a well-known baj. In another program, a musician is described as a "well-known tabla player of Delhi. He belongs to the Delhi gharana of musicians." In the first of these three examples, both primary meanings of "gharana" could be understood, style and social group. In the second, "gharana" can only mean style, since there is no gharana of this name and the performer is in fact a member of the Moradabad biradari. In the last example, "gharana" clearly refers to the Delhi biradari, a social group.[6]

Charismatic Authorities

A person who has had many disciples and who has exerted a profound influence separate from pre-existing traditions may sometimes have a gharana named after him, such as the Atrauli (or Jaipur) gharana of Alladiya Khan (1855–1946). Alladiya Khan studied with many different ustads and created a unique style. He had many disciples, including Kesarbai Kekar, considered by many to be India's greatest vocalist until her recent death. His is a separate gharana, sometimes referred to as the Alladiya Khan gharana, even though he did not want it named after himself but rather after his birthplace, Jaipur (Deshpande 1972:26). Because his ancestral home is Atrauli, it is also sometimes referred to as Jaipur-Atrauli, and even as the Kolhapur gharana after the town in which he was court musician for many years.

The politics of pedigree is well-illustrated in the writings of Deshpande, a disciple of the Alladiya Khan gharana. He states that Alladiya Khan's family was originally Hindu and "traces its ancestry to one Baba Vishwambharadas, the ancestor of Swami Haridas, the guru of the famous Tansen." In other words it was a family, originally Brahman Hindu, of traditional musicians *ancestral* to Tansen (1972:26–27).

For instrumentalists, especially, gharanas named after charismatic authorities relate ultimately to Tansen in one way or another. The several ways to reach Tansen are often complex. Table 24 illustrates the genealogical connections between Wazir Khan—the ustad of Hafeez Ali Khan and Allaudin Khan—and Tansen, through his daughter Saraswati. On the list also are Sadarang and Adarang, the developers of the modern khayal style of vocal music, and perhaps also the originators of solo instrumental music. Vocalists often (but not always) trace a disciple connection to Sadarang-Adarang, and through them to Tansen as well. But for contemporary instrumentalists, the connection to Tansen is particularly important.

Table 25 illustrates the genealogy of the Seniyas, descendants of Tansen through his son Bilas Khan. Descendants of Tansen's daughter are known also as sadarangiyas (after Sadarang) and as binkars, the bīn having been a specialty of their lineage from the time of Naubat Khan, Tansen's son-in-law. Descendants of Tansen's sons were also known as rababiyas, since the rabab was their particular specialty. The Seniyas themselves branched off into two sections after the disintegration of the Mughal Empire; one group went to the western part of India, putting themselves under the patronage of Rajput princes, and becoming known as *Pachhaōs* or *Pachhawālās* ("Westerners").

The other group travelled east, joining the courts of Hindu and Muslim princes in Oudh, Rewa, Gwalior, Banaras, Bengal, and elsewhere, becoming known as *Purabiyās* ("Easterners") (Sen 1972:171, 252, 253; Prajnanananda 1960:17). The last rababiya at the Mughal court was Chajju Khan, who left during the "Time of Troubles" just before Shah Alam became the last titular emperor in 1759 (Sen 1972: 252; Spear 1951:8–10, 120–22).

As mentioned earlier, no living musicians claim direct descent from Tansen through any line, although musicians do claim discipleship. Ustad Mushtaq Ali Khan, one of India's most respected musicians, is considered an exponent of the pure Seniya style. His father studied with a disciple of Amrit Sen, a disciple (possibly a son) of the great Rahim Sen, famous as the leading sitarist of his time (Imam 1959b:23). Rahim Sen was a direct descendant (either son, grandson or great-grandson, depending on which genealogy one checks) of Maseet Khan, the originator of the Maseet Khani baj, himself said to be a descendant of Bilas Khan, one of Tansen's sons.

There are then a variety of interpretive frames for the concept of gharana. The important point is that the concept of gharana, somewhat like the concept of caste, exists at several levels. There is no way to enumerate gharanas since different people have different ideas about what they are and how the concept of gharana should be used. (Table 26 compares the gharana lists of six authors to illustrate this point.)

Pedigrees

Above all, a gharana identity provides a shorthand notation for a musician's pedigree, be it a biological or a cultural inheritance or both. Sometimes, both modes of inheritance are indicated to establish a more precise identity. In Table 8, for example, No. 43 (Ustad Sharafat Hussein Khan), a famous vocalist, is shown as descended from Atrauli khandans through both parents. Yet he was a disciple of Fayyaz Khan (No. 49), his mother's sister's husband (who, it will be recalled, was himself descended from the Rangile gharana through his father). In concert programs, Sharafat Hussein Khan is identified either as representing the

Agra gharana style or as being a member of the Agra-Atrauli gharana.

The genealogical depth of a musician's pedigree is commonly stressed although consistency seems to dissolve at a certain point, usually three generations back from the present. As we have seen in Chapter 4, Wahid Hussein Khan's long pedigree agrees with the one given by Vilayat Hussein Khan, except that the version I received from Wahid Hussein Khan has two extra generations (Khan 1959:191–93). For the Gwalior gharana several contradictory genealogies are given by authorities. The genealogy in Table 7 is based largely on interviews with Zia Mohiuddin Dagar, but differs in details from a version I published earlier, demonstrating how pedigrees can become distorted in even a few years (cf. Neuman 1978a:190).[7] Aggarwal's information on the Gwalior gharana is quite at variance from Vilayat Hussein Khan's account and others by creating a kinship connection between Haddu and Hassu Khan and Bade Muhammad Khan and making the grandfather of the two brothers (in Khan's version) their father (1966:25–27).

Pedigrees become distorted because of faulty memory particularly, as one goes back in generations. A set of brothers are sometimes remembered as ancestral to one another, telescoping the pedigree, or the opposite occurs, in which two or three generations are collapsed into one, making three brothers out of a grandfather, father, and son. This phenomenon has been studied in some detail in other Muslim communities outside of India, and it showed up repeatedly in my own research (cf. Peters 1960).

Pedigrees are sometimes consciously manipulated, although it is difficult to document such instances. I know of one ancestor who was dropped from a Kalawant pedigree because he associated with accompanists and singing girls, and there are several instances where individuals appear in a pedigree, only to be disputed by other musicians who claim they are artificial additions to bring (unjustified) honor to a family.

Since gharanadar musicians are considered by some to be the monopolists of the music tradition and by others as its preservers, we can conclude that the politics of pedigree revolves around attempts to demonstrate the authenticity, age, and consequent purity of a lineage and the body of knowledge associated with it. This is accomplished through two strategies: one historical, which involves the presentation of an extant pedigree to affirm the legitimacy of a given gharana, and the other social, which requires the arrangement of proper marriages for the maintenance of a proper pedigree. In this way the present generation sustains its relationship to its past and assumes responsibility for its future.

6. Adaptive Strategies of Hindustani Music Culture

A politically united India has yet to find in its heart the unity of spirit that can establish that reciprocity of created and shared values where artist, patron, and public are integrated in the pattern of its traditional civilization.

Stella Kramrisch

The introduction of India's railway and telegraph system in the early 1850s, the great uprising of 1857 with its concomitant social dislocations, and a slow but steady increase in urbanization set the stage for the evolution of gharanas. Their rise can be understood as an adaptive response to a changed social and cultural environment after the mid-nineteenth century.[1]

The gharana as a sociomusical institution provided two important functions. First, it served as a carefully controlled pool of individuals from which highly specialized musicians could be recruited. Since gharanas were in the first instance based on family descent, the direction and extent of musical transmission could be carefully controlled, monitored, and nurtured through a complex web of kinship obligations and responsibilites. Because the families were Muslim, members could, unlike their Hindu neighbors, marry cousins close and distant, thereby maintaining direct control over the property of the gharana, their musical knowledge.

Aside from providing a social organization of specialized knowledge, gharanas provided a sociomusical identity for musicians, who, with the advent of modern means of quick transportation and communication, were exposed to a wider, and more diverse and anonymous, public. The name of a gharana did not leave the musician similarly anonymous.

Before the 1850s, communication and movement between courts was often a matter of weeks and months; afterwards, it became a matter of hours and days. Although musicians were still largely patronized by the nobility and the newly rich merchants, their family residences became autonomous, constant, and eventually ancestral. Musicians travelled to different places and often stayed for months and even years, but they always had an ancestral home, now invariably located in urban areas. Centers of transportation, communication, and a visiting public, towns and cities also gave gharanas their names.

It appears that almost as soon as gharanas were formed, they themselves underwent changes to adapt to a rapidly changing social environment. New gharanas formed out of older ones, such as the aforementioned Patiala gharana, and the notion of a gharana as sociomusical identity expanded to include solo instrumentalists and, eventually, accompanists.

Perhaps the most fundamental change in the social environment of Hindustani music was the forms which patronage has taken in this century. A hundred years ago, professional musicians in India, as in other parts of the world, were maintained by the aristocracy, a pattern of support that continued well into the 1900s. In an article published in 1919, Basanta K. Roy describes the progressive patronage of the Gaekwar (ruler) of Baroda, contrasting it favorably with the absence of state support for music in America.[2]

Musicians today can still recollect the era of private patronage. Ustad Sabri Khan, for example, remembers going at night with his grandfather to the house of a wealthy businessman, his grandfather's patron. Whenever the patron decided to have a musical party, Sabri Khan's grandfather, on call every night, was summoned to accompany the vocalists. For the nobility, musical parties were a desideratum of rank, as Satyajit Ray's film *Jalsaghar* ("The Music Room") so aptly illustrates, a prestige symbol which was utilized in a similar manner in Europe (cf. Raynor 1972:75 and *passim*).

Older informants still remember their roles in the courts, viewing a position there as the apex of a musician's career. The late Ahmed Jan Thirakwa spent twenty-six years as a court musician in Rampur. Before this period he had been associated with a theater company. He left the theater company when he was called to Rampur, "because it was a court service, and a respectable one." Musicians were provided with their own quarters where they lived with their families. Every evening they had to be present, whether or not music was to be performed. According to Ahmed Jan, musicians arrived after the Nawab of Rampur had finished dinner—about nine o'clock—and stayed until twelve, playing for him and his friends. "Common men were not allowed in."

Court musicians were paid a monthly salary. Ahmed Jan Thirakwa received Rs. 200/– per month ("but Rs. 200/– of those days is equivalent to Rs. 1000/– today"). In addition, a house supplied with electricity and water was included, along with gifts of money on ceremonial occasions.

Members of the nobility—at least those who are now musicians—claim that musicians were treated with great respect. The late Birendra Kishore Roy Choudhary described for me the condition of musicians whom both his father and later he patronized, in his court at Gauripur in Bengal:

> All zamindars [landlords] used to have court musicians employed by them, so we had many musicians under our employment. From my boyhood I used to listen to their music. Actually I only started learning serious music after my graduation from Calcutta University in 1924. . . . There were two permanent musicians in our court (it was very small) but other great musicians used to come and stay for three to four months of the year. . . . [The two permanent musicians] performed every day, that is according to their own convenience, my father's, and mine. They were like family members. When a guest was coming and if he [the musician] was in the house and playing,

then he would play, like that. It was settled informally . . . we gave them permission to go outside and perform. In those days [the salary of musicians] was very cheap. One received Rs. 250/– and the other Rs. 100/– [per month]. Those days the cost of living was cheap. Rs. 250/– means today Rs. 1000/–. Musicians who came from outside were given a lump sum, Rs. 500/– to Rs. 600/– like that. . . .

A recently published work by Joan Erdman (1978) provides the first detailed study of the social organization of musicians in an Indian court. From it we learn that musicians were incorporated into the bureaucracy of the Jaipur court, in departments called *karkhānās*. Not only classical musicians were included but also local musicians from the countryside. In contrast to the Mughal practice of honoring individual musicians, the maharajas of Jaipur incorporated musicians and other cultural specialists into their households, providing them their livelihood with salaries and sometimes with income from villages.

The influence of musicians in the court life of nineteenth-century India reached its apogee in the Lucknow court of Wajid Ali Shah, where a contemporary observer reported that a coterie of musicians practically ran the state for a time.

The most powerful favorites were two eunuchs, two fiddlers [sarangiyas?], two poetasters, and the Minister and his creatures. The Minister could not stand a moment without the eunuchs, fiddlers and poets, and he is obliged to acquiesce in all the orders given by the king for their benefit. The fiddlers have the control over administration of civil justice; the eunuchs over that of criminal justice, public buildings, etc. The Minister has the land revenue; and all are making enormous fortunes. [Quoted in Edwardes 1960:155].

Although interpretations of the Lucknow court vary in details (cf. Imam 1959 and Sharar 1975), the point of the musicians' importance is the same. Imam, relating a story from his own past, notes that court musicians demanded and were accorded great respect, and that at any sign of disrespect, they sent in their resignations (1959a:17).

With the cessation of princely patronage, which began to decline at about the middle of the nineteenth century but lasted in some cases until Independence in 1947, musicians had to look elsewhere for support. In the first three decades of this century three institutions emerged which eventually came to provide the basis of patronage today: radio, public concerts, and teaching institutions. They are important not only as providers of income for musicians, but as influences on the totality of Hindustani music culture.

All India Radio: The State as Patron

The first regular broadcasting station in India began service in 1927. Initially a commercial station, it was taken over by the government in the early thirties and by 1939 there were nine radio stations located in Delhi, Bombay, Calcutta, Madras, Peshawar, Lahore, Lucknow, Dacca, and Tiruchirapalli (Mullick 1974:13–16).

K. S. Mullick, formerly an All India Radio administrator, recalls the difficulty of persuading musicians to perform for radio in the early days. The grand ustads were reluctant to have their art transmitted to just anyone, and amateurs did not perform in public. Consequently, most early musicians were recruited from the salon districts. Because of this practice the Delhi radio station was nicknamed " 'Sarkari Chawri Bazaar' (official Chawri Bazaar)—after the well-known street where singing and dancing women carried on their profession." This reputation had the unfortunate effect of discouraging participation either by "respectable musicians" or by amateurs from respectable social backgrounds. After Independence a ban prohibiting anyone "whose private life is a public scandal" was introduced by Sardar Patel when he became Minister of Broadcasting. This opened the way for "non-professional artistes to offer themselves for broadcast engagements" (1974:33–34).

As of 1961, 10,000 musicians filled the rolls of All India Radio (Mathur, 1965:127). Among them were many "men and women from educated and 'respectable' families who [were] no longer shy of giving performances and receiving fees" (ibid.). J. C. Mathur, also formerly with A.I.R., thinks that this has changed the status of the professional musician, who is no longer "subject to the whims of his patron. The only distinction now between the amateur and the professional musician is that the former is obviously unable to devote as much time to music as the latter" (ibid.).

In 1969, All India Radio in New Delhi had 713 "Casual/ Staff Artists (music)" listed on its rolls.[3] Of these, 146 were listed as Karnatak artists, ten as composers, two as chief music producers (one each for Hindustani and Karnatak music), one as an instrumental caretaker, and the remaining 554 as Hindustani music artists. The distinction between "staff" and "casual" is the difference between musicians who work full-time at All India Radio (and in a few instances at the Television Center next to A.I.R. New Delhi), and other artists who occasionally come to broadcast recitals for which they receive remuneration, but who are not regular employees of the radio station.

Of the 554 "Hindustani" music artists, 96 (17 percent) are on the staff, and 458 (83 percent) are casual (see Table 27). A further distinction in the A.I.R. list is between "classical" musicians and "light classical" musicians. Listed as classical are 289 musicians; 63 (22 percent) on the staff and 226 (78 percent) casual. The light classical category is itself broken down into "light classical vocal" and the Light Classical Orchestra. The former category includes one staff artist and 232 casual artists, while the latter contains 32 staff artists and no casual artists.

Vocalists at A.I.R.

Few vocalists are staff artists at All India Radio, the vast majority being casual artists who come from time to time to broadcast performances (see Tables 28 and 30). Because vocalists are musically so highly specialized there is very little they can do as vocalists on a regular basis. And in fact no vocalist staff artist performs vocal music as a primary activity at A.I.R. Rather, they perform either of two major functions: playing the tanpura or being administrative officers. In terms of social rank, these activities are graded at opposite ends, being respectively the lowest and highest positions in the staff artist hierarchy.

The drone is of fundamental importance in Indian classical

music, and when provided by a tanpura, the tanpura player's musical function is basic (Deva 1967:17–82). Yet, perhaps paradoxically, no sociomusical identity corresponds to "tanpura player." No one studies the tanpura or performs riaz to perfect a technique, although musicians do have standards by which to judge it. For example, good tanpura players can maintain an unwavering drone, consistent dynamic range and tempo, and, perhaps most importantly, they can sustain their patience for non-stop strumming through a two-hour, non-stop performance. Nevertheless, to play the tanpura requires no formal training, indicates no special talents, and consequently justifies no professional status.

This is something which Western students have difficulty understanding. They are typically as interested in the tanpura as the solo instrument and want to know how it is played, how long it takes to learn, and whether it is difficult to play. When told that it is not in fact learned in any formal sense, they are amazed, a reaction which never ceases to amuse Indian musicians.

The tanpura player thus has a musical role to play without a corresponding social identity to sustain that role. Traditionally, the tanpura was played by the vocalist and by disciples. Another musician must be available to play the tanpura for vocalists who do not play it themselves while singing or desire more than one tanpura, also for vocalists and instrumentalists who bring no disciples to the studio. In the unusual contexts of a radio studio or in performances abroad, providing a tanpura player can be difficult since typically no disciple or relations of the performer are in attendance. Performing in the West, Ravi Shankar pioneered one kind of solution by employing his instrument maker as the tanpura player. Abroad, the tanpura player has thus gained an identity--on the back of album covers—which has never actually existed in India. It is more usual nowadays to have expatriate Indians with some musical training provide tanpura accompaniment for concerts abroad.

At A.I.R. this problem has been solved by the hiring of vocalists whose primary function is to play the tanpura. There are seven musicians listed in Table 32 who play tanpura in the Light Classical Orchestra at the Delhi radio station. Four have no specialties classified other than tanpura playing, while of the other three two are listed as vocalists and one as a *jaltarang* player. The first four, however, do not personally identify themselves as tanpura players, but as vocalists. The one staff artist listed in the table of "light vocal music" artists (Table 30) is functionally a tanpura player, but classifies himself as a disciple of the Kirana gharana and a classical music vocalist.

At the other end of the hierarchy, vocalists function in an administrative and executive capacity. All seven such vocalists at A.I.R. are fairly well-known performers: two are "producers of music," three are "assistant music producers," one is a composer, and the other is at the Television Center.

The music producer organizes and schedules the programs to be aired in the following weeks. He sees to the notification of casual artists, sending them a letter which gives them the name of the rāg they are to play, as well as the time and place where the program will be taped or broadcast. It is also his function to arrange the schedule of staff artists, making sure that they are in the studios on time. Not all music producers are vocalists. At the time of the study there were also a flutist and a jaltarang player who were music producers.

Instrumentalists at A.I.R.

The rubric "instrumentalist" comprises the other specialist category in the A.I.R. directory. The twenty-eight accompanists compose just one half of the staff artists of classical music. Discounting three solo instrumentalists whose primary function is that of music producer, and one other who is a composer, accompanists make up somewhat more than half of the performing staff artists at All India Radio (see Table 31).

As the remaining staff artists are solo instrumental performers, the question arises, what do soloists *do*? If they were all to perform solo, there would be very little for any one of them to do, and no time whatsoever available for casual artists. All India Radio's solution for keeping soloists reasonably occupied is the National Orchestra, *Vadya Vrindan* (cf. Joshi 1963: 9–13; Mullick 1974: 39–40).

Every morning from about ten until twelve noon, the performers of solo instruments (along with some accompanists and Karnatak musicians) rehearse orchestral compositions created by A.I.R. composers, which are later broadcast. Compositions are written in solfège notation, and copies are distributed to the performers at the time of rehearsals. Following explicit directions from the conductor, musicians work out a piece of music section by section. Taped performances ranging between ten and thirty minutes in length are broadcast almost every evening.

Delhi radio has four channels, one of which, Delhi A, regularly broadcasts classical Indian music. The accompanying schedule illustrates the programming heard with some variation every day of the week.

Sample Program Schedule at All India Radio (Delhi)[4]

*Delhi A**

7:10–7:30 A.M.
Anant Lal and Party
Shahnai: *Bhairav* [Rāg]

8:15–8:45 A.M.
J. Mattoo
Khayal *Mian Ki Todi*

11:00–11:30 A.M.
Ghulam Ahmed
Khayal *Ramkali*

11:30 A.M.–12:00 M.
R. K. Suryanarayanam
Vina Recital (Karnatak)

12:00 M.–12:30 P.M.
Bade Ghulam Ali Khan
Phonograph Records

1:30–1:40 P.M.
Ajai Kumar Khanna
Sitar: *Dhun* [classicized folk tune]

5:30–5:50 P.M.
J. Mattoo
Khayal *Patdeep*

5:50–6:05 P.M.
Ajai Kumar Khanna
Sitar: Rāg *Pilu*

8:15–8:35 P.M.
Anant Lal and Party
Shahnai: Apni Pasand ka Rāg
[Your Favorite Rāg]

9:45–10:00 P.M.
Ajai Rumar Khanna
Sitar: Rāg *Desh*

10:40–11:10 P.M.
Anant Lal and Party
Shahnai

11:10–11:20 P.M.
Vadya Vrindan
[National Orchestra]

11:20–11:50 P.M.
Ghulam Ahmed
Khayal *Bageshri*

*Total 190 minutes of Hindustani classical (exclusive of records); 10 minutes orchestra; 30 minutes Karnatak

A given artist is usually featured two or three times a day. Two of the artists in the sample schedule are on the staff (Anant Lal and J. Mattoo). As staff artists, they receive no extra remuneration for performing over the air. The members of the party accompanying Anant Lal are casual artists, receiving fees for their performances.

Fees are determined by a grading system at A.I.R. A panel of experts listens to the auditions of musicians and assigns the grades. Both staff and casual artists are assigned grades which ideally reflect their merits, although political considerations sometimes influence the results (cf. Mullick 1974:37). For example, if some members of the experts panel belong to the same gharana as the auditioner, he may expect a more favorable outcome than he could otherwise count on.

Fee ranges for the grades are illustrated for casual artists in Table 29. (The fees pertain to 1969 and have been substantially increased since.) The "top-class" rank is reserved for eminent musicians, with very few achieving this grade—only ten from a total of 554. No top-class grade category exists for light classical music artists, and their fees are proportionately lower. A and B-high grades are assigned to the professionally competent musicians. Those having an A grade usually enjoy an established reputation, whereas those with a B-high grade are either younger artists "coming up" or older "hacks." The B grade is assigned to 60 percent of all musicians and 21 percent of the staff artists. Assignees of the B grade consist of young artists just beginning their careers, the vast majority of whom are light vocal music artists (Table 30). This category includes many amateurs who sing folk music (*lok gīt*), ghazals, qawwali, and other "light" song types.

Some musicians have more than one grade if they are proficient in more than one category of music. Thus A.K. is a top-class vocalist for khayal and receives Rs. 140/– for a day's broadcast. He is also graded B-high as a thumri and dadra singer, for which he receives Rs. 60/–. The grade which a casual artist achieves also determines the number of programs which he gives in a particular year. A musician of B grade has three programs a year, a B-high musician gives four to six programs a year, an

177

artist of A grade presents ten programs a year, and an artist graded top-class broadcasts twelve programs a year.

Casual artists are recruited from essentially two classes of musicians, those who are too good to be staff artists and those who are not good enough. It is noteworthy that all the top-class musicians save one are casual, the one exception being an accompanist. At the other end of the scale (Table 28), 139 out of a total of 154 B-grade artists are casual artists.

In 1969 the monthly salary for staff artists ranged from a maximum of Rs. 350/– for B-grade musicians to Rs. 540/– for A-grade musicians. Top-class musicians used to receive Rs. 50/– above the maximum Rs. 540/– per month, but this amount was later cut, so that they now receive the same maximum as an A-grade musician.[5]

Life at All India Radio

Staff artists, like court musicians of an earlier time, are on duty for a specified number of hours every day. There are two shifts at the station, the first beginning technically at six in the morning and lasting until two or two-thirty in the afternoon, when both Delhi A and B channels close down. I do not know the reason for the interruption in broadcasting, but it is probably due to a combination of budget considerations and siestas. The second shift begins at four in the afternoon and lasts until midnight.

In practice, musicians are rarely on duty during the whole shift, simply because there is nothing to do for most of the day. Live music programming does not begin before 7:00 A.M. for the morning shift, and not before 5:30 P.M. for the evening shift. Accompanists, that is sarangi or tabla players, usually perform at least once a day, but sometimes only as a five-minute filler between regularly scheduled programs.

Some musicians attempt to practice during their free time, but the only available spaces are empty studios, which do not remain free for very long. Also, since many musicians are on duty at any one time and usually not more than two or three studios are available, there is very little opportunity to accomplish a real riaz.

178

The main meeting place is the A.I.R. canteen, where staff artists and other employees gather for tea and biscuits. This is the place to find musicians throughout the day. Between 4:30 and 5:00 P.M., the second shift gathers here, after having both checked in with the duty officer and noted the day's schedule on the way to the canteen in the rear. A clipboard on the wall lists the programs—who is to perform when, with whom, and in which studio.

Visiting All India Radio with sarangi player Ali Ahmed, I observe a typical evening shift.[6] Ali Ahmed, the sarangiya, finds that he is scheduled for the "Spotlight" program. This means that he must perform for a few minutes after a news commentary which begins at 9:15 P.M. but rarely lasts until the next scheduled program at 9:30. As he has nothing scheduled before the "Spotlight" program, he has to wait around for five hours. Rather than do this he approaches his friend, Nazir Ali, and asks him to substitute. "Look, Nazir bhai, I've got the 'Spotlight' program tonight, but I have to visit a friend of mine whose wife is ill. Why don't you take it for me?" Nazir gives a little growl as he always does when asked, because this happens regularly between musicians, and the reactions are variations on the basic theme. "I can't take it tonight," he answers. "I'm on at 8:15 and I want to get home early tonight. Anyway, why don't you go to your friend's house a little later?" He smiles sardonically and winks at me, while dragging on his biri. They both know the routine, which includes the invariable bantering back and forth. Ali Ahmed persists. "Brother, it's really true what I'm saying. His wife is ill. He came by this morning and asked if I could bring him some medicine from my friend, the doctor; I really have to go!" Nazir gives me another knowing and disbelieving look as he readies his response. Just then Mr. Kapoor comes rushing out of the studios and exclaims how glad he is to see Ali Ahmed and Nazir Ali.

Mr. Kapoor is a vocalist, but his main duties are administrative. As an assistant music producer, he is responsible for seeing that the programs get on the air, on time and correctly, with no mix-ups. Sometimes he has to find a substitute at the last minute, as he must tonight. A staff artist just called in—it was hard for him to get to a phone earlier—saying that he could not come; now they need someone to take his place. The program is scheduled in twenty-five minutes. Can Ali Ahmed fill in? Ali Ahmed would be glad to fill in for the missing accompanist. There's only one thing: he really can't stay for the "Spotlight" program, as a friend of his needs some medicine for his sick wife and so he has to leave early to get the medicine. Why doesn't Kapoor Sahib find someone to fill his night slot, and he will play in the next slot? Kapoor pleads with him, saying that already one man isn't there and where is he going to find someone else to do it. And so it goes. Ali Ahmed finally convinces Nazir to do the "Spotlight," and he goes into the studio to substitute for the missing accompanist.

A light vocal casual artist scheduled for a program arrives half an hour ahead of time. He sings his song, perhaps a poem by Ghalib set to his own music. The staff composer must arrange an orchestral accompaniment for it. (The Light Music Orchestra is a small ensemble having between five and fifteen performers.) After listening to the vocalist the composer sings (or plays on the piano) a background for him, a melodic accompaniment. Then the orchestra follows suit. The composer introduces variations by indicating where an instrumental solo should come or by telling the violinist, for example, to play an octave above the rest with ornaments. This preparation is called a rehearsal; it is all done orally with no written score for the ensemble, which is ready for live broadcast in less than thirty minutes.

Interaction

The ambience at All India Radio is casual and comparatively egalitarian. Accompanists tend to interact more often and more intensely with each other than with soloists. There is, however, a marked hierarchical distinction between the extreme graded ranks. Staff artists of A-grade are indistinguishable from those of B-high grade. But the relationship between staff artists of A grade and those of B grade is marked by hierarchical distinctions. This is exemplified most markedly in the canteen. Ali Ahmed (sarangi, A), Nazir Ali (sarangi, B-high), and Gopal Khanna (tabla, A) regularly sit together. They are always joined by others (or in their turn join the group already sitting at the table). They sit down without ceremony, next to or across from one another. When musicians such as Vinod Sharma (sarangi, B) or Zakir Ahmed (tanpura, B) approach the table, however, they ask for permission and usually seat themselves at some distance from the main group. Theirs is clearly a subordinate rank expressed by the fact that they rarely speak unless spoken to, otherwise simply listening to (and nodding with) the conversation of the central group.

As the sun begins to be less oppressive in the early evening, musicians often sit in little clusters on the lawn within the grounds of the station. About this time some Muslim musicians may be seen praying together; Ali Ahmed, Nazir Ali, Barkat Ali and Imtiaz Hussein form one such group. This does not always occur; often some members of the group are missing, and others join in.

In other social situations, Barkat Ali will limit his interactions with other accompanists. He is the only top-class staff artist at the station and expresses his rank by maintaining distance. He sits occasionally with the others in the canteen, but always "isolated," sitting at the head of the table, or at an unoccupied side where no one sits next to him. He is respected by all, but is considered "very proud" by some. Recognized as a prominent artist, he is at the same time older than most other staff artists. He gives his age as fifty-five years, but he is known to be quite a bit older. If his real age were known he would have been retired at the mandatory sixty years.[7]

Interaction between the higher-grade accompanists and soloist-administrators is manifested by outward mutual respect. Some balancing prestige factors operate at this level. Soloists, by virtue of their sociomusical identity, occupy a higher rank than do accompanists. But in the context of A.I.R. they do not practice their traditional specialty because they are the administrators and producers. Even the staff soloists are engaged in a form of musical activity which is not traditional, the National Orchestra and the Light Music Orchestra. Only accompanists practice their traditional occupation of performing classical Indian music. Theirs is a position which, structurally, appears identical to that of the court musician in the past, and not only in terms of being on duty for a certain period of time. They are also the "resident" musicians who are on call to accompany "guest" soloists, just as musicians resident at court performed for their patrons. They are the regulars—the musical members of the household—whereas even the administrators who appear on A.I.R. broadcasts do so as guests, not as a part of their regular activity.

All other things being equal, these inverted hierarchical elements result in a balance between administrative soloists and performing accompanists. Both are servants of A.I.R., and only at the higher administrative levels, such as the Chief Producer of Music, is there no ambivalence in status. The Chief Producer is in control, and the few occasions where he and the staff artists interact exhibit the wide difference of rank between them. The Chief Producer of Music for Hindustani music is also director of the National Orchestra. He is usually not present at rehearsals, but when he walks into the room, the bustle of rehearsal activity is transformed into immediate quiet. The conductor and the administrators of lower rank politely make requests of a staff artist; the Chief Producer commands.

Being a staff artist is also part of the sociomusical identity of a musician, but it has different kinds of significance for soloists and accompanists. In a public performance, a staff artist's position at All India Radio will invariably be announced. Soloists who have "made it" as concert performers, it will be recalled, are never staff artists. For a soloist serious about a concert career, performing in an orchestra or arranging light classical music is demeaning and musically unsatisfactory. Thus, on the concert stage the identity of A.I.R. staff artist is at best an ambivalent prestige factor for a soloist. The accompanist is not in the same position, since being "in service" with respect to his traditional rank is already a significant move upward. He is, after all, a staff *artist.*

For any musician, be he soloist or accompanist, a position at A.I.R. is often seen as an impediment to a concert career. This is less true for the sarangi player, who has a much narrower choice, for a solo concert career, limited as he is to vocal accompaniment. All musicians, however, require tabla players and, as we have already indicated, their importance has increased in the last few decades. Muhammad Hussein Khan, for example, could have joined the staff several years ago. But he explains that having to be on duty six days a week would keep him so busy that he would have no time to practice, maintain his contacts, and keep up a busy concert career. He can earn the equivalent of a month's income at A.I.R. in one or two nights on the stage.

Staff artists, especially those of A rank, may give public performances, augmenting their regular income—sometimes considerably. Gopal Khanna, for example, earns the maximum for an A-grade staff artist (Rs. 540/– per month). During the season he performs publicly in Delhi and outside at several music festivals, and in a good year he earns Rs. 5000/– extra. Staff artists are given one month's leave per year, which they are free to take at any time and in any sequence. Extensive concertizing requires leaving the security of a regular income as a staff artist to attempt a career as a concert artist.

All India Radio turns out to be the major source of support for the rank-and-file musicians regularly employed there. Its patronage of casual artists is also considered important for those who live on otherwise infrequent engagements plus a few tuition fees. Sitarist Mubarak Ali for example, performs for A.I.R. ten times a year. He receives Rs. 120/– for each performance, which gives him Rs. 1200/– a year. He also earns about Rs. 1000/– to 1500/– per year from public performances. In addition, he has three students—two who are Westerners—from whom he earns about Rs. 500/– per month or Rs. 6000/– annually. His total annual income comes to about Rs. 8500/–, only 14 percent of which comes from his fees as a casual artist at A.I.R. However, its significance is greater than shown by the percentage, since the income from A.I.R. is regular and dependable. Disciples come and go, particularly Western ones, and there can be lean years for public performances.

All India Radio's effect on the music culture of India generally, and Delhi in particular, is not limited to its economic support of musicians, although this is considerable. A.I.R.'s patronage has had an effect on the social status of musicians (Mathur 1965). Addressing all Muslim musicians—in other words, most hereditary musicians—as "Khan Sahib," an honorific extending to accompanists as well as soloists, was a practice begun at A.I.R. Sarangi players and tabla players in the old days were called "sarangiwalla" and "tabalchi," terms of address and reference which were demeaning. "Sarangiya" and "tabliya" are now used as polite terms of reference, and "Khan Sahib" as a polite term of address.[8]

Another marked influence of All India Radio has been the ban on the harmonium. Although it has been commonly believed (myself included) that B. V. Keshkar, Minister for Information and Broadcasting in the early 1950s, was responsible for this ban, it was actually instituted by John Foulds, an Englishman who had come to India to study its music and was appointed head of the Delhi station's Western music section in the 1930s (Mullick 1974:38). Many theorists have argued that the harmonium negatively affected the tonality of Indian vocalists because of its tempered tuning and its inability to simulate the various ornamental structures such as the mir and gamak so basic to classical Indian music. Foulds himself believed that, when broadcast, the harmonium overshadowed the singer.[9] One of the challenging ethnomusicological puzzles is that the limitations of the harmonium did not inhibit the greatest vocalists of India from utilizing it regularly as the accompanying instrument. The harmonium has the advantage that a vocalist can accompany himself, something he cannot do, for musical *and* social reasons, on the sarangi. The difference in timbre and intonation does not seem to have been crucial, in spite of the (verbal) premium put on the sarangi's ability to match the human voice, and the very high premium on exact intonation.

The harmonium has been popular in India since the nineteenth century. As early as the seventeenth century, an English traveler, John Fryer, reported that the organ attracted special attention there:

> In what perfection [Indian] music stands (as I am no competent judge) I could never give my ears the trouble to examine, it seeming loud and barbarous; yet they observe time and measure in their singing and dancing, and are mightily delighted with their tumbling

and noise. They as much dislike our shriller music, hardly allowing our waits fit to play to bears, and our stringed instruments strike not their hard-to-be-raised fancies; but our organs are the music of the spheres with them, charming them to listen as long as they play. [1698:191, spelling and capitalization modernized]

Even now the harmonium is customarily used for teaching purposes and is commonly found in "musical" households. In October 1970, A.I.R. organized a symposium around the question of the harmonium and Indian music. At that time, the harmonium was still banned from A.I.R. although criticism of the ban was growing. During the discussions, one musician noted that great artists such as Ustad Fayyaz Khan used the harmonium for accompaniment. Another authority stated, however, that "he did not favor it and if he ever used it, that was for playing to the gallery" (see the *Statesman,* October 23 and 24, 1970). Others argued that it was necessary for teaching, but it could be dispensed with for the performance of classical music. Still others felt that the harmonium was good for light classical music, but not for classical music.

The seminar on the harmonium was published as a special issue of the *Journal of the Sangeet Natak Akademi* (No. 20, 1971) with a postscript of no little interest, stating that All India Radio (which sponsored the seminar) had partially removed the ban.

i. Top grade and A-grade artistes may use the Harmonium as an accompanying instrument in classical, light classical and light vocal music.

ii. Approved Quawaali [sic] parties of all grades who utilise the Harmonium in public performances may also use it in broadcasts.

iii. Approved choral groups for classical, light classical and light music may use the Harmonium with permission from the Director of the Station concerned.

iv. Specially produced items in classical, light classical and light programmes may use the Harmonium on the advice of the producer concerned.

The ban on the use of the Harmonium will remain in programmes of other lower grade artistes. No solo performances of the Harmonium will be broadcast. This directive will operate for a period of one year after which the position will again be reviewed.

The ban, later completely lifted, kept many sarangi accompanists "in business," although all of them are capable of providing harmonium accompaniment as well. In this same seminar Ratanjankar, the well-known music educator and performer, prefaced his discussion of the harmonium's role with the suggestion that since sarangi players have been largely absorbed by A.I.R. and they are consequently hard to get for public performances, others should take up the instrument and learn it. He concluded that the sarangi is "also passing out of vogue" (1971:11).

In public performances, the harmonium is used widely, sometimes with sarangi. From the vocal performer's perspective, its intonation, if not exact, is more dependable than that of many sarangiyas.

B. V. Keshkar was responsible for instituting the National Program of Music, the Radio Sangeet Sammelan, the grading of artists, and the National Orchestra. Although his tenure of office as Minister for Information and Broadcasting did not last longer than the fifties, his influence is felt even now. A strong believer in state patronage and control of music, he disliked gharanas and the secrecy of ustads. He is believed by some to have democratized the status of musicians. His policies are still controversial, but his support for Indian musicians is not (see J. Singh's foreword to Keshkar 1967).

Public Performances

The public concert season in Delhi begins in October and extends through April. Between May and September the capital is relatively quiet as the summer and monsoon seasons prevail.

A variety of organizations sponsor regular musical events in Delhi, most of them having been instituted in the 1960s and 1970s. From 1969 to 1971, the major annual music event in Delhi was the Shankar Lal Festival of Music, which began in 1963 and is held annually in March or April. Musicians from all over North India are invited to the three-day festival. More recently, other annual conferences have been started. One of the most prominent is the Ustad Hafiz Ali Khan Memorial

Music Festival, held annually in Bombay and Calcutta as well as Delhi. It was first held in Calcutta for two weeks in December 1973, with sixty-three musicians participating. The published program is actually a book with photographs and short biographical sketches of all participating musicians and several articles about Ustad Hafiz Ali Khan. It is now a collector's item among connoisseurs.

Two other important organizations in Delhi are the Indian Cultural Society (founded 1963), devoted to music and dance, and Raag Rang (founded 1962), an organization of prominent artists and "music lovers" which sponsors twelve recitals a year. In addition to a number of less prominent musical societies, other organizations sponsor a musical event from time to time. For example, the "Youth of India" society, based at Delhi University, sponsors drama, mime, dance, and, very occasionally, a music recital by a prominent artist.[10]

The musicians in Delhi who rely most on such public performances to augment their incomes are accompanists. Except for the very few stars of the musical world such as Vilayat Khan, Ravi Shankar, Ali Akbar Khan, and a handful of others, soloists cannot depend exclusively on concert engagements. Soloists who are not prominent often perform gratis or for a nominal sum just to appear on stage. Accompanists, however, must always be paid. For example, an annual concert of "budding artists" is sponsored by the Sangīt Sabha (founded 1967). The soloists are all young artists, coming from both educational institutions and hereditary families of musicians in Delhi. They are not paid for their performances, but their accompanists are.

Well-known accompanists are also in demand outside Delhi. Lesser-known accompanists will accept jobs whenever offered and for virtually any fee. The strategy of determining fees is a delicate one. Traditionally, since the role of the accompanist was necessary but interchangeable, real bargaining was usually not feasible. But with the increasing importance of the accompanist as part of the total performance, those who have managed to adapt to the requirements of the stage have become fairly successful. The following sections consider several strategies for succeeding as a public performer.

How a Musician "Makes It"

Fixing Fees. Muhammad Ali Khan is a well-known accompanist in Delhi and other parts of North India. A staff artist at A.I.R., he has also performed abroad on several occasions. During the season he receives about a dozen invitations to participate in music conferences from Panjab to Bihar. The letters from conference organizers are personally written, following a common format. After inviting him to participate in the conference, they ask him to consider the nature of the conference; it is either a charitable function, located in a small area, or just starting up. Would Ustad Muhammad Ali Khan please take these economic facts into consideration when—if he accepts—he establishes a fee? In other words, the sponsors write an exceedingly flattering letter describing how honored and happy they would be to have a musician of such eminence appear, acknowledging that he demands and receives high fees, and asking if perhaps he could make an exception in their case. If M. A. Khan has performed at the same place before, the suggested fee is often the same previously offered by the sponsors.

Muhammad Ali Khan has several things to consider. He must be able to estimate his own worth in the context of different conditions. The amount of the fee is important not only for the obvious economic reasons, but also as a precedent for other engagements. If his fees are too high he prices himself out of the market. Settling for lesser fees puts him among rank-and-file accompanists, a situation from which he would find it difficult to emerge.

Fees are generally fixed per sitting. For one music conference, M. A. Khan was scheduled to accompany soloists in three separate performances for which he was to receive Rs. 400/– for each, for a total of Rs. 1200/–. As it happened, he accompanied four soloists, thus receiving another Rs. 400/– for the extra sitting.[11] The accompanist tries to fix the fee per sitting so that he is not exploited by the organizers. If he accepts a flat fee, then he may be requested to accompany many soloists, a request to which he would ordinarily have to accede. If he can arrange to have fees fixed per sitting, he then attempts to be scheduled as often as possible since his earnings are comparatively high. For their part, sponsors try to have as many different artists on the program as they can manage. It is better to have two prominent accompanists like Muhammad Ali Khan giving three performances each, rather than to have only one giving six performances.

Muhammad Ali complains that other accompanists sell themselves cheaply; when they agree to play for Rs. 30/– just for the money, he believes they show no self-respect and that they make it difficult for other accompanists to demand high fees. Even prominent accompanists sometimes accept relatively low fees. Thus Sunil Misra, a famous accompanist, is always in demand by the star solo performers and is somewhat of a star himself. Yet he asks only Rs. 600/– per sitting, whereas he should be getting at least Rs. 1000/–, in M.A.K.'s opinion. If Misra is accompanying at a given conference, then Latafat Ali Khan, another well-known, but not so famous, accompanist cannot demand his customary Rs. 500/–, but must settle for Rs. 300/– per sitting.

Accompanists also complain that the stars are paid too much, and indeed some fees are astronomical. The top musicians typically receive between Rs. 6000/– and Rs. 7000/– per performance, sometimes receiving as much as Rs. 10,000/–. Some accompanists feel that this is inequitable and that they should receive a higher proportion per performance.

Sometimes Muhammad Ali Khan will accept a job even if there is only one sitting and the fees are not very good. He may agree to this because he is a friend of the organizer, or wants to get out of Delhi for a few days, or is scheduled to accompany a famous artist, which raises his own prestige as well. Sponsors pay for hotel, food, and rail fare. Muhammad Ali Kahn demands and receives first class rail fare, but usually travels second class, saving the difference.

In Delhi, Muhammad Ali Khan finds himself in competition with many other accompanists. So far as fees are concerned, he competes with able but far less expensive accompanists, while in terms of prestige he is in competition with other well-known accompanists. When festivals or music recitals are held in Delhi, the famous artists from outside often bring along their own accompanists. Other less prominent artists from Delhi or outside are accompanied by Delhi musicians, many of whom play for relatively little. As a result Muhammad Ali does not perform nearly as often as he could if he were to price himself more modestly. He feels that to lower his fees would be a mistake because in the end he would probably not make as much money. Since there is a difference in fees on the order of a factor between five and ten, he would have to perform in that many more concerts to make an equivalent amount. Muhammad Ali, like Gopal Khanna, makes about Rs. 5000/– annually from public performances. Both of them say that they were able to start commanding higher fees after they had toured abroad.

The "Foreign Returned" Artist. Ravi Shankar's pioneering success in concert tours abroad has had a profound impact on the music culture of India. A surprising number of musicians listed in the *Who's Who of Indian Musicians* (1968) have been abroad, many to Afghanistan, where the king was an enthusiastic patron. In the years 1969 to 1971, ten of the seventy-five musicians listed in Tables 1–6 had already been to the West on concert/teaching tours. In the following five years about twenty more toured abroad. Several have left their staff positions at A.I.R. to go to Europe and America where they have been freelancing. Others have spent extensive periods in teaching positions coupled with giving recitals. One musician has opened a successful school in Europe.

One of the ironies of Indian music culture results from the musician's having gone abroad and being "foreign returned." The tour abroad has proved to be the most notable symbol of success—a new, important kind of prestige factor (Keshkar 1968: 73–77). Both soloists and accompanists have "made their names" by performing abroad and advertising that fact. In concert programs, reviews of the artist in Western newspapers are often reprinted; and in this sense audiences (or at least critics) in the West have made their influence felt in Indian music culture.

The reasons for success after foreign tours can only be suggested here. Generally a high premium exists on foreign manufactured goods and foreign degrees, especially among the urban middle class, a significant portion of whom supply much of the new audience for music. This xenophilia attaches itself to musicians as well. If an artist has been accepted abroad, the argument perhaps runs, then he must be good, and good enough to be patronized here. The high cultural premium on foreign things is an old tradition in India; for example, the higher rank accorded to foreign-originated Muslims. The following paragraphs recount how the experience of being foreign-returned has affected the life of a musician.[12]

Yusuf Ali is a young and extremely talented accompanist, coming from a family of musicians and living with them in Old Delhi. When I first met him, he was shy and unassuming, "a simple man," as one would say in India. He gave occasional performances and accompanied students of vocal and instrumental music. He was treated well, but it was clear that his social rank was quite modest.

The world of Old Delhi, where Yusuf lived when I first met him in 1969, is very different from that of New Delhi, and in another age from that of the West. Typically, the buildings in Old Delhi are large. At street level, godowns (warehouses) and tea shops open into the little alleyways; living quarters are on the second and third floors. Yusuf lived with his family on the top floor of such a building. When I visited him, I entered from the stairway into a large open courtyard, on three sides of which were three rooms. Yusuf's uncle was sitting in the room on the left. He was very old and had to be cared for, although he could still carry on an animated conversation.

I was invited to sit on a thin rug in the room on the right, where Yusuf and his brothers sleep. This room contained a double bed, a radio, a tanpura, a harmonium, two sets of tabla, and a sitar. Two cupboards held eating utensils and other knick-knacks. On an open shelf extending from the back wall adjacent to the cupboard stood a photo of Yusuf's deceased father, a hand mirror, and a small brass container holding lampblack that is applied to the eyes of little children to ward off the evil eye and used as a cosmetic by musicians onstage.

Yusuf was one of many musicians in this old Delhi ward. His older brother, thirty-two years old, was a B-grade accompanist at A.I.R., while his younger brother, eighteen, was studying sitar and earning no income. Yusuf earned about Rs. 150/– monthly, accompanying students and giving occasional programs, while his brother received Rs. 280/– from A.I.R. From this Rs. 430/– a month income, twelve members of the family had to be supported, not including other relatives who came to stay from time to time for a few months. At the time of my visit, Yusuf's sister's husband's brother from Lucknow was staying with them in Delhi while he tried to secure a transfer from Lucknow A.I.R. to Delhi A.I.R.

Yusuf, who was twenty-two at the time, had only recently begun to earn an income. His older brother had supported the family since the death of their father when Yusuf was only ten years old. The uncle who stayed with them was an old man even then and had no income and no children. This was the situation until early 1969, when Yusuf was invited by the prominent soloist, Hyder Ali Khan, to accompany him abroad. He had been recommended by another soloist who had heard Yusuf at several private performances. Yusuf accepted with delight.

In Europe, he concertized with the soloist for three weeks and then returned. He told me that he had enjoyed the tour very much, having earned over Rs. 1000/– ($150.00); he bought some clothes, gifts for relatives, and a watch for himself. On his return he was offered a few jobs, two with prominent artists for which he was paid Rs. 200/– each; previously his highest fee, on only one occasion, had been Rs. 100/–.

At the end of the summer, Hyder Ali again offered Yusuf the chance to go abroad, this time for an extended period from December until April. This offer included both a contract as artist-in-residence at a college in Europe, and several concert tours. Although it looked as though he had several good possibilities in India, he decided to go since such an opportunity was rare.

In Europe, where I again met him several months later, he was staying with some European admirers of his, and Hyder Ali was a guest elsewhere. Their relationship had become strained and Yusuf was extremely homesick. Although he was surrounded by Western admirers, he felt completely alone. He vowed never to leave India again, and would have returned, except that it would have meant leaving Hyder Ali stranded. The stay had been extended, and yet concerts were scheduled for still another month.

The sources of conflict between Hyder Ali and Yusuf were both economic and social. When a soloist goes abroad, it is his responsibility to provide his own accompanist, and when fees are settled, they always include the services of the accompanist. A contract is made between the soloist, his agent, and the sponsor. The soloist pays the accompanist's fees out of his own earnings. On the basis of examples which I know, accompanists then receive 10 percent or less of the soloist's earnings, *after* expenses.[13] Usually the soloist and the accompanist come to a verbal agreement after the tour; during it the soloist provides only pocket money. Because this second tour lasted longer (it was very successful), Yusuf was at times so low on funds that he even had to ask for cigarette money. He had the opportunity, but not the wherewithal, to go shopping or do other things on his own. This was one source of tension between the two.

The other was a change in the status relationship between them. As mentioned earlier, there are obligations on the part of the accompanist and corresponding rights belonging to the soloist. But audiences in the West are not sensitive to the differences in status and rank of soloist and acompanist. The accompanist is perceived as an equal (or near-equal) of the soloist. During a concert, ovations are accorded to the accompanist as often as to the soloist—and sometimes more often. In India, the soloist receives the lion's share of backstage attention while the accompanist is surrounded by a more modest coterie composed often of relatives and close associates. In the West, after a concert, admirers hang around both the soloist and accompanist (and even the tanpura player—if there is one), asking questions and poking at instruments. Yusuf had become a personality in his own right, so that by the time I met him he was often surrounded by a number of European admirers, both men and women. Being at the center of the stage as a performer was a new and somewhat dizzying experience for him. Consequently, when the soloist asked him to bring cigarettes from the green room after a concert one night—

something an accompanist would always do—Yusuf Ali Khan refused, not verbally but just by ignoring the request.

I had already been back in India for a month when Yusuf returned from Europe, and he came to visit me a week after he arrived. We were pleased to see each other since we had become rather close. He had come to ask me a favor. He wanted help in finding an apartment in New Delhi. Why? Well, people would be visiting him now and he needed a place where he could meet them. Who? Music critics, people who request interviews, those who were important contacts and so forth. He couldn't have them come to his flat in Old Delhi. It was crowded, dirty, and noisy; they would not find their way in the lanes; it wouldn't look good.

Yusuf Ali Khan is now a celebrated accompanist. He performs throughout India and makes a good income. He is sponsoring his younger brother, making sure that he has some exposure. His older brother also gets more jobs. Yusuf now lives in New Delhi, but often visits his relatives in Old Delhi. He is still very polite to others, but clearly no longer an innocent. Some of his old associates accuse him of becoming proud, "his head has grown big," and it is true that he walks now with an air of confidence and poise. He still expresses humility, but whereas formerly it derived from his modest station it is now projected as polite behavior and is perhaps a consciously articulated image of the artist as a humble man.

I do not intend to offer psychological or aesthetic evaluations of a foreign-returned musician. There is, however, an attitude expressed among certain informed listeners and some musicians that a trip West is a mixed blessing. One old master, invited by a disciple, went to England to stay for several months. After two weeks he returned, extremely distraught by the behavior of another disciple, an Indian, who smoked and drank in front of him and treated him not as his guru, but just as another friend. Ravi Shankar himself is often criticized for having become Westernized, a charge which he vigorously denies (Danielou 1971; also Shankar 1966:44–48).

Although going abroad, especially to the West, can have possibly deleterious effects on an artist's psyche and his music, many musicians are willing to take the chance. Some have been able to stay in the West for several months at a time, earning a living by giving lessons and private concerts. However successful they might actually be, they rarely return to India empty-handed. (For a rare exception, see Sharman 1970:174–75.) For a musician who has not been abroad, or who went very long ago, a trip out is at worst an occasion to make money; at best it enhances his prestige among his associates and audiences. For the enterprising younger artists, going West is seen as a successful if somewhat circuitous route to succeeding back East.

Contacts. Musicians, whether soloists or accompanists, find it necessary to know many kinds of people. No single individual, or even group of individuals, acts as a music broker in Delhi. There are, however, influential people whom it helps to know. The ways in which such acquaintances help are difficult to generalize about. Relationships are cultivated because they may lead to other contacts and eventually to a booking. Some radio artists, for example, seek out those who judge on the evaluation committees, so that when their auditions for upgrading are given, they are not performing for strangers or judges to whom they are an unknown.

Newspaper music critics are other important persons to know. Soloists and sometimes accompanists cultivate them as well. If an accompanist is known to the critics, something more than the standard one-liner may be written about him—perhaps a sympathetic discourse that provides an *artist's* identity. Merely knowing powerful people in the government with little or no connection to the musical world can be helpful. If an artist knows someone in the Ministry of Tourism, he may get his passport processed with little red tape. He may even be recorded by Indian Airlines, having his music broadcast during flights.

For musicians coming from hereditary families, interaction with a *barā ādmī* (*lit.*, "big man") requires entering into a network of relationships very different from those of his family, khandan, biradari, or mohalla. The transition from the web of alleyways in Old Delhi, where all call one another "bhai," to the boulevards of New Delhi, where people are not "family" and are addressed as "Sir," is more than just a move from a crowded old city to a spacious new one. It is also a move from individuals whose identity, role, and status are interlinked with one's own to unknown individuals who occupy important and powerful positions. The rules for interaction are formal, resulting in highly stylized role-playing.

The difficulties of moving from the traditional world of Old Delhi to the contemporary world of New Delhi are poignantly exemplified by Walter Kaufmann's recollections. When he was working at A.I.R. in the 1930s, he encountered old, distinguished musicians who could sing in the most complex rhythms, but had to have a disciple count the money they received for their performing fees since they did not know how (1968:8). Even today, hereditary musicians are usually accompanied by "sidekicks," often disciples or younger relatives, who also perform the role of the intermediary in their relations with outsiders. The sidekick plays the interpreter. In conversation, the musician may need to turn to his sidekick for corroboration about an event or idea, or ask him to clarify a point or remind him of a detail. In this way the sidekick often acts as a translator or enhancer of the messages being communicated to or received from outsiders. Important also is that a coterie of disciple-brothers lends dignity to the musician in the otherwise unfamiliar contexts in which social interaction with "big men" takes place.

Music Education

Music education as a source of patronage is primarily of three kinds. First is the guru-disciple institution. Second are "tuitions." (This term is commonly used and refers not to the fee but to the pupil himself. If a teacher has ten tuitions, he means that he has ten pupils from whom he receives a fixed amount.) Third are music schools, in which musicians serve as either teachers or accompanists.

Gifts

Estimation of what a particular artist receives from his disciples is difficult since it is not considered an economic exchange or a matter for discussion. On certain occasions, such as the ustad's birthday or a disciple's initiation, the disciple presents his ustad with an offering of money in varying amounts. One disciple may offer Rs. 11/– on the occasion of the guru's birthday while another may offer Rs. 101/–. The amount includes an extra rupee, which is given to signify something special, above and beyond an ordinary exchange. It is partially a function of the disciple's ability to make a given contribution, and partially the degree of intensity of the relationship between disciple and guru. In an ideal sense, no guru supports himself entirely by the gifts of his disciples, and this is probably true in practice. A more standard income is derived from pupils who pay for their instruction.

Tuitions

If a musician is visibly unemployed, as are several whom I interviewed, he always says that he earns at least some of his income from tuitions. Again, it is difficult to estimate to what degree this statement is true since one cannot always verify it by meeting the pupils. In at least one case known to me, the response of "tuitions" is a euphemism for being virtually unemployed; in another it is a cover for the musician's work as a tabla player in a salon of singing and dancing girls.

Some well-established musicians earn a considerable portion of their total income from pupils, giving lessons in their own homes. The more standard practice is that the teacher goes to his pupil's house. This is particularly true when a male musician has a female pupil.

The distinction between a disciple and a pupil is established when the pupil undergoes the ganda-bandhan, after which he is ritually established as a disciple. In the past this ceremony is said to have been reserved for only the most outstanding and devoted disciples. Musicians nowadays are sometimes accused of being indiscriminate, accepting as a disciple anyone who pays for instruction. In practice, this is probably not done by artists enjoying a high reputation, and in any event they would not do it overtly. An unrecognized musician is merely a teacher who has tuitions only, usually young beginners, and he charges a prescribed fee for each session. An ustad usually accepts only more advanced students as tuitions and receives a fixed amount as well. Of these tuitions, several may remain with him over an extended period of time, in which case he may initiate them as disciples. After this, prescribed fees supposedly stop, although in practice a disciple typically continues giving a fixed amount to his ustad (cf. Deodhar 1973).

In the past, specialists on accompanying instruments rarely taught persons outside their families. This situation has changed, for tabla at least, and now disciples from outside are studying it. There is even a female tabla player—unheard of before—who has joined the Department of Music at Delhi University. To my knowledge there are no Indian sarangi students who do not come from a hereditary family of musicians. (But see Table 31 for a possible exception.) One Brahman I met in Banaras began to study the sarangi many years ago, but found himself under extreme social pressure to abandon it. This was because of the social stigma on sarangi players and also because, to a Brahman, the skin and gut strings of the instrument are polluting. He finally gave up the sarangi, but only after he had constructed a similar instrument which had frets and was made entirely of wood with no skin cover. Although he said that he invented it himself, a similar instrument, although unfretted, is illustrated in Popley's *Music of India* (1921:109).

It should be emphasized that the rather widespread system of tuitions is due to the rehabilitation of and interest in classical music. This change from the former attitude that music professionalization is not respectable has been noted by Mathur above, as well as by many others, including Keshkar. Under the former patronage of an aristocracy, the explanation goes, music had ceased to be a spiritual activity and had become erotic, sensual, and vulgar. "No respectable middle class parent would have liked his boy or girl going in for music and dance" (Keshkar 1967: 8–9). Keshkar assigns credit for the reversal in attitude to Rabindranath Tagore, V. N. Bhatkhande, and Vishnu Digambar Paluskar (ibid.). All three founded educational institutions, those of the last two being devoted exclusively to music.

Music Schools

In Delhi several kinds of educational institutions are devoted to teaching music: a music department at Delhi University, other departments at separate music colleges, and neighborhood music schools. Most musicians who teach at such institutions are soloists, and they are not usually from hereditary families. Accompanists are members of the staff as accompanists, rarely as teachers. Tabla is taught as an auxiliary subject, the knowledge about (but not of) which is considered necessary for all soloists. The sarangi, to my knowledge, is not institutionally taught anywhere in India.[14]

No student receiving his or her training exclusively from a music college has ever become a recognized performer of Indian classical music. Music education in India is oriented toward teaching young men and women the rudiments of theory and practice so as to make them informed and sympathetic listeners, and in some cases teachers, as indicated by the prospectus of the Gandharva Mahavidyalaya, an important music school in Delhi:

> The institution was established in 1939 by its founder Principal, Shri Vinaya Chandra, Sangītlankar, disciple of the veteran musician, Pandit Vinayakrao Narayan Patwardhan. The Vidyalaya came into being to perpetuate the sacred memory of the saint musician of India Pt. [Pandit] Vishnu Digambar Paluskar, the great resuscitator of Hindustani music, and to keep up the ideals set down by him in order to popularize the Indian classical music among the masses by:
>
> (a) modernized method of instruction;
> (b) training qualified teachers; and
> (c) restoring to music its rightful place as an integral part of our culture.

Bhatkhande and Paluskar viewed the revival of Hindustani music as concomitant with its reemergence as a respectable branch of knowledge and its dissemination to a wide listening public. At the end of a speech delivered in 1916, in Baroda, upon the occasion of the first All-India Music Conference, Bhatkhande envisaged the future of Indian classical music once again open to all:

I cannot but hope that in a few years more there will be an easy system for the instruction of our music which will lend itself to mass education. Then will the ambition of India be fulfilled, for then the Indians will have music in the curricula of their Universities and music instruction will be common and universal. And if it please Providence to so dispense that there is a fusion between the two systems of the North and the South, then there will be a National music for the whole country and the last of our ambitions will be reached, for then the great Nation will sing one song. Once there is a system for music the gates of instruction will be thrown open and compulsory music education will immediately follow as a natural consequence (1934:50).

But a half century later, musician and scholar J. L. Mattoo tempered his praise of music schools with a question:

There are some thousands of music schools in North India today, but out of these very few, say five or six, have really been founded and managed on certain set principles. . . . There is no doubt that these institutions have done pioneer work in popularizing music and enhancing its prestige. . . . There must be thousands who have quali-fied from these institutions during the last thirty years. . . . But the point is, are there any among them who by their performance have won such a name in the musical world that they have really become indispensable for conferences of Hindustani music? (1965:19)

Music schools then have mixed attributes: they support musicians and create an informed listening public, but their teaching methods are, in large part, antithetical to the spirit of the guru-shishya system. Students in music schools learn ten to fifteen rāgs a year, a set of compositions (bandish) set to those rāgs, and a certain number of tals. Instruction is usually in groups, and what students learn is generally considered quite superficial. The idea of learning a large number of rāgs, for instance, is viewed by traditional musicians as a fundamental misunderstand-ing of the nature of a rāg. Professional musicians are often heard to say that it is far better to concentrate on one or a very few rāgs, exploring each in depth to enable the disciple to extend his understanding of many other rāgs quickly. "If you practice rāg Yaman intensely, and come to really know it, then the knowl-edge of other rāgs will come of itself." Thus, when traditonal musicians are asked what they think about learning music in schools, they consider it a laudable, but misguided, effort on the part of teachers and students. Schools make friends for classical Indian music, but no one learns much about music making in schools. On the other hand, some authorities like Keshkar—who is a connoisseur but not a performer—feel that the guru-shishya manner of learning music has become, like gharanas, politicized and unnecessarily sancrosanct:

> Music is an art and should not be converted into a religion. I am mentioning this because I find some of the defects of the guru-shishya tradition creeping into music. When a student learns from a teacher in music, he is not getting a religious message or tradition. He is learning an art. There is nothing sancrosanct about a musical tradition that is learned from a particular guru. . . . The art of practical performance is something different from theory. Indian musicians have developed the defect of treating it as a religious cult and they fight with anybody and everybody belonging to another guru. [1967:41]

Even so, Keshkar sees the primary function of music schools as institutions for training informed listeners rather than performers or teachers (ibid.:43).

7. The Ecology of Hindustani Music Culture

There have been more changes in Indian Music in the twenty years after Independence than in the two hundred years before it.

Chetan Karnani, *Listening to Hindustani Music*

 The question of changes in the culture and sound of Hindustani music has been for me a fundamental intellectual problem. Accordingly, much of my research and many of my discussions with musicians and informed listeners has been directed towards indigenous perceptions of music culture change. Although I have found a wide range of responses about details, the general conclusion is that no fundamental change has taken place. To be sure, the use of the microphone, the loss of courtly patronage, and the spread of film music are mentioned as having altered the traditional terrain in which Hindustani music once thrived. Yet the musical effects of such changes are considered largely peripheral: the landscape has changed, but the essential sounds in it are untouched. True, the microphone has enabled weak-voiced singers to perform in public and has allowed tabla solos to reach an aural prominence they otherwise would not have achieved. The absence of courtly patronage (which older musicians particularly miss) means fewer discriminating listeners and an uninformed appreciation of artists. And film music draws away potential listeners from the art tradition and threatens to infect the musical sensibilities of the younger generation. But despite these and other changes, the tradition, it is generally averred, remains intact.

What these kinds of descriptions have in common is a concern with the circumstances of performance, not the performance itself. The performance, like the tradition underlying it, remains in its abstract conception still true and still persistent, although perhaps now weakened. Taking a cue from the indigenous concern with the circumstances of performance, I would like to suggest that a useful approach to the dynamics of Hindustani music is to view it ecologically. Music, in this sense, is interpreted as "intricately interrelated to societies; as a commodity sold, purchased and consumed; as an artifact—probably the most important one in most cases—of a culture; in short, as anything but pure, abstract and self-contained" (Archer 1964:28). What are the primary features of an ecology of music? I can think of four general components of a music culture in addition to the music itself: the producers of music, the consumers of music, the contexts of music events, and the technology of music production and reproduction. Considered analytically distinct, each of these has undergone many changes which have affected not only their internal organization and interrelationships, but the shape of music sound itself. The following pages present an initial (and tentative) attempt to elucidate what I have elsewhere called the ethnomusicology of culture change (Neuman 1976).

The Producers of Music

I have shown a fundamental distinction between hereditary and non-hereditary musicians. Only in part can it be understood as a Muslim-Hindu polarity. Although privately expressed and publicly denied, the communal prejudice of musicians is an important phenomenon, but one that has yet to be systematically explored. Sociologically more fundamental than communal differences, however, is the fact that music specialization, in the shift from

Hindu to Muslim hegemony, underwent a transformation from avocation to occupation. By virtue of the guild-like organization of hereditary musician families, the art became increasingly separated from the former carriers of the tradition, the priestly class. The professionalization of music and its subsequent insulation from outsiders is rightly interpreted as a means to control competition; music had now become a discrete commodity, separated from its former role as an adjunct activity of priests, genealogists, and jugglers. As fewer musicians were imported from outside India and the provincial capitals became politically and economically more powerful, an inevitable—and sometimes insatiable—increase in the consumption of music arose, as the Lucknow of Wajid Ali Shah so aptly demonstrates.

It is no accident that gharanas, as sociomusical phenomena, emerged at a point when India was beginning to undergo its own transformation into a modern society. Gharanas provided a more general social identity, an identity which distinguished not only musical styles, but groups of musicians and their disciples. At the same time, it is not as surprising as it may seem that the gharana, bearing so many characteristic features of a caste, was essentially a Muslim creation. Because marriage between close relations was not only permitted but encouraged, in marked contrast to Hindu practice, it allowed the formation of a relatively small circle of specialists. They succeeded for a time in cornering the art music market, a market which was highly competitive by virtue of being limited to a small and discriminating public. As the circle of listeners began to expand, particularly in urban areas, around the turn of the century, the nature of competition for patronage must also have shifted as it moved towards a public venue. Born as they were during this very same period, gharanas can be usefully thought of as "quality control" centers. They controlled a product, music, which, unlike most other products in India, was inherently the result of an achievement-oriented dynamic, as exhibited in the musical competitions between specialists. Gharanas did not prevent competition; they controlled it among themselves. And they controlled the achievement-oriented recruitment of specialists by subordinating it to the principle of ascriptive recruitment through the medium of hereditary lineages and select disciples. It is in this sense that gharanas acted as guardians of the tradition.

Since Independence, however, a profound shift has occurred in attitudes about public and remunerated performances of music, which is coincident with and related to the awakening of a national consciousness and the decline of traditional patronage forms. The result has been a change in the social organization of musicians: their recruitment, their training, and their roles. As a dramatic movement, it is very recent, culminating with the vast population exchanges following Partition. Parallel with like changes in other sectors of contemporary urban Indian society, it exemplifies the decreased emphasis on equating an occupational category with a social identity. Music has become a profession in which recruitment rules are increasingly a matter of economics, social rank, and "personality." It has also become a profession incorporating a wider range of occupational roles, many of them distinctly modern ones such as teacher (in music colleges), administrator, concert and film music artist, radio artist, and music critic. One musician may perform several of these roles. The important point is the existence of a much wider range of professional possibilities—respectable possibilities—than before.

Today's gharanas have in the totality of their characteristics a reality that seems a microcosm of what the highly pluralistic society of India ideally wants to become. They include as their members both men and women, who come from a variety of religions (although principally Muslim and Hindu), castes (although tending to the extremes of high and low), and ethnic groups (everything from Kasmiris to Bengalis to Rajasthanis). There are individuals who are ultimately derived from a gharana background and who have subsequently rejected it (like the renouncer of the caste system) and "gharanas" of individuals who have rejected the idea of gharanas. In these guises, gharanas assume forms and meanings that mirror the history of caste in India and perhaps anticipate ethnic pluralities even now in the making.

The musical niches not only allow a greater diversity of occupational possibilities, but also require a refinement of roles which musicians enact in presenting themselves. For example, the role of orthodox artist requires a new support structure since maintaining a "traditionalist" stance limits the range of remunerative possibilities to what is properly traditional. Concertizing abroad, playing light classical music, teaching in schools, and seeking fame are, by the most orthodox, conceived as compromising activities. This attitude tends to be true of some hereditary musicians coming from soloist backgrounds, who, as torchbearers of a musical tradition, must maintain its integrity, including behavior onstage and off. As one vocalist told me, accepting an offer to perform a program consisting entirely of ghazals would be very profitable; however, people would then say, "See that Khan Sahib, see what he does for money!"

Another major role, performed typically by non-hereditary and younger musicians, is that of "popularizing" classical music for the masses. Although claiming the source of their knowledge as the traditional guru or ustad, they are not bound by the same restraints. In principle they are required, as good disciples, to carry the purity of the tradition forward. Yet they can rationalize the compromises they make in terms of accommodating and "uplifting" the masses—awakening them to their cultural heritage while making the products of the Great Tradition accessible to a wider public.

Both the orthodox and the didactic roles, seemingly contradictory in spirit, can be mutually reinforcing as they are performed by individuals. Through the representations of his disciples, the orthodox artist can achieve fame without seeking it; the disciples can claim fame through these same representations.

To evaluate changes resulting from a shift in the basis of social recruitment is not simple. To deny differences in the way hereditary and non-hereditary musicians conceptualize their social, occupational, and aesthetic identities would be naive. Perhaps the only valid generalization is that non-hereditary musicians are not as closely tied to the mystique of the profession. Certainly, little remains of the sense of ownership and secrecy of musical knowledge which was so characteristic of older hereditary musicians. A more open willingness to share musical knowledge is evident. On the other hand, older musicians feel that what the younger musician has to share is in fact nothing much: for them the secrets and the idea of secrets still remain.

The recruitment of musicians from non-hereditary backgrounds extends to all specialists except sarangi players. There are few if any instances of non-hereditary musicians becoming sarangiyas. That speciality alone still retains the stigma of its brothel identity. It is in part because of this lingering association that sarangiyas themselves are not teaching their sons the instrument. Sons are learning to become tabliyas and soloists, or are being directed out of the music profession entirely. The sarangi is not taught in music institutions, and it may very well become extinct in another generation (Deshpande 1971:18; Neuman 1977) and all classical vocal performance practices will then have to accommodate to either harmonium or violin accompaniment or perhaps even to no melodic accompaniment. Singing unaccompanied is already suggested as a practice by the late Ustad Amir Khan of Indore. In spite (or because) of coming from a sarangi family and having played the instrument, he refused to have any accompaniment at all.

Concomitant with the increased respectability of music as a profession is the attendant increase in the number of female performers coming from "respectable," middle- and upper-class families. The appearance of the professional woman musician from such backgrounds is a very recent phenomenon, becoming significant only since the 1960s. From it a number of interesting problems arise.

First is the competition that these women give to the hereditary women performers. In 1977 I conducted an interview with an elderly tawaif who bitterly complained that since the "housewives" had entered the profession, the hereditary women vocalists were as a class being nudged out.

The change to a respectable social origin is also connected to the shift in repertoire forms. Although female hereditary musicians like the great Kesarbai Kekar sang khayal only, most women singers were identified with the lighter varieties of art music, such as thumri and ghazal. There was in other words not a complete, but certainly a partial, division of musical labor between men and women. There were (and are) virtually no men in the classical tradition exclusively associated with thumri or ghazal,[1] and there were virtually no women instrumentalists, either soloists or accompanists. This separation of specialties is no longer as prevalent today, and it promises to be even less so in the future. Certainly a motive for women to abandon the specialization in lighter forms is related to the social identification of these lighter repertoires with the courtesan tradition. Classical forms are now being more generally adopted by the contemporary younger women vocalists of hereditary families as well.

The whole question of the history, attitudes, and social organization of hereditary women musicians is obscure, and has been systematically pursued by only one scholar, whose works are as yet unpublished.[2] What impact the entrance of non-hereditary women musicians into Hindustani music has and will have is still an open question.

The renewed interest in and respectability of music have greatly increased the demand for music instruction, which, in turn, has resulted in a patronage system for musicians that has little to do with performance. As I have indicated, numerous musicians in Delhi earn at least some of their income from teaching. For many soloists it is the only source of regular income. But in formal educational institutions, hereditary musicians play only a marginal role. Music colleges and departments of music in universities place a high premium on formal degrees, with the consequence that many younger musicians pursue degrees, although not always in music. Non-hereditary musicians in particular have joined the search for academic credentials and consequently have gained a competitive edge over hereditary musicians in these same institutions, even though they may be musically less competent. But there is evidence that younger hereditary musicians also recognize the importance of an advanced degree. A study of one family of sitarists notes that the youngest son of the lineage, although a sitarist, plans to study for a B.A. degree because "his chances for success as a sitarist . . . will be very much enhanced by a good education" (Silver 1976:45). Musicians in South India take degrees in such areas as law, to insure against an uncertain career as a musician (Higgins 1976:22).

In terms of musical enculturation, the most profound changes exist within the guru-shishya institution. It is no longer possible to live as well as learn with a guru, unless you are one of his kinsmen. The guru himself is either busy concertizing, which involves much travel, or busy teaching many disciples in order to earn a living. A modified guru-shishya system has developed in response to these exigencies. Sometimes a disciple spends two or three months of the year studying intensively with his guru, while perhaps teaching the rest of the year. Or he may have a specified time when he visits his guru every day over a number of years. Depending on the time available and the nature of the relationship, an ustad will give a disciple either group or private instruction, and in many cases both. One disciple, for example, went to college (where he was studying music) during the week, and then commuted to stay with his ustad during the weekend over a period of four years. During some of the day he was instructed with other students, but he also received private instruction.

Whatever the variations in this modified system, there is general agreement that it is a necessity of the modern urban life style, though far from the ideal of the past. The disciple is only intermittently incorporated into the ustad's ambience, and then must leave it to attend to everyday concerns. The disciple no longer breathes, eats, drinks, and lives music full time. This is perhaps the most pressing and depressing concern of the traditional master. More disturbing to him than new and changing styles, or the shift in patronage from "the good old days," is the disappearance of a way of life and along with it, perhaps, its music.

It is difficult to convey to the reader what this life of music must once have been like, but it most certainly involved a more rhythmically graceful pace. Today there is no time: no time to practice, no time to sit with other musicians, play cards, and gossip about other musicians, no time to sit down and teach one's sons, no time to tune up, to finish one's alap, or to finish one's concert. It takes time to wander through the back alleys of Old Delhi and stop to chat with friends on the way, to breathe the air and smell the smells and dream the music that eventually will turn a disciple into a genuinely learned musician, himself an ustad.[3]

Other than in a general sense that the tempo of music is now much faster, the manner in which changes in the use and

Ustad Mushtaq Ali Khan giving a lesson to his disciple, Sharmistha Sen, a professional sitarist as well as a lecturer in music at Daulat Ram College, Delhi University.

Vocalist Janki Bai, accompanied by two sarangiyas and a tabliya at a recording session circa 1902. For her performance she received Rs. 3000/-, considered a princely sum at that time, as it still would be today. *Photograph by F. W. Gaisberg from his book* The Music Goes Round *(1942).*

Srimati Laxmi Shankar singing at the Hardballabh Music Conference. She is accompanied on the sarangi by Ram Swaroop.

A vocalist from Kabul, Afghanistan, singing at the Hardballabh Music Conference. He is accompanied on the sarangi by Ustad Sabri Khan and on tabla by Sri Shankar Ghosh. The visible tanpura player is Sri Sharma, who performs the same role as a staff artist at All India Radio, Delhi.

conception of time and environment affect music is not easy to stipulate. But recently Peter Row (1978) has suggested that the music training received by hereditary musicians is fundamentally different from that of non-hereditary musicians, with important musical consequences arising from the difference. The method of internalizing the conceptions of different rāgs, for example, was less formal among hereditary musicians. For them, learning rāgs was like learning to speak: the rules of syntax were absorbed through listening and performing, but they were not explicitly formulated. Non-hereditary musicians who have had their earlier training in music schools have learned rāgs as others learn a foreign language in school. Rules of rāg structure have been abstracted, and they are conveyed to the student as a basis for learning rāgs. Unfortunately, what is vital in speech and music—the subtleties, the numerous exceptions, and the rules for breaking rules—are less easily transmitted through a formal system. The result is a more concrete understanding of particular rāgs: rāgs as formulas rather than dynamic processes. To the extent that non-hereditary musicians enter the ranks of professionals, it would appear that their musicianship will alter the cultural definition and musical significance of rāgs. When rāg *Malkauns* ceases to be the rāg of jinns and becomes a pentatonic scale, the music *becomes* something different because it *means* something different.

The Consumers of Music

The most obvious changes in the music culture of India concern the consumers of music. I use "consumers" here as an inclusive category to refer not only to the listening public but also to others who directly or indirectly utilize music—manipulating, controlling, directing, patronizing, and therefore consuming it. One important consumer is the advertiser.

In Delhi, which has no commercial radio stations sponsoring classical music, advertising patronage is found in the program notes of public concerts. Indeed, many public concerts are heavily subsidized by the advertisers featured in program notes, since the purchase price of tickets usually covers only a portion of operating expenditures. Were it not for advertisements, most public musical functions would not be economically feasible. Advertising occasionally makes unpaid admissions possible, where tickets would in any event be difficult to sell. In the program of young artists mentioned previously, where soloists were paid nothing, there were, besides the fees of accompanists, other production expenses which were met entirely from the proceeds of advertisements. Usually the treasurer of a music society solicits these printed advertisements, the products of which are addressed to explicitly middle-class demands. For the businesses involved, this is seen not only as advertising a product, but, even more importantly, as good public relations. Indeed, many advertisements do not promote a product in so many words, but merely state the name of the manufacturer "with best compliments."[4]

More recently, private businesses have even become involved in sponsoring an entire festival. Since 1971 the Indian Tobacco Company has sponsored an annual festival of music known as the ITC Festival, featuring noted artists, generous fees and, in 1976, ticket prices ranging up to Rs. 100/–. In that year the proceeds of the concerts were donated to the Prime Minister's National Relief Fund.

Other consumers of music are organizations which sponsor musical events as celebrations of meaningful occasions or as part of a series of cultural events. The Gandhi Centenary, for example, sponsored a "Cultural Program of Music and Dance" in 1970 which featured (over a two-day period) a chorus of students of the Gandharva Mahavidyalaya, two recitals by soloists from North and South India, as well as several dance programs. The Press Club of India celebrated its twelfth anniversary in 1970 by featuring a sitarist and tabliya. Many music recitals by big-name artists in Delhi are sponsored by organizations having nothing to do with music, but interested in celebrating themselves with cultural events such as concerts. Private individuals also consume music by celebrating their anniversaries with musical concerts, although these events are now quite rare.

The most important consumer of music is the state. Aside from owning the radio network, the state views music as a means of developing cultural unity and subsidizes it, officially at least, with this as the explicit purpose.[5] When politicians or governmental functionaries are recruited to addresss a state-supported musical event, such as the Sangeet Sammelan of All India Radio, the theme of national and cultural unity is invariable. Both the inaugural address for the 1970 Sangeet Sammelan and the musical performance (by Hindu and Muslim Karnatak artists) were reported in the *Hindustan Times* as exemplifying this unity:

> National Integration through music was the main theme of Dr. A. N. Jha's inaugural address. Evidence of a pan-Indian music consciousness, cutting across region and religion was available in plenty of the occasions. Many passages of Chinnamoula's Sindhu Bhairavi piece were reminiscent at once of the Hindustani Bhairavi and of Bismillah Khan. Here was a Muslim playing item after item of Hindu devotional music. The supporting player on the Nagaswaram was also a Muslim, but both the drummers were Hindu. [October 19, 1970]

However, in a review of the same concert, the *Statesman* music critic gave a more realistic appraisal of the event:

> The Chief Advisor, Hindustani Music [at A.I.R.] Mr. Brahaspathi, who welcomed the Lt. Governor of Delhi, Mr. A. N. Jha, presiding dignitary, spoke extempore as at a public meeting. Mr. Jha having paid his dutiful tribute to the power and influence of music and the need to preserve its pristine appeal through all forms of patronage and recognition walked out even before the opening item began.
>
> There was a change of program announced half-way during Chinna Moula Saheb's nagaswaram recital. The artist of the second half Manik Verma could not come and Chinna Moula was to continue with his nagaswaram. The announcement was greeted by half the house making a beeline for the exit. That much for the power of national integration which music has to which eloquent reference was made by Mr. Jha. [October 18, 1970]

Whatever the motivation, the state, through All India Radio and other institutional media, supports a large musical establishment, including, for example, the Division of Music, Dance and Drama, which is supported at both national and state levels. During the national elections of 1977, artists in this division were sent to the villages of Haryana (and I presume other states) as part of the political campaign. Frequently, they form troupes to entertain and communicate government messages, such as the desirability of family planning, to villagers.

Classical musicians are sometimes sent out as goodwill ambassadors to foreign countries at government expense. The earlier travels of Indian art musicians in the 1950s were made possible, I believe, largely through such government sponsorship.

So far we have not considered the listening public as a type of consumer. The radio listening public is not a well-known entity, although it seems clear that the actual number of listeners for "classical" radio broadcasts is very small. R. D. Lambert (1967), in a review of Mathur's *Lamps of Aladdin* (1965), remarks that most listeners in India tune in Radio Ceylon to hear popular film music, the broadcasting of which was until recently discouraged by the government. We can thus consider the category of people who pay their license fees to operate a receiver as a majority who are "patrons" of classical music though certainly not "consumers."

There is still the small minority which consumes classical music, few who actually listen and others who "overhear" the music, especially when there is no other programming available. As indicated before, playing in a radio studio is not wholly satisfying for many musicians, and one suspects that if there were no audience, the artists would have to invent one. The only audience response perceived by the artist is that which he witnesses in the studio itself or, occasionally, in the columns of music critics.

Another kind of consumer is the purchaser of records. Although no data are available about the current recording scene, my strong impression is that, as a source of patronage, recordings are only marginally significant for all but the most famous artists. Records are expensive in India, an LP in 1978 costing Rs. 42/50, and even for the middle classes, building a collection is expensive. There is also a virtual monopoly, the vast majority of classical recordings being produced by the Gramophone Company of India.

The history of recording in India has yet to be written, but an account by F. W. Gaisberg, the first representative of the Gramophone Company to reach India, gives us a fascinating glimpse of the initial period (Gaisberg 1942:54–59). The first commercial recordings on wax discs were made in Europe in early 1902, and by the end of that year Gaisberg went to India and produced the first commercial recordings made there. To listen to the performers, he had to utilize the good offices of the superintendent of Calcutta Police, who provided an officer to guide him through the entertainment district. He apparently recorded only women singers, who in those days were all of the courtesan class. Only one or two male singers had been recommended to him, but they "had only high-pitched effeminate voices" and he therefore did not record them (ibid.:56).

Two of the artists Gaisberg recorded are still remembered today: Goura Jan, "an Armenian-Jewess who could sing in twenty languages and dialects," and Janki Bai, who received a fee of Rs. 3000/- for a recording session. A particularly interesting observation Gaisberg made was that when artists of the courtesan tradition "began to make names for themselves, many of them insisted that the word 'amateur' should be printed on the record label" (ibid.:57). A similar valuation on amateur status as a symbol of respectability is currently found in Iran and Afghanistan.

Although there is a fairly respectable catalogue of recordings now available (see Barnett, 1975), I believe that the importance for the artist in having a recording is primarily as a symbol of success, a fairly accurate gauge, since with few exceptions only successful musicians are commercially recorded.[6]

The most visible and important consumers of art music are those attending live programs of music, forming what Erving Goffman has called a "focused gathering" (1961). These are the consumers who (usually) pay for or at the least attend musical events, follow the careers of artists, and in listening are musically appreciative.

Artists conceive of two kinds of such listeners; these do not exactly correspond to sophisticated and unsophisticated audiences, although there is a degree of overlap. One is the person who addresses his attention primarily to the musical performance. He may be a student or an old connoisseur, but the main point of his attendance is the absorption of music. He follows the music, nods his head in assent, and if moved indicates as much by the responses described. The other kind addresses himself to the totality of the performance, which includes not only onstage activity, but also everything around it. This consumer is, ironically, often another musician, monitoring the music and the audience response. Depending on the musical event, these consumers often gather into clusters outside the boundaries of the listening space, but within the boundaries of the event space. Typically this is where the concession stands operate, whether outside next to the large tent or inside within the vestibule of the concert hall. In the concert hall, such as one finds in Sapru House, there are doors which can be closed, separating the music space from the lobby. Whether or not the doors are kept closed depends on the rules for a particular recital. In contrast to other musicians, these consumers want to be seen at such gatherings. They are usually either members of the organization which sponsored the performance, or persons connected in some way with music-making in Delhi, part of the music circle. Of course, the same person may be one or the other type of consumer, listening carefully to one artist, and enjoying a recess while another performs.

Still another consumer of music is the "fan." There are a few musicians—perhaps only two, Vilayat Kahn and Ravi Shankar—who have become virtual stars attracting large numbers of listeners who will not otherwise be seen at concerts. Other lesser-known artists also have their fans, although these do not assume crowd proportions.

What is fundamentally important about all these types of consumers is the very diversity being described, which has two major implications for Hindustani music. First, there are presumably a variety of musical tastes to be accommodated among the different kinds of consumers associated with different listening publics. The music performed before a large, uninformed audience is believed by musicians to require an adjustment of traditional performance practices. Showy virtuosity, light rāgs, short performances, and perhaps even explaining to the listeners what is to happen musically are phenomena incorporated for the mass audience. A more general result, which I shall discuss later, is the manipulation of rāgs: mixing two or more rāgs to make what is known as a *misra rāg* or stringing a series of rāgs together in one performance to produce a *rāgmālā*. These are not new musical phenomena, but the degree to which they are now used, even in the last decade, is unprecedented.

The other implication of a heterogeneous listening public is the rise in importance of the tabla accompanist. It appears that, like his Western counterpart, the tabla player has increasingly been defined as part of a duet and his virtuoso performance is now a fundamentally important part of a concert, at least of a solo instrumental concert. If the widely-held folk hypothesis is true—that rhythm is more immediately accessible to the untrained sensibility of a naive audience—it would explain in musical terms the increased importance of the tabla player.

The one other kind of consumer to be considered is the music critic writing for the newspaper. Although few in number, critics have in a sense become the pubic connoisseurs as well as connoisseurs for the public. Karnani claims that artists prefer performing in urban centers because their concerts are reviewed in the press, and then "are discussed, and this is one of the easy ways to success" (1976:60). I am not sure this is an easy way or the primary reason for performing in urban centers (where else to perform?), but it is certainly quite true that musicians read what is written about them, particularly in the English press (in which case some may have to have it read to them). They are quite sensitive to what is written about them even though they often claim that critics do not know much about music. (This view, I might add, is not totally unfounded. I remember one review of a sarangi concert written by a South Indian critic which betrayed his total lack of understanding of sarangi performance. Among other things, he conveyed his amazement that a sarangi player could perform longer than an hour. He believed that since sarangi players play with their knuckles, they easily become exhausted and are unable to play for extended periods of time, an interpretation of course which is total nonsense.) More important, however, is the politics of criticism. Critics are usually closely tied to musicians, and very unfavorable reviews are rare. An exception, which became a cause célèbre a few years ago, was a highly unfavorable review of an artist married to an important official in the musical world of Delhi, who brought pressure to have the critic removed from the newspaper's staff.

In sum, the distinctions among listening publics are important to the performer, because he receives critical attention and gratification from earnest listeners, and through them perhaps a reputation. For the others his performance acts as a catalyst in creating a social event. For the one type of consumer, the music is the product and for the other, the personality of the musician or the event itself becomes the product.

The Contexts of Performance

When All India Radio in Delhi decided to reintroduce live audiences for the National Program of Music on Saturday night, it was responding to something that is transparently obvious to any Indian musician: the importance of an audience which receives his message and transmits its own to him. It is noteworthy that whereas in the West authenticity is defined in terms of simulating performance practices, for example, the reintroduction of a Bach trumpet, in India authenticity is attempted through a simulation of the traditional context of the performance such as the mehfil.

In the vast majority of cases, however, the particular performance milieu has changed markedly. There is precious little information on the details of performance contexts a century ago. We do not know, for example, if musicians carefully balanced their repertoire of compositions and rāgs, making sure that these would not be repeated too often in a short period of time. We also do not know if, with many musicians attached to a court, there was a fixed organization of program presentation—if esteemed artists performed earlier for example, and less esteemed later on. We do not know if morning and afternoon rāgs were regularly presented since, in descriptions, musical performances are typically reported as held in the evening hours. What sparse knowledge we do have on the more public musical occasions— the salons of courtesans—provides little information on the kind of music produced (e.g., MacMunn, 1932:82–89).

The modern consumer and the contemporary contexts of musical performances clearly mark changes in the social and cultural environment of musical occasions. The extent to which music—as a manifestation of India's cultural tradition—is produced and consumed, whether in celebration of the Press Club of India's anniversary or as an exhibition for the "Youth of India" society, indicates a novel interpretation of the role of classical music. In response, the musician has moved from the role of purveyor of aesthetic and other delights to the role of mediator and interpreter of India's Great Tradition. This is the impetus behind the popularization of classical music, and the explicit rationale for virtually any public musical function. As Narayanon Menon rightly points out, the move to the concert platform signals the shift of patronage to the public; it also resembles, as he says, the place from which "one lectures" (1963:18). Menon also mentions the necessity of adjusting to a larger audience and inferior sound amplification systems. But the comparison to a lecture should not be lost. At the most general level, musical occasions in India are ritual occasions, celebrating the renewal of national consciousness and giving shape to this consciousness through the total event, of which the music performance is only a part. This encompasses the widest sense, for as we have seen there are a variety of contexts, audiences, and consumers which the musician engages and speaks to, "saying something of something" through a specialized medium designed for the higherly informed few but adapting to the variously informed many (Geertz, 1972:26).

The aesthetic decisions which musicians make—utilizing a serious or light rāg, ending performances on a light note, introducing the explicit competition, play and cooperation in the jawal-sawab and jugalbandi forms—vary according to their perceptions of the audience. But these decision strategies constitute only one class of changes or modifications which musicians have employed in adapting to a different sociocultural context. In the light of changes in the ecological circumstances of music culture, there have been and continue to be a variety of responses oriented toward "saying something of something" more effectively. One way of investigating this is to consider what might be called, paraphrasing Erving Goffman, the presentation of artistic self in concert life.

Models for Performance

In an illuminating article, William Weber has shown how the notion of musical masters of the past raised to musical sainthood was a European phenomenon of the mid-nineteenth century concomitant with the rise of a mass public; and how conductors of symphony orchestras "all made themselves into charismatic figures at the podium and devised grand programs which made the music of the masters seem awesome rather than esoteric" (Weber 1977:5, 19).

The *movement* of a performer can be a visual representation of the *manner* of a piece. The public personality of an artist also contributes to an interpretive context creating meaning in the music through extramusical messages. Put another way, stage presentation should tell us something about what is happening musically, or rather what the artist means to convey.

My observations lead me to think that in North India there are two primary models from which cultural cues of stage presentation are derived: the courtly (*darbār*) and the devotional (*bhakti*). It is no accident that these models also represent the bipolar traditions of music as a way for and a way of life. They continue a fundamental ambivalence in the meaning of musicianship which I would suggest mirrors all facets of Indian culture; an ambivalence, I should add, which is in itself not there interpreted as a contradiction or a paradox but rather as a natural reality of being.

The darbar model simulates the contemporary idea of the court performance. The performer enters the stage with a flourish of *salāms*, slow and dignified. His costume (for it is not everyday dress) can be extravagant or muted, but it is complete in its elegance. Draped on his shoulder and, when seated, covering his legs and exposed feet is a delicately embroidered Pashminar, the most refined of Kashmiri shawls.

On the stage is still another platform, raised a few inches above the stage floor. The platform is covered with an oriental rug and, if particularly elaborate, may have a little banister around the two sides and back, decorated with garlands of flowers. The spotlights focus the attention of all on the artist.

The musician will sit tall and straight, dignified and serious, look-ing carefully at the audience—scrutinizing it—for perhaps no rea-son other than letting the audience know that he is taking them into account and that his performance demands silence, atten-tion, and respect.

The darbar model is that of the refined monarch who is authority personified. It is a model more characteristically uti-lized by hereditary musicians, Muslim artists who still celebrate the glories of the royal dynasties. It is also more characteristic of instrumentalists, specialists who through their virtuosity captivate the listeners and inspire their imagination, to dream perhaps in their bourgeois consciousness of an aristocratic past.

The whole ambience is one of majesty.

For other kinds of listeners and perhaps for those we have just left as well, it is important to know that the performer is personally a *devoted* person; to his music and to Supreme Being. To know this is to anticipate a deep relationship between the performer and his music. The *bhakti* presentation simulates above all the idea of authentic performance of pure devotion. The listeners are not so much attending to as they are corporate witnesses of the performance: what in India would be called a *darshān*. The performer, here more typically a vocalist, addresses himself to God, raising his hands in supplication as he sings his devotion. He wears no costume, but the ordinary everyday dress of the loosely fitting shirt (*kurtā*) and loose slacks (*pajāmas*).

Performers utilizing the bhakti model, or aspects of it, will tend to be non-hereditary musicians, usually Hindus. The de-meanor in contrast to the darbar model is one of humility, not pride.

There is still a third model I wish to consider, the salon model of the courtesan class. In this model one finds aspects of both the courtly and the devotional. The performance of a hered-itary woman vocalist can stress one or the other because of the particular nature of the song types which have as their central theme, love, either earthly or devotional. There is a fundamental ambiguity in the texts of the light classical music forms which allows speeches of love to be addressed to a lord, and it is up to the performer and the listener to determine if the lord is human or divine. I think that, in most performances, what sets this salon model apart from the others is that the interpretation of the text is kept deliberately ambiguous, utilizing both the worldly darbar and the divine bhakti as a combined model—a model of ambivalence?

Why do there have to be such models? And why are the two models the operant metaphors? The history of public stage performances is still recent enough and the music still connected enough to its immediate tradition, that the darbar and the bhakti models are the only meaningful models upon which contemporary performances can be based. They involve the audience—in their separate ways—in a contextual structure which provides an interpretive frame for the intelligibility of the performance and the listeners' relationship to the performance. Such an interpretation corroborates the findings of other social scientists working in India: that Indian society adapts to the exigencies of contemporary life through the utilization of traditional forms and symbols, remolded for novel demands.

The Technology of Music Production and Reproduction

In the 1930s, Walter Benjamin outlined the impact of technology on art in his prescient article "The Work of Art in the Age of Mechanical Reproduction." Benjamin was concerned with the authenticity of a work of art, its "aura" as a unique "presence in space and time." With mechanical reproduction, such a unique presence was lost or weakened as a "historical testimony," and consequently the work of art lost its "authority." This loss of authority led in turn to a "tremendous shattering of tradition" (Benjamin 1969: 220–21). One can hardly do justice to Benjamin's rich flow of ideas with these few excerpts, but they seem immediately and highly relevant to the present condition of Hindustani art music. The concern with authenticity and tradition underlies what might be termed the problem for Hindustani music today.

In the West, the mechanical reproduction of music has led to obvious changes in performance practices. Confining ourselves to the classical tradition, we experience in the generation raised on recordings an expectation of live performances based on these recordings. The recorded version has in one sense become the original experience, and a live performance is from the point of view of LP listeners the reproduced object. An obvious effect of such an obverse arrangement is that technical flaws, edited out of the recording and thus unavailable as experience, assume magnified significance in live performances. A high aesthetic premium on technical perfection results. The nature of aesthetic effects within the recording context can be further explored in the current controversy regarding "direct to disc" recordings in which mistakes cannot be edited out. Critics of this technique argue that musicians under enormous pressure not to make mistakes (because otherwise the recording has to be repeated) focus all their attention on this problem and thus lose spontaneity. The "like live" conditions of the performing studio result in mechanical performances. Defenders of this technique argue that performers, because of the pressure upon them, produce their most creative efforts, as in the context of a concert hall performance. They do not become creatively "lazy" in the studio from knowing that they can splice together the products of many takes.

For the most part, Hindustani performances are also recorded without editing within discrete sections, although if a performer does not like his performance he can usually repeat it from the beginning. Yet the knowledge that a performance will be preserved usually affects an artist's attitude to his performance. Some artists, it is claimed, will only provide a bare-bones version of what they are capable of presenting, in order to keep special knowledge out of the public domain. This is a common belief of connoisseurs concerning contemporary long-playing records. Curiously, however, the three-minute "78s" of old masters are universally admired. In these recordings, so people say, the old masters squeezed the essence of a rāg into three minutes, and what we hear are perfect miniatures of rāgs. Even today, listeners sometimes feel that a particular recording represents an archetypal performance. This possibility raises intriguing questions. To what extent, if any, will such recordings become models for performances in live contexts? Already one can hear discussions among informed listeners, who speak of Amir Khan's *Marwa* or Vilayat Khan's *Yaman,* referring to now classic recordngs. Definitive renderings may create definitive versions of a rāg, crystallizing the conception of a rāg on a recording. This was earlier not merely impossible, but irrelevant as a possibility. However, now it can happen and, if it does, it will radically transform the fundamental notion of what a rāg is, as well as the basis of Hindustani performance practices.

This became clear to me at a recent performance (1977) by Ali Akbar Khan in Delhi. About three quarters of an hour into the program I heard a series of snaps and clicks just behind me. Looking around, I saw several people quickly changing their cassette tapes. For these people and probably many more, a live Ali Akbar Khan performance was captured to be heard and reheard. The cassette recorder, basically an innovation of the 1970s, is already being manufactured in India and offered at moderate prices (about Rs. 300/– in 1977). Also a few commercial cassette recordings are available for about half the price of discs. There are probably few live performances by major artists today which go completely unrecorded. All these recordings, coupled with those available on commercial discs, make at least the major artists more widely and more commonly heard than previously possible. What can we expect from these new circumstances of reproduction and "reconsumption"? Along with Benjamin we can hypothesize that the aura of a live performance recorded and reheard is diminished. But it is equally admissible to say the aura can be transferred from presence in a live performance to preservation in a recorded one. Some collectors in India (and in the West) keep their private recordings under lock and key, to be from time to time "displayed" to their friends. These collections may in the future perform the role of gharanas in the past, not as social but as mechanical embodiments of tradition.[7]

The aura of Hindustani performances has been transferred to another locale as well, to unique presences in space and time today, the star performers. It is they who are able to maintain authority by their established claims to authenticity through hereditary traditions (even when, strictly speaking, they are not hereditary musicians). And it is through their own embodiment of tradition that they are able, and find it necessary, to introduce musical innovations. The demand for innovations is a consequence of their sustained exposure through recordings and public concerts. Their ability to produce innovations is a function of their musicianship of course, but just as important is their impunity to accusations of being non-traditional. They are the definers of tradition.

Certainly, in the public concerts of artists such as Ali Akbar Khan and Vilayat Khan, the standard format of two or three distinct rāgs is no longer regularly followed. Instead, new rāgs— discovered, borrowed, or invented—are brought before the public. Modulation between rāgs or mixing rāgs is also becoming more common, as I earlier indicated. Vilayat Khan, for example, usually ends his concerts with his justly famous rāg *Bairavi* (which is indeed the traditional closing rāg of a concert). However, he has introduced the idea of modulating the tonic through some or all of the twelve semitones to end with his beginning tonic. In his "Modulation in Hindustani Art Music," Row claims that "anyone who has heard Ustad Ali Akbar Khan, Pandit Ravi Shankar and Sri Nikhil Banerjee play *rāg Shyam Kalyan* in successive performances over the last 10 to 12 years should be aware of the very discernible increases in modulation devices applied to it" (1977:119).

Performing a ragmala (in effect a medley of rāgs) is considered a virtual desecration by some older orthodox musicians ("like mixing castes"), but it is a musical solution, I think, for listeners who have become surfeited with standard rāgs too commonly available through mechanical reproductions. In the modulation connecting different rāgs in a "string," the focus of aesthetic interest in Hindustani music moves from a concern with relationships between intervals to that existing (or being created) between rāgs. Aesthetic interest is similarly focused where a new rāg is created from elements of two established rāgs.[8] Like any creative act, the mixing of rāgs is an attempt to discover new relationships between existing elements, resulting in the creation of new structures, which in turn become existing elements through convention. We can perhaps usefully consider this a musical metaphoric process.[9]

Other rather more concrete changes have of course occurred, owing to the new technological environment. For example, the obvious constraint in both the radio and recording studios is time, both its measure and its duration. There is an absolute limit on the length of the performance, which has to fit within the timetable of the radio schedule or the limitations of an LP; there is also the musician's allocation of time to different parts of a performance so that he may present what he regards as its totality. The problem of duration is exemplified in an account of the early days of All India Radio. A famous musician agreed, after much persuasion, to broadcast a program. He was offered an hour of air time which he refused, saying it took that long just for him to warm up. He could not be dissuaded from this idea, but he finally agreed to minimally a three-hour performance. There still was no possibility of allowing him this much time since other regularly scheduled programs had to be broadcast; so the studio personnel tricked him. He started singing at six o'clock in Studio one, thinking he was being broadcast, whereas in reality the previously scheduled work was on the air. At seven o'clock they switched in the artist, who was by now "warmed up," and gave him the following two hours, until nine. At a few minutes before nine, the producer came into the studio and pointed to the clock, whereupon the musician wrapped up his performance (Mullick 1974:30–32).

The idea of a time-bound performance has undoubtedly affected public performances as well. Ravi Shankar indicates this when he writes that "performing within a specific time limit was excellent training for the concerts I was to give later." He adds that "each day I spent at the radio station's studio, I did three or four sessions, and my programs were well-proportioned and included a variety of styles" (1968:75).

Studio sessions for commercial discs allow capabilities and experimentation not ordinarily available. For example, Vilayat Khan utilizes a slight echo in some of his recordings to simulate a certain ambience. Thus the recording "Night at the Taj" in which he is playing with his younger brother Imrat Khan (on the surbahar), the performance is supposed to evoke the romance of Emperor Shah Jahan and Mumtaz for whom he built the Taj Mahal.

The interior of the all-marble Taj has a high dome and voices are echoed in the interior. Tourists are regularly presented a performance of the echo by one of the wards of the Taj Mahal, an effect that is simulated in the recording.

The recording studio affects non-classical forms perhaps even more markedly. In one session I attended, a woman vocalist from Rajasthan was singing a *Mānd,* a Rajasthani folk form which is perhaps now undergoing classicization. She was accompanied by an ensemble which consisted of harmonium, violin, sitar, sarangi, and tabla. The ensemble was led by a conductor-arranger, who organized the actual compositions for the instruments around her performance. But the real artist—as he himself exclaimed—was the engineer at the tape board who, dancing at his dials, balanced the instrumentation and voice and was responsible for the final effect.

Technological innovations have affected another important element of Hindustani music culture: musical instruments. For example, Ustad Zia M. Dagar has added another bass string to his bīn, as well as extra-wide frets on which he can pull his string for a wider intervallic portamento. He sometimes attaches a contact microphone to his instrument so that it can be heard by a larger audience. Ram Narayan, the first and only musician to perform solo sarangi exclusively, uses harp strings purchased abroad instead of homemade gut, so as to produce the smoother, faster, and clearer tone for which his performances are renowned. These are not isolated examples; they are part of a long tradition of technological experimentation on instruments. The two major solo instruments played today, the sitar and sarod, are in their present forms probably less than a century old. The vichitr vina was invented in this century. Other innovations which are adopted technologies are the violin, harmonium, and Hawaiian guitar, borrowed from the West and integrated to varying degrees in the Hindustani tradition.

Other innovations are essentially stylistic, requiring no technological modifications and yet entering into a technological environment. For example, probably the most important stylistic innovation in instrumental music in this century has been the development of the gayaki (vocal) style adapted to instrumental music. Vilayat Khan has perfected the gayaki style on sitar, bringing it very close to its vocal counterpart (cf. Jairazbhoy 1971). Such an innovation is not lost on younger musicians, for whom the successful musicians of today are important models. It is an open secret that there are a host of young instrumentalists, who, whatever their stylistic loyalties to their gurus ought to be, patently copy either Ravi Shankar or Vilayat Khan. Instead of listening behind curtains as did the musicians of yesteryear, they tape the programs of the contemporary master (still surreptitiously), and copy the intricacies of his style in their own performances. It is probably this practice, rather than a concern for commercial pirating, which leads many of the master musicians to prohibit recordings of their public concerts.

Because of the influence of a few masters who now provide the major patterns copied by other musicians, there has probably been a *decrease* in the diversity of performance styles. At the same time there has been an *increase* in the variety of musical experiments and forms that musicians perform. The variety of stylistic novelties as exhibited in the different performance practices of different gharanas has been greatly reduced, but the forms—borrowing new rāgs, utilizing folk music, and presenting unusual combinations of performers—seem to have greatly increased in comparison with past practice. One would expect such a dynamic in a musical environment in which the flow of ideas has been speeded up through the mass media, and the sensibilities of the listening public redirected from the traditional "novelty" of depth to the modern one of breadth.

If we learn anything from this, it is that music systems, even those which put a high premium on stability, can be highly labile and can change by any measure quite dramatically. The changing organization of procedures and consumers, the new contexts of performances, and the modern technological environment all arise out of and reflect the dynamics of Indian society in this century. Whether they will culminate in a "tremendous shattering of tradition" remains to be seen. So far I believe, they have not.

8. The Cultural Structure and Social Organization of a Music Tradition

Earlier, I questioned how a traditional system of music can survive in a world which seems to undermine the basis upon which it has existed. What I have found is that musicians as individuals, and as social groups, have been highly resilient while appearing to be highly resistant. Singer suggests that "Indian civilization has built into it adaptive mechanisms for incorporating new techniques, new ideas, and newcomers with only a gradual displacement of the old" (1968:xi). Like the pedigrees of musicians which beyond the third generation allow for reinterpretations of connections, the "tradition" of the past is also open for a continuing revaluation in light of contemporary circumstances. This becomes particularly clear in the concepts of historical time and space which musicians have concerning their own tradition.

When speaking of this past, hereditary musicians move inevitably toward it, assembling their ancestors and reviving their memories. They describe their pedigrees and, if one insists, draw sequential lines of fathers and sons, but in their minds the most distant and most recent ancestors occupy the same plane in time. Historical time and historical geography are juxtaposed so that those units which bear significant relationships to one another

are placed not in terms of their absolute distance, but in terms of their relative importance. A hundred years or a thousand years may be as close or far as the frozen events which define them. Their conception of historical time—which readers familiar with India will recognize—gives the participants an immediacy and close identity with a past and a place, which are always equidistant from oneself.

It is this kind of past which the participant invokes as a model and a justification for his present actions and behavior. Such a perception, moreover, is by no means characteristic of today only. Imam, who it will be recalled was writing in the middle of the last century about his contemporaries, now the legendary giants of the past, said of his own traditional past:

> Let it not be hidden from the listeners, singers and lovers of music that among the present-day musicians I have undoubtably seen a few who are effective in their singing and whose *Alap* or exposition had transported the listeners now into a sedate state of enchantment and now into a restless state of awakening. But the spectacular effects produced by the earlier musicians as described above have remained in the dreamland of the past only. [1959b:7]

Apparently there is, then, not only a past which molds and personifies the "tradition" but also a tradition of representing a past which, however unreachable, is always available as a model for the present. So commonly is one assaulted, sometimes assuaged, with the perpetual sighs of what always was but never is— a collective remembrance of things past. Whether it is the sixteen hours of riaz shaping a living legend or the musical battles of a thousand years past, these all exist for musicians and their disciples as the tradition which lies at the root of the present.

The tradition of Hindustani music as now conceived rests on a number of different loci from which differing shades of its reality emerge upon interpretation. Those associated with the micro-traditions of hereditary musicians and their gharanas, and those who eschew these identities, looking to a more distant past of a pan-Indian musical tradition, share the same repertoire of historical elements defining that tradition. But, by a rejuxtaposition of the relationships among these elements, a different definition of the significance of points past is put forth to interpret the strategies for the present. One discovers, then, an ideational system built upon the foundations of a historical system, the elements of each system having an isomorphic relationship with those of the other. The assortment and reassortment of these elements allow for a continual renewal, at the level of ideas, of what at its base appears a constant past.

This is well-exemplified in the guru-shishya system of learning, a model adopted by Muslim musicians. But whereas in the Sanskritic tradition only the guru's role was based on ascriptive principles, with the professionalization of music the disciple was included as well (cf. Mookerji, 1951:200). The critical difference of course was that the latter-day disciple was being trained for performance, whereas the classical shishya sought only competence. This probably explains the Urdu term for this system as *ustad-shagird* rather than *shaikh-murid.*

Professional musicians insist that the guru-shishya manner of learning is still the only way to train performers and to keep the tradition alive—the chief concern of all musicians today. Although there have always been some doubts about the authenticity of particular traditions, today professional musicians point to the fundamental change in the musical enculturative process. The music schools are not geared to train performers, and the times do not allow the traditional guru-shishya system to operate.

However, the evidence from my work in Delhi indicates that this is perhaps not so fundamental a problem as it seems to the ustads, although their apprehension makes a great deal of sense. Were younger musicians trained to perform before an audience of the extinct aristocracy with their highly refined and special sensibilities, then their modern training would be inappropriate and, in that sense, inadequate. They would, for example, not have the enormous repertoire of compositions and skills at extemporizing required to keep the same small audience interested over an extended period of time. In terms of the relative performer-listener ratio at that time, there must have been a much higher per-capita level of music consumption than there is now, and of course there must have been a very different kind of consumption pattern characterized by a homogenity of tastes and a more relaxed pace. As Lully was with Louis XIV, artists must have been highly responsive to the tastes of their small and articulate audience. The consumption patterns of to-day's listeners àre naturally quite different, the most important difference being the heterogenity of tastes, requiring a greater diversity of styles in order to communicate to them.

For this, artists of today are much better adapted than their forefathers would have been. All professional performers go through a period of intensive training with one or, more com-monly, several gurus. In addition, as we have seen, younger art-ists have and utilize the replication capacities of tape-recording and phonograph records in order to copy their particular models. As it is, younger artists do borrow a great deal and come on stage with a large repertoire of styles, forms, and idioms—modes through which novelty is introduced. Diversity is thus created laterally to accommodate a receptive public consisting of differ-ent kinds of audiences, each being offered something according to its tastes and abilities. This explains the exploitation of techni-cal and musical resources such as the increased popularity of tabla solos, lighter "classicized" forms like the dhun, and musical combats like the sawal-jawab. There is indeed a whole set of experiments on the stage which would be anathema to the ortho-dox but which are viewed with interest by the public. Taking a somewhat longer historical perspective, the evolution and adop-tion of new instruments, the separation of vocal and instrumental styles, the entrance of folk traditions into the classical, and con-comitant musical developments such as the khayal and thumri suggest earlier adaptive strategies of Hindustani music for a then-changing society. To do more than speculate, however, will re-quire a history of early eighteenth-century music culture yet to be written. But it seems reasonable to suggest that the history of Hindustani music from the beginnings of its professionalization will not be understood without a consideration of the changing social and cultural contexts to which it spoke. To the extent that music, or any cultural expression for that matter, exists, it must arise out of a tradition. When, as in India, we discover a tradition of looking to a past encompassing vast ranges of space and time as a verification for actions in the present, the circle becomes complete. Strategies can be adopted as long as they have validity in the past, a past which can be selected and brought forward like an obscure rāg to answer the demands of the present.

The adage that "in order for things to remain the same they have to change" finds its mirror image in India. There we might say that "in order for things to change, they have to appear the same."

This work has been an attempt to utilize what might be called a bifocal perspective; alternating the frame of reference, I have tried to indicate what an ethnomusicological approach— itself somewhat of a bifocal discipline—can reveal about a socio-cultural system as it reflects on and is reflected by its music culture.

Through one half of the lens, we see the contribution of an ethnomusicological approach to a better understanding of the relationship between the great and little traditions of a civilization, particularly in the context of modernity. Indicated in the results of this study are the adaptive processes which have been occurring in other areas of Indian society: an ability, in its most general sense, of the social system to undergo the necessary modifications and structural changes requisite of a modernizing society without sacrificing a corresponding cultural structure conceived as traditional. This is the force of Harold Gould's insistence that we make a more rigorous distinction between idea systems and social systems when considering the complementary or contradictory models of modernity and tradition:

> We must therefore distinguish between traditional social structures which *qua* structures are patently incapable of assimilation to modern social structures and the mobilization of traditional values, skills or artifacts in behalf of modernization and nation building. Social systems cannot be mutually reinforcing when they rest on different mutually exclusive levels of social evolution, but idea systems can. [1970:3]

In the proliferation of new occupational and performance roles, innovations in training, and expanded rules of recruitment, in the diversification of listening public and patron and the changed role relations and social identities of musicians, the social organization of the musical tradition can indeed be said to have changed. Although viewed from one perspective these changes might appear as radical alterations, seen from within they seem logical extensions of the cultural structure of Indian civilization. The social organization has not so much been dramatically reshaped as enlarged, using past units as seeds for developing the present elements. Thus, the recruitment of musicians from hereditary families continues but is augmented from other sources. The guru-shishya system persists and remains the fundamental institution for providing performers, but it is increasingly coupled to some training in music colleges. Perhaps this system works through what Singer, in another context, has called "vicarious ritualization" by which the guru and shishya relationship, though compressed in time, succeeds nevertheless, like the universally admired rāgs heard in the 78 rpm recordings of past masters and the reduced five-hour riaz routines for present ones (1968:439).

The "idea system," or what I have called the cultural structure, can adapt to changing social conditions because it is constructed from elements which allow both contradictory interpretations and a continuing potential for revision; witness the tabliya who refused to play the subordinate role to the soloist, or the two observers of the esteemed Ustad Fayaz Khan who could not agree whether or not he used a harmonium, and if he did what he thought—or ought to have thought—about it.

The disjunction between social and cultural changes does not always result in a harmonious equilibrium between the two. But so far, it seems to me, Indian music as a cultural tradition has had, by virtue of the manner in which its history has been constructed (and reconstructed), the ability to encompass particular contradictions and thereby resolve them. The cyclical nature of the Hindustani rhythmic system where the *sam* is counted as the first beat but musically perceived as the end, the conceptualization of historical time and space as encircling the subject and giving him equal access to all points, and the cycle of births and rebirths are all, I would suggest, expressions of the integration of

Indian cultural structure, and are also in various senses contradictory. But this very contradictoriness is certainly distinctive of, if not unique to, Indian thought and is self-consciously extended to encompass the supposed dichotomy of tradition and modernity.

Looking through the other half of the lens, we can consider for a moment the more direct ethnomusicological question of how all this bears on the music itself. For one thing, we have seen how using indirect kinds of data such as the restructuring of instruments, or the utilization of novel media, gives us insights into the dynamics of musical style and value. From changes in the social organization of musical specialists we can infer changes in the organization of the music itself: the recruitment of bowed accompanists in the vocal tradition, the bifurcation of hereditary families into solo instrumentalists and vocalists, and the changing musical conceptions brought in by folk musicians of the past and non-hereditary musicians of the present.

Like the cultural structure of Indian civilization, the art music of India as a cultural expression draws on the particles and perceptions of the past. As a symbolic system, it conveys meaning through the expression of affect; and as some meanings always change either in content or in their distribution, the symbols which carry them also seem to change accordingly. In an ultimate sense, a musical system is arbitrary, like language, and its intelligibility coupled with its untranslatability can only suggest an adumbrated "how" for its ineffability. But so pervasive, eminently human, and fundamentally non-utilitarian a cultural product as music leaves in its wake—like an atom its trail in a cloud chamber—a tantalizing hint or a passageway, as Lévi-Strauss believes, for the discovery of something essential to the mystery of ourselves.

I have here attempted to build a kind of cloud chamber, where the element itself, music, has been for the most part excluded, except for the reflection of its image in its environment. Because musicians are the mediators of the phenomenon, it has seemed most worthwhile to fix attention on them, their ideas as they state them, and their ideas as they enact them. I have also concentrated on the context of performance, looking for signs in the new media and uses to which they are put which might enhance my understanding of the role of music in Indian society. Clifford Geertz, in his eloquent and incisive analysis of the Balinese cockfight, reminds us how art forms generally have a role in social life.

> Enacted and reenacted, so far without end, the cockfight enables the Balinese, as, read and reread, *Macbeth* enables us, to see a dimension of his own subjectivity. As he watches fight after fight, with the active watching of an owner and bettor (for cockfighting has no more interest as a pure spectator sport than does croquet or dog racing) he grows familiar with it and what it has to say to him, much as the attentive listener to string quartets or the absorbed viewer of still life grows slowly more familiar with them in a way which opens his subjectivity to himself.
>
> Yet, because—in another of those paradoxes, along with painted feelings and unconsequenced acts, which haunt aesthetics—that subjectivity does not properly exist until it is thus organized, art forms generate and regenerate the very subjectivity they pretend only to display. Quartets, still lifes, and cockfights are not merely reflections of a pre-existing sensibility analogically represented; they are positive agents in the creation and maintenance of such a sensibility. . . . It is in such a way, coloring experience with the light they cast it in, rather than through whatever material effects they may have, that the arts play their role, as arts, in social life. [1972:28]

For the participant in the musical culture of India— whether passive or active, knowledgeable or not—the musical event as social act and cultural construct, heard and reheard, creates its meanings and provides its interpretations of the Indian experience. And beyond the jealousies proverbial among musicians, the paternalism of government patronage, the aesthetic innocence of many listeners, and the yearnings for a sensibility long past, there remains always the hope that a given performance will not merely evoke, through sympathetic resonance as it were, a sentiment or a sense of feeling of what has been, but will produce, if only for a moment, the reality of what always is.

Tables

Note: The musicians listed in Tables 1 through 6 are musicians whom I interviewed. The information included there is based largely on these interviews, supplemented by genealogies and interviews with other musicians and connoisseurs not listed in the tables. Ages are often approximate and are listed as of 1969–70. Caste designations are, in most instances, quite reliable since they are either based on common knowledge or have been cross-checked. Caste designations refer only to the most inclusive category of such designations and do not indicate specific caste groupings. Where there is doubt about a caste designation a question mark is entered. For Muslim musicians, no caste designation has been given in several instances, even though a musician's origin might be ascribed to one or another caste category. The designation is omitted because such a musician really belongs only to his immediate family group and marries either within or completely outside the family. A marriage outside the family is usually with a Hindu woman, and one can consider the Muslim who contracts such a marriage as truly "caste-less."

Occupations are listed in condensed form in Tables 1 through 6. These listings are to be interpreted as follows:

University Lecturer or *Professor*: A musician whose primary musical activity is teaching in a university.

Music College Teacher: A musician who teaches in an institution devoted only to music instruction.

Teacher: a musician who has "tuitions" (pupils). He or she is self-employed.

Staff Artist, A.I.R.: a musician who is a full-time employee of All India Radio.

Staff Artist (Tanpura, A.I.R.): a musician with any one of a variety of musical specialties, whose primary function at All India Radio is to play the tanpura.

Orchestra Musician: a musician who performs in one of the hotel or entertainment orchestras.

Ustad: This is not properly an occupation as such, but because of his status an ustad is typically supported by his disciples and/or relatives.

Concert Artist: a musician whose primary musical activity is giving public concerts.

Student: a musician who is taking an advanced degree. Since my research began, the one person listed as such has become a lecturer in a college.

Freelance: a designation referring only to accompanists. Such musicians are often unemployed, but receive "gigs" from time to time either in respectable public concerts or as accompanists for female singers and dancers in the few salons still operating.

Table 1. Vocalists

	Religion	Caste	Musician Family	Vocalist Family	Occupation	Age	Sex
1.	Hindu	Brahman	No	No	University Lecturer	50	F
2.	Hindu	Brahman	Yes	Yes	Staff Artist, A.I.R. (Tanpura)	35	M
3.	Hindu	Brahman	No	No	Music Advisor, A.I.R. Musicologist	70	M
4.	Hindu	Brahman	No	No	Staff Artist, A.I.R. (Tanpura)	40	M
5.	Hindu	Brahman	No	No	Music College Teacher	70	M
6.	Hindu	Brahman	No	No	Music College Teacher	50	M
7.	Hindu	Brahman	No	No	Music Producer, A.I.R.	35	M
8.	Muslim	Mirasi	Yes	No	Staff Artist, A.I.R. (Tanpura)	30	M
9.	Muslim	Mirasi	Yes	No	Staff Artist, A.I.R. (Tanpura)	40	M
10.	Muslim	Mirasi	Yes	Yes		70	M
11.	Muslim	Kalawant	Yes	Yes	University Lecturer	45	M
12.	Muslim	Kalawant	Yes	Yes	Teacher	50	M
13.	Hindu	——	Yes	Yes	Music College Teacher	60	F

Table 2. Sitar Players

	Religion	Caste	Musician Family	Occupation	Age	Sex
1.	Muslim	Mirasi	Yes	Orchestra Musician	25	M
2.	Muslim	Mirasi	Yes	Teacher	35	M
3.	Muslim	————	Yes	Staff Artist, A.I.R.	30	M
4.	Muslim	————	Yes	Concert Artist	30	M
5.	Muslim	————	Yes	Concert Artist	35	M
6.	Muslim	————	Yes	Staff Artist, A.I.R.	35	M
7.	Muslim	————	Yes	Ustad	60	M
8.	Hindu	Brahman	No	Teacher; Concert Artist	35	M
9.	Hindu	Brahman	No	University Professor	55	M
10.	Hindu	Brahman	No		55	M
11.	Hindu	Vaidya	No	Student	25	F
12.	Hindu	Kayasth	No	Teacher	50	M

Table 3. Sarod Players

	Religion	Caste	Musician Family	Occupation	Age	Sex
1.	Hindu	Brahman	No	Teacher; Concert Artist	55	M
2.	Hindu	Kayasth	No	Concert Artist	40	F
3.	Hindu	Brahman	No	*	25	M
4.	Hindu	Kayasth	No	Staff Artist, A.I.R.	50	M
5.	Muslim	Mirasi	Yes	None	20	M

*He is quasi-professional and gives occasional recitals. Main source of income and primary occupation is a poultry business.

Table 4. Sarangi Players

	Religion	Caste	Musician Family	Occupation	Age	Sex
1.	Muslim	Mirasi	Yes	A.I.R.*	45	M
2.	Muslim	Mirasi	Yes	A.I.R.	50	M
3.	Muslim	Mirasi	Yes	A.I.R.	50	M
4.	Muslim	Mirasi	Yes	A.I.R.	55	M
5.	Muslim	Mirasi	Yes	Freelance	60	M
6.	Muslim	Mirasi	Yes	A.I.R.	35	M
7.	Muslim	Mirasi	Yes	A.I.R.	45	M
8.	Muslim	Mirasi	Yes	A.I.R.	30	M
9.	Muslim	Mirasi	Yes	A.I.R.	55	M
10.	Muslim	Mirasi	Yes	A.I.R.	35	M
11.	Muslim	Mirasi	Yes	A.I.R.	45	M
12.	Muslim	Mirasi	Yes	A.I.R.	55	M
13.	Muslim	Mirasi	Yes	Freelance	25	M
14.	Muslim	Mirasi	Yes	Freelance	35	M
15.	Hindu	?	Yes	Freelance	50	M
16.	Hindu	?	?	A.I.R.	40	M
17.	Hindu	Katthak	Yes	Freelance	65	M
18.	Hindu	Dholi	Yes	A.I.R.	40	M
19.	Hindu	Katthak	Yes	Freelance	50	M
20.	Hindu	Dholi	Yes	Freelance	45	M

*A.I.R. indicates a staff artist, All India Radio.

243

Table 5. Tabla Players

	Religion	Caste	Musician Family	Occupation	Age	Sex
1.	Muslim	Mirasi	Yes	Freelance	30	M
2.	Muslim	Mirasi	Yes	A.I.R.*	30	M
3.	Muslim	Mirasi	Yes	Retired	80	M
4.	Muslim	Mirasi	Yes	A.I.R.	35	M
5.	Muslim	Mirasi	Yes	A.I.R.	35	M
6.	Muslim	Mirasi	Yes	A.I.R.	55	M
7.	Muslim	Mirasi	Yes	A.I.R.	55	M
8.	Muslim	Mirasi	Yes	Ustad	60	M
9.	Muslim	Mirasi	Yes	A.I.R.	55	M
10.	Hindu	?	Yes	A.I.R.	50	M
11.	Hindu	Brahman(?)	Yes	A.I.R.	50	M
12.	Hindu	Rajput	?	A.I.R.	35	M

*A.I.R. indicates a staff artist, All India Radio.

Table 6. Other Instrumentalists

	Religion	Caste	Musician Family	Occupation	Age	Sex
			Bin			
1.	Muslim	————	Yes	Teacher	35	M
2.	Muslim	————	Yes	A.I.R.*	30	M
3.	Muslim		Yes	Teacher	40	M
4.	Hindu	Brahman	No	————	70?	M
			Vichitr Vina			
1.	Muslim	Mirasi	Yes	A.I.R.	50	M
2.	Hindu		No	Composer; Advertising	40	M
			Violin			
1.	Muslim	Mirasi	Yes	A.I.R.	30	M
2.	Hindu	?	No	Composer; Orchestra Musician	45	M
3.	Hindu	?	No	A.I.R.	35	M
			Dilruba			
1.	Hindu	Brahman	No	A.I.R.	40	M
2.	Sikh	?	No	A.I.R.	35	M
			Esraj			
1.	Muslim	Mirasi	Yes	Hotel Orchestra Musician	25	M
			Guitar			
1.	Christian	————	No	A.I.R.	40	M

*A.I.R. indicates a staff artist, All India Radio.

245

Table 7. The Gwalior Gharana and Its Connections

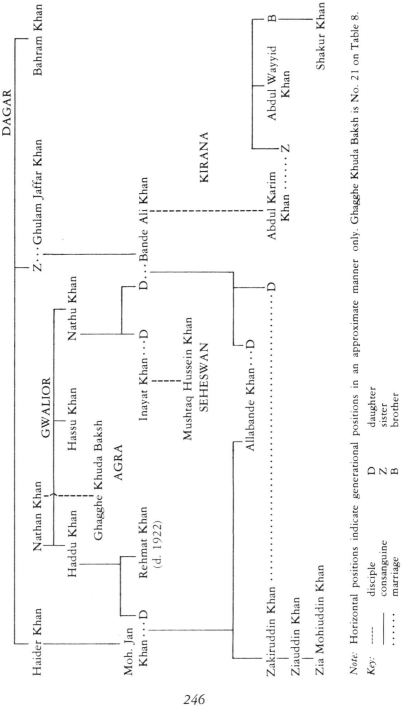

Note: Horizontal positions indicate generational positions in an approximate manner only. Ghagghe Khuda Baksh is No. 21 on Table 8.

Key:

-----	disciple	D
———	consanguine	Z
·······	marriage	B

daughter	
sister	
brother	

246

Table 8. The Agra Gharana and Its Connections

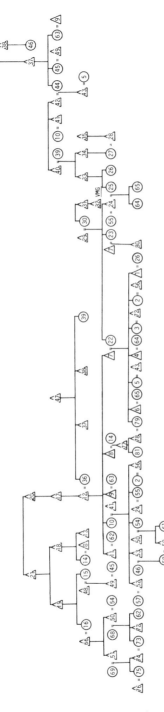

Note: Numbers are the "names" of individuals. No. 1 (Ego) is Ustad Yunus Hussein Khan. Many names appear twice, once as descendants and once as linked by marriage. For example, No. 2 is the daughter of No. 7 and the wife of No. 56, who is himself the son of No. 10, who is the brother of No. 7. No. 47, the founder of a closely related gharana (Attrauli), is located twice for reasons of space.

Table 9. Marriage Links between Atrauli and Agra Khandans

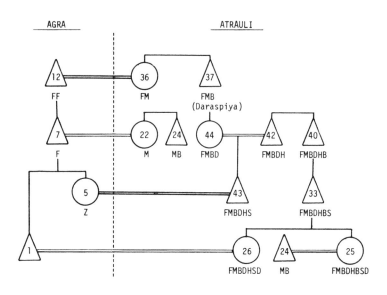

Note: Numbers correspond to those given in Table 8. All relationships are indicated relative to No. 1, Ustad Yunus Hussein Khan. No. 43 is Sharafat Hussein Khan.

Key:
F father D daughter
M mother S son
B brother H husband
Z sister

Table 10. Marriage Relations between Agra and Khurja Khandans

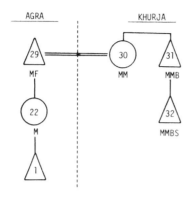

Note: Numbers correspond to those given in Table 8. Relationships are indicated relative to No. 1, Ustad Yunus Hussein Khan. No. 31 is Altaf Hussein Khan. No. 32 is Wahid Hussein Khan.

Key: F   father
M   mother
B   brother
S   son

Table 11. Exchange of Daughters between Agra and Atrauli

Atrauli Daughters to Agra			Agra Daughters to Atrauli		
Atrauli	=	Agra	Agra	=	Atrauli
26	=	1	2	=	56
64	=	4	5	=	43
65	=	6	10	=	41
22	=	7			
63	=	9			
36	=	12			
46	=	53			
45	=	49			

Note: Numbers correspond to those given in Table 8.

Table 12. Agra Marriage Links (1 = FMZSD/MBWZ)

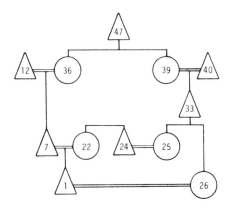

Note: In Tables 12–22, numbers correspond to those given in Table 8. No. 1 is Ustad Yunus Hussein Khan.

Key:
F	father	D	daughter
M	mother	S	son
B	brother	H	husband
Z	sister	W	wife

Table 13. Agra Marriage Links (1 = FZHBSD; 2 = FZS)

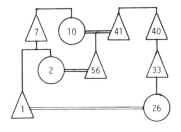

Table 14. Agra Marriage Links (3 = FFFFBSDSS)

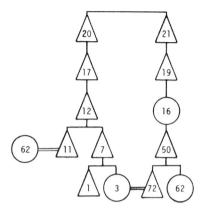

Table 15. Agra Marriage Links (4 = MBD; 6 = MBD)

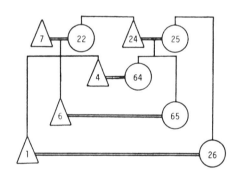

Table 16. Agra Marriage Links (5 = FZHBS)

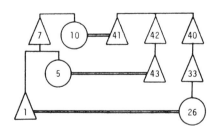

Table 17. Agra Marriage Links (79 = FBSS)

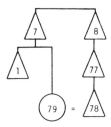

Table 18. Agra Marriage Links (7 = 22, 23)

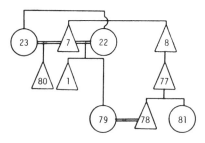

Table 19. Agra Marriage Links (10 = MBDHB)

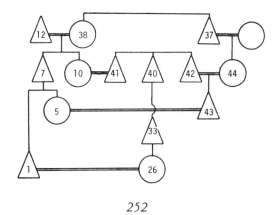

Table 20. Agra Marriage Links (9 = MBD)

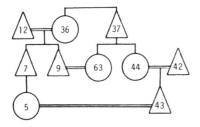

Table 21. Agra Marriage Links (8 = FFFBSD)

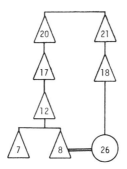

Table 22. Agra Marriage Links (11 = FFFBSDSD)

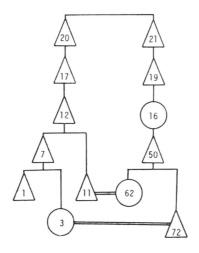

Table 23. The Delhi Gharana of Mamman Khan

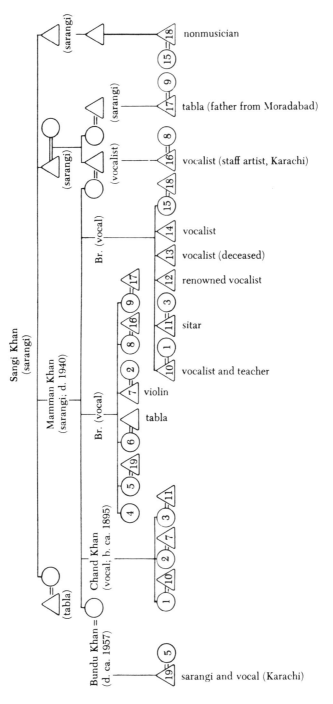

Source: *Eight Urban Musical Cultures*, ed. Bruno Nettl. Urbana: University of Illinois Press, 1978. Reproduced by permission.

Note: A repeated number indicates that an individual is both a descendant and linked by marriage.

Key: Br. brother

Table 24. Tansen's Daughter's Descendants

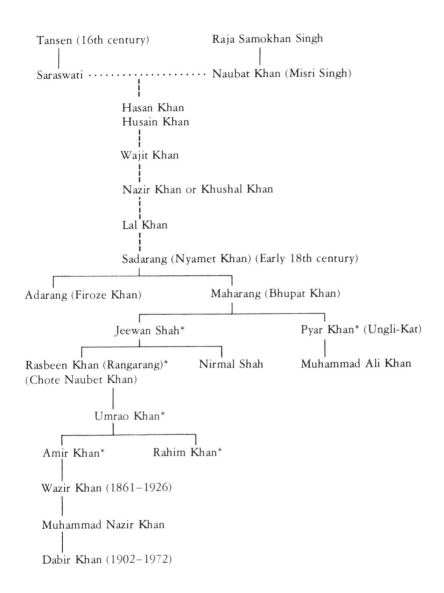

Source: Adapted from Sharmistha Sen, interview with Dabir Khan, in "The String Instruments of North India," unpublished Ph.D. dissertation, Visva-Bharati University, 1972. Used by permission.
*Mentioned in Imam (1959b).

Table 25. Seniya Sitar Lineage

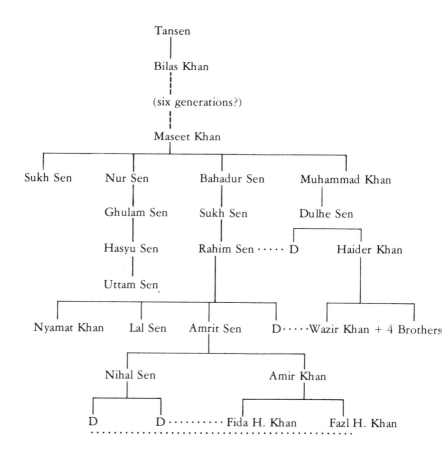

Source: Adapted from Sharmistha Sen, "The String Instruments of North India," unpublished Ph.D. dissertation, Visva-Bharati University, 1972. Used by permission.

Table 26. Vocal Gharanas as Listed by Six Authors

Deshpande (1973)	Chaubey (1945)	Trikha (1967)	Aggrawal (1966)	Sen (1972)	Kaufmann (1968)
Gwalior	Gwalior	Gwalior	Gwalior	Gwalior	Gwalior
Agra	Agra	Agra	Agra	Agra-Atrauli	Agra
Kirana	Kirana	Kirana	Kirana	Kirana	Kirana
Jaipur	Delhi	Jaipur	Delhi	Jaipur-Atrauli	Indore
Patiala	Patiala	Patiala	Patiala	Patiala	Patiala
Indore		Sham Chaurasi	Indore	Delhi	Lahore
Bindibazar		Sehaswan	Atrauli	Atrauli	Alladiya Khan
		Mathura		Rampur-Sehaswan	Rampur
		Delhi Gharana of Mamman Khan			Agra-Rangile
		Delhi Gharana			
		Khurja			
		Atrauli			
		Indore (listed as "technique of Music")			
		Saharanpur			

257

Table 27. Hindustani Music Performers at Delhi All India Radio (1969)

All Categories of Music		Classical Music Only	
Staff	96 (17%)	Staff	63 (22%)
Casual	458 (83%)	Casual	226 (78%)
Total	554	Total	289

Note: Tables 27–32 are compiled from an unpublished list of musicians at All India Radio, Delhi, 1969.

Table 28. Hindustani Musicians at Delhi All India Radio (1969) by Grade and Institutional Status

Grade	Vocal		Instrumental		Total
	Staff	Casual	Staff	Casual	
Top	0	3	1	6	10
A	4	20	15	13	52
B-high	3	19	25	26	73
B	0	67	15	72	154
Total	7	109	56	117	289

Table 29. Fee Scales for Casual Artists at All India Radio (1969) per Performance Day

Grade	Range (Classical)	Light Classical
Top Class	Rs. 125/- to 200/-	Rs. ———
A	80/- to 120/-	75/- to 90/-
B-high	60/- to 75/-	50/- to 70/-
B	40/- to 55/-	30/- to 45/-

Table 30. Light Vocal Music Artists at Delhi All India Radio (1969) by Grade and Institutional Status

Grade	Staff Artist	Casual Artist	
A	0	14	
B-high	0	31	
B	1	187	
Total	1	232	233

Grand Total, Tables 28 and 30: 522 musicians

Table 31. Staff Artists at All India Radio by Instrumental Specialty and Grade

Specialty			Grade			Hereditary*	
	Top	A	B-high	B	Total	Yes	No
Sarangi	1	2	8	3	14	13	1(?)
Tabla		4	4	5	13	7	6
Pakhawaj			1		1	1	
Subtotal, Accompanists					(28)	(21)	(7)
Sitar		2	1	2	5	1	4
Sarod		1	3	1	5	2	3
Vichitr Vina		2			2	1	1
Shahnai		1			1	1	
Flute		1	1	3	5		5?
Esraj		1	1		2		2
Violin		1	3		4	1	3
Clarinet			1		1		1
Jaltarang			1	1	2	1(?)	1(?)
Dilruba			1		1		1
Bīn			1		1	1	
Subtotal, Soloists					(28)**	(8)	(21)
Total	1	15	25**	15	56**	28	28

*The "yes" column is quite certain except where indicated with a question mark. The "no" column includes those whom I know to be from non-hereditary families of musicians plus those I strongly suspect are not. Those indicated by a question mark are less certain, although likely.

**The bīn player is listed twice, once as a sitarist; hence the totals reflect one fewer than indicated.

Table 32. Staff Artists: Light Classical Orchestra Membership

Specialty	Number	Comments
Tanpura	7	2 also listed as vocalists, 1 as jaltarang player
Tabla	3	
Cello	2	
Flute	2	
Dholak & Naqqara	1	
Composer	4	
Clarinet	3	
Sitar	1	
Jaltarang	1	Also listed as a tanpura player
Mandolin	2	
Guitar	1	Hawaiian and electric
Violin	3	One listed as a music producer
Vocal	2	Listed above as tanpura players
Dilruba	1	
Sarangi	1	
Double bass	1	
Subtotal	35	
3 listed twice	−3	
Total	32	

Notes

Chapter 1

1. The extent to which it is difficult to generalize about India is illustrated by the variation in the interpretation of these terms. *Chiz* is the Persian word for "thing," and in my own experience with musicians I have heard it used in the sense of "musical thing," which could include anything from a vocal composition to any particular musical element or combination of elements. In the literature it is always identified as the song composition. *Bandish* is synonymous with either a vocal or an instrumental composition, according to Powers (1979), and my own experience corroborates this usage. But Deshpande makes a point of distinguishing chiz from bandish, claiming that the former is the actual composition, whereas the latter is the form of the composition, by which he means the manner of singing the composition (1973:32). On All India Radio, program announcements commonly use the sanskritized *rachanā* for instrumental compositions. These variations in usage are undoubtedly a function of actual variations in usage and not merely different interpretations of usage.

2. Row's definition continues: "These musical materials include:

   1. The tonal material
   2. The characteristic ascending and descending patterns (which are often loosely referred to as scales). Depending on the rāg the ascending pattern may employ either (a) stepwise motion, (b) combinations of steps and leaps, (c) oblique motion or (d) alternate possibilities such as primarily (b) but sometimes (c). The descending pattern will also employ one of the above but rarely simply the reverse of the ascending motion.
   3. Prescribed tonal functions such as tonal centers, finals, weak or passing tones, special ornaments applied to certain tones, etc.
   4. Thematic material which is a set of basic motivic patterns that in fact represent the essence of a rāg.
   5. Finally the all important drone which always accompanies the performance of a rāg. The drone consists of the tonic plus one, two, and sometimes three additional tones such as the fifth (most common), the fourth, a combination of the fifth and the seventh, or the fifth and the third and so on. The drone serves to reinforce the tonic and thereby offer a constant point of reference to which all other tones are related and when combined with one or more additional tones creates a framework of tonality for the rāg" (1977:104).

3. A somewhat different version of the following paragraphs is found in Neuman (1976).

Chapter 2

1. *Chilla,* it should be noted, is widely used for a variety of ritual forty-day waiting periods. Among the Chishtiyya order of Sufis, for example, the chilla was practiced as secluded worship (Aziz Ahmed 1969:38).
2. Imdad Khan was the grandfather of the great sitar maestro, Ustad Vilayat Khan. There is a similar story concerning the Lucknow author Mirza Mohammad Ruswa (1857–1931), which can be found in his *Courtesan of Lucknow (Umrao Jan Ada),* translated by Khushwant Singh and M. A. Husaini (Delhi: Hind Pocket Books, n.d.), p. 11.
3. See, for example, an article in *Overseas Hindustan Times,* September 7, 1972, p. 5, in which Vishnu Digambar Paluskar is described as practicing twelve hours a day from the time when he was twelve years old.
4. William Kay Archer (personal communication).
5. One hears, especially from those outside the hereditary families, that certain musicians coming from a long line "have music in their blood." Yet I do not think that individuals think of talent as being inherited. Musicians themselves never make this claim, explaining quality in musicians in terms of inheriting an old and valued tradition. Musicians will make cultural differentiations, as when a Muslim musician will say of Hindus that since they do not eat meat they do not have enough strength for doing a lot of practice and becoming great musicians. Yet there are enough examples of both Hindu and Muslim musical genius of which all participants are quite aware so as to invalidate any such argument for biological and cultural characteristics.
6. This was a good point made in a bad film, *Guru.*
7. There are of course several systems of notation which are used for teaching in music schools and instructing pupils at an elementary level. But ustads typically feel that notations are either harmful or at best useful only as mnemonic devices for learning basic structures, and that real learning must be received orally.
8. The English word *hotel* is used in India as a synonym for *restaurant.* The Hakim Hotel, near Jama Masjid, serves Mughal style food, but provides no lodging.
9. This is the Urdu term, which is commonly used. The Hindi term is *pat-shishya.*

Chapter 3

1. For a comprehensive discussion of music and Islam see Choudhury (1957). On Sufism and music see Hazrat Inayat Khan (1973).
2. A description of this urs can be found in *The Census of India* (1961).
3. The theory of ras in a musical context concerns the relationship between music and the emotional states it communicates. See Pandey (1959).
4. Ustad Karamatalla Khan (d. 1977) was another virtuoso of the tabla. Robert Gottlieb's research on the tabla (1977) was based in large part on Karamatalla Khan's knowledge and on his performance of tabla, which can be heard on the accompanying recordings.
5. A recently built auditorium, Kamani Hall, located next to the Sangeet Natak Akademi on one side and Bharatiya Kala Kendra (school of music and dance) on the other, is now the most important venue of concerts in Delhi.
6. Outstanding full-length performances by Vilayat Khan can be heard on two EMI recordings: EASD-1332 "Supreme Genius of Ustad Vilayat Khan" in which he performs rāg *Darbari,* and EASD-1350 "Ustad Vilayat Khan" in which he performs rāg *Yaman.* The record notes by Nazir Jairazbhoy include an interesting description of the recording session. For more on Vilayat Khan see Jairazbhoy (1971), which in-

cludes a recording of Vilayat Khan demonstrating a variety of rāgs. For one view on the objective measurements of intonation in Hindustani music, see Jairazbhoy and Stone (1963).

Chapter 4

1. Sufis generally were reticent about connections of worldliness, particulary in connection with the court. For a brief discussion of this see Mujeeb (1967:139–43). For a discussion of general Sufi influence on Indian music in the North, see Brahaspati (1975).
2. There was an opposite movement of Indian musicians to Afghanistan when Amir Sher Ali Khan (1869–79) imported a few leading vocalists from India—known as ustads—supplanting the previous Persian monopoly of urban court music (Slobin 1976:34).
3. In a solo tabla performance, however, the tabla player will be accompanied by a melodic instrument, usually either the sarangi or harmonium, playing a *laharā,* a set piece within the rhythmic cycle of the performance, and repeated throughout the duration of the performance.
4. On rare occasions one hears three or more instruments together, but this is highly unusual and distinctly experimental. These kinds of experiments are usually heard over All India Radio.
5. This is a somewhat contentious assertion since there are some tabla players who will insist that they are soloists, an interpretation that is given some credence by the fact that tabla players are becoming increasingly important in contemporary concert situations. Shepard (1976) discusses the Banaras tabla style only with reference to solo performance. Her guru, Sharda Sahai, objected strongly to the idea that tabla players were accompanists, insisting that there is a long tradition of tabla solo playing, and that consequently tabla players should also be considered soloists. My own information from tabla players in Delhi is that the idea of tabla solo playing in public is very recent. According to Stewart (1974:162), the development of a solo repertoire is an early twentieth-century phenomenon. As I have argued elsewhere, the very divergence of such interpretations constitutes an important datum for the study of music culture change (Neuman 1977:239).
6. Being a well-known accompanist enabled him to have a steady source of income. As a soloist he did not initially have as many opportunities since the demand for solo sarangi had not yet been created. Many individuals, knowing that I was studying the sarangi, were polite about it, but revealed that they just did not like to listen to solo sarangi. "It is only good for *sangat,*" that is, as an accompanying instrument.
7. Peter Row informs me that there are some exceptions to this rule among well-educated non-hereditary musicians in Bengal (personal communication 1978).
8. According to Platts (1965), *khalifa* is used in India to refer to Muslim cooks, tailors, and barbers. Sakata notes that in some parts of Afghanistan, *khalifa* (along with *ustad)* is used as a term of address for hereditary musicians. Interestingly, *khalifa* in the context of musicians is a pejorative term for a *dalāk,* a low-ranking barber-musician in Afghanistan (Sakata 1976:7).
9. The concept of khandan is not constant, and a systematic study of the use of the term among South Asian Muslims remains to be done. It is used by musicians to refer strictly to the patrilineage descent group, as well as to all blood relatives; it will sometimes overlap with the concept of biradari among South Asian Muslims (see Alavi 1976) and will sometimes have the connotation of "family."
10. Because of the opprobrium attached to such marriages they are little talked about to outsiders, but are not uncommonly the source of scandal and gossip within the

community. I know of three cases. In one a well-known musician took a tawaif for a second wife. In another a young musician fell in love with a tawaif and married her, thereby breaking off his betrothal to another woman in his community. Because of this incident, the brotherhood of which he was a member split into two: on the one side were families supporting the scorned bride-to-be and demanding compensation, and on the other was the immediate lineage descent group of the young man, refusing to pay compensation. In the third case I have genealogical evidence of a musician-tawaif marriage given to me by the tawaif herself, but vehemently denied as fact by members of the musician's community.

11. Other women musicians recruited from musician castes did play on musical instruments. Sharar discusses the *Domnis,* who "were great innovators. Giving up dhols [barrel drum] they adopted tablas, sarangis and cymbals, as was the practice with male and courtesan musicians" (1975:145). These performances, however, were for exclusively female audiences. The practice of women performing before women is still maintained by some rural communities of Mirasis, but apparently is now greatly diminished as a custom, and is interpreted as a distinctly low-ranking custom.

12. Among Shia Muslims, temporary marriages called *mutah* are sometimes contracted. I do not know whether *mutah* is used as a euphemism for what is actually concubinage, or whether its meaning is literal.

13. The eminent vocalist and musicologist, Vamamrao Deshpande, wrote about his own teacher, the great Mogubai Kurdikar, that for some time she suffered from rumors that she was not an official disciple of Ustad Alladiya Khan, until he confirmed that fact in a public announcement. "Those were times when the status of an artist was defined by his being a gandabanda shagirda [a formally initiated disciple] and not being one almost amounted to being labelled illegitimate progeny" (Deshpande 1974). I would like to thank Jennifer Post for this and other valuable references on women musicians in India.

14. See for example V. H. Khan's (1959:221) story about two sarangi players who went on to become famous vocalists.

15. The paragraph following is a paraphrased translation by Harbans Mathur from the original Urdu.

16. Islamic society in India is divided at the most general level between those who are former Hindus converted to Islam and those who entered India as Muslims. The significance of this ancestry is that "original" Muslims are higher in social rank than converts.

17. Bundu Khan's music is discussed in Jairazbhoy and Stone (1963).

18. That is, there are no ancestral lines of Brahman musicians, although temple musicians are said to inherit their positions in the temple.

19. There has been a similar Hinduization among certain isolated rural Mirasi families in the state of Haryana. This is described in Neuman 1979 and in a forthcoming work on rural Mirasis.

20. A similar phenomenon is found in the Karnatak tradition, where most musicians claim some kind of disciple connection to the great Tyāgarāja (Powers 1979).

21. Like Ibrahim Adil Shah, there apparently were many in the nobility who studied music seriously (Ahmed 1956:51). Imam discusses musicians of the nobility as a separate category (1959a, 1959b:*passim*). A classic account is that of the famous Baz Bahadur, the King of Malwa, who, after he lost his kingdom to the Mughals, joined Akbar's court as one of his court musicians.

22. According to my informant, playing only a bayan "perhaps showed that he [the tabla player] did not respect him [the shahnai player]." In India the left hand is impure; only the right hand is used for actually inserting food in the mouth. The low rank of shahnai players is mirrored by clarinet players in the folk tradition, for both put the instruments in their mouths, which in India is a polluting act. Interestingly, similar attitudes were noted in Afghanistan by Sakata. She quotes Clebert (1963:202) to the

effect that spittle and semen are identified with each other among gypsies, and adds that "the association of spit and semen is suggested in our own expression: 'he is the spitting image of his father' " (1976:5).

23. B. C. Deva reports that the sarangi is little known in the South, where it is used by *"oduvars* who are musicians who sing *tevarams,* an ancient Tamil hymnody." He adds that it is not used in classical South India music (1977:106). In another work, Deva puts the introduction of the violin a bit later, attributing it to a musician who lived between 1786 and 1858 (1978:171).

24. Bols are the characteristic timbres that plucked and percussive instruments are capable of. Occasionally tabla players perhaps accompany bīn players, since this is what one sees in a photograph in Fox-Strangways' book (1965:86, plate 10).

25. One measure of familiarity is that in at least three published works on the sarangi, the label *sarangi* is attached to illustrations of other instruments. It is confused with a *sārindā* in Shankar (1968:38) and Sachs (1940:227) and with a dilruba in Curtiss (n.d.:29).

26. A similar function is given by Bachmann for bowed instrumentalists in the Western minstrel tradition. From a manuscript of the first half of the thirteenth century he finds evidence that "the fiddle's main role . . . was to give the singer his note by providing short preludes and interludes, to keep him in tune, and to allow him to rest between verses" (1969:126). What is markedly different from the contemporary Indian performance practice is the absence of any kind of heterophony.

27. There are three helpful sources on tabla styles which have become recently available. The more general sources are Stewart (1974) and Gottlieb (1977); Shepard (1976) focuses on one tabla baj. Interestingly, although there are several dissertations on drums in India (for the South see Brown's study of the *mridangam,* 1965) there is to my knowledge no specific work on any melodic instrument written by a westerner.

28. As Ansari (1960: 38, 45, 46) points out, the Mirasi ("musicians") were one of three Muslim castes who designated themselves with a new caste name, *Shaikh,* for the 1931 Census (Census Reports, U.P., 1931, p. 531, table).

29. The whole question of whether Muslims in India can be said to have caste is the subject of some controversy. See Dumont (1970), Marriott and Inden (1974), Madan (1976), and Ahmed (1973) for a range of interpretations.

30. The premium on cousin marriage in Islam is sometimes explained in terms of the peculiarities of Islamic inheritance law, in which daughters share (to a certain degree) with sons. The most effective method of keeping property within the descent group is to practice patrilateral parallel cousin marriage, which is called *b'int'am* (Levy 1957:96–98, 101, 144–46). According to Basu and Roy, the incidence of consanguineous marriages for a sample of Delhi Muslims increased from 15.90 percent in pre-Partition (i.e., before 1947) India to 37.84 percent after Partition (1972:21–27; *Eastern Anthropologist* 25[1]).

31. Blunt sees this process working in somewhat the opposite way: two groups establish an affinal relationship which leads to the prevalence of cousin marriage. "The natural result of this custom [i.e., marrying within the marriage circle] is that the marriages of cousins is extremely common" (1931:196–97).

32. There are sometimes problems of succession if the son is too young, incompetent, or otherwise unable to assume office. Also, if the biradari bifurcates, one segment will have to choose a new chaudhari.

33. According to W. Crooke, Katthak are considered Brahmans by low-caste Hindus, while H. H. Risley considers them a subcaste of Brahmans from Bihar (Crooke 1896:IV, 172–76; Risley 1891:433). According to M. A. Sherring however (1872), the Katthak consider themselves Rajputs. E. A. H. Blunt describes them as religious troubadours who "carefully preserve their ancient ballads, allowing nobody to tamper with them" (1931:234). Risley also states that the name Katthak is applied to any musician who plays the violin (sarangi?), no matter what caste or creed. Some of

India's greatest tabla players come from this community, representing the Banaras baj, the history and style of which has been treated by Shepard (1976).

34. The reference to Muhammad Safdar Hussein Khan's *Qanun-e-sitar* (1871?), was given to me by Brian Silver (in a letter dated November 25, 1973), who translates the relevant passage as follows: "Moreover, the difficulty is this, that teachers of it [music] are usually mirasis, kalavants, etc. So, first of all they are without knowledge; second, by greed of gold or some other reason, they practice neglect or avarice. Because of this, the learner himself becomes dizzy [is left in turmoil] and does not reach the stage of his goal." I should add that there is one older reference I have been able to find about Mirasis. It is in Richard Burton's account of Sindh, published in 1851. In it he mentions Kalwat (Kalawant), whom he describes as "respectable singers," and Langha or Mirasi, "the bards of the country" (Burton 1973:302). His description accords well with Tandon's, mentioned below. (The term *Langha* as a reference to a particular kind of Mirasi is still used in Rajasthan.) According to Burton, the music they performed was closer to Persian than Indian, a judgment corroborated by a photograph of Sindhi Mirasis, to be found in Taylor (1872: VI, Plate 335-2), where one musician is seen holding what looks like a Persian setar (although it has eleven tuning pegs). Yet according to Burton, the Mirasi and Kalawant "have a great and almost religious respect for the name of Tansen" (Burton 1973:304). These observations suggest that Sindh was an avenue for Persian influences, lying as it does between Baluchistan and Rajasthan. In his writings, Burton considers Sindh a distinct cultural area separate from India and Persia.

35. Blunt suggests that Mirasis and Dharis were originally separate groups that intermarried so that eventually they were no longer distinguishable, an interpretation I am in agreement with and which I expand below (Blunt 1931:205). Crooke treats the Dhari as a separate caste divided into Hindu and Muslim sections (1896:II, 276–78). This I think is also true. There were and probably still are Hindu Dharis. The famous sixteenth-century Hindu poet, Surdass, referred to himself as a Dhari in one of his poems (Bryant 1978:151), and Joep Boer in a personal communication states he has been told that in smaller places in Uttar Pradesh musicians still refer to themselves as Dharis. In the caste compilations, Dhari are also listed as one of the sections of the Katthak (Crooke 1896: III, 174) converts from the *Nat* group (Blunt 1931:205); yet Crooke elsewhere considers them a separate caste (ibid.:IV,60). Ibbetson at one point notes that Dharis have been included in a census enumeration with the Mirasis, but that since they are said not to intermarry, they should be considered separate castes (1916:234–35).

　　Crooke discusses Mirasis as a kind of tawaif, whose daughters are not allowed to marry but must learn to sing and dance from a Dhari or Katthak. The sons marry women from "some low Hindu or Muhammadan tribe," who are not allowed to become prostitutes. The males "are supported by the earnings of the girls and act as their pimps and attendant musicians (bhanruā). They wander about from one inn *(sarai)* and town to another in search of business, and attend marriages and festivals where they sing and dance." He adds that Tansen is the patron saint of the dancing girls, which suggests their connection with the art music tradition (1896:IV,367–69). Further references to Mirasis can be found in Briggs (1953:93), Crooke (1907: 105,129,187), and Ibbetson (1970:III,105–19). Ibbetson's four-page discussion on Mirasis is the most complete account and a valuable source. He seems to be using Mirasi as a very large caste category, because he includes all types of caste terms under the Mirasi rubric, including both Kalawant and Dhari. Insofar as I have been able to determine, his information is quite reliable. For example, the list of clan names *(got)* and locations of caste officers of rural Mirasis in the Haryana area are still to be found today, almost a century later.

36. The practice of musicians living in particular wards in Delhi can be traced back at least to the fourteenth century, when Ibn Batuta reported a community of musicians

near Hauz Kaus (in present-day New Delhi) during Muhammad Tughlak's reign (1325–1351). When Muhammad Tughlak moved his capital to Daulatabad in 1327, a musician's ward was located there and musicians, both men and women, came and paid their respects to their "chowdri" by performing before him (Rizvi 1941:335, Sharar 1975:133).

37. See Sambamoorthy (1959:II,268–77), who discusses the "rights, privileges and duties" of the principal (soloist) and "duties and rights of accompanists" in the South Indian classical music tradition.

38. Until the 1930s virtually all compositions were performed in tintal (Peter Row: personal communication).

39. The former greeting would be performed by a Muslim and the latter by a Hindu.

40. According to Naina Devi (1974), accompanists occupied opposite places several decades earlier, which signifies a change in their respective musical importance (personal communication).

41. The other exception of course is where soloist and accompanist come from the same family.

42. For a discussion of conceptual levels for the term *biradari* among Muslims in Pakistan, see Alavi (1976).

Chapter 5

1. Although the founders of the earliest gharanas lived in the mid-nineteenth century, the term seems not to have appeared until the twentieth. For an account of the origin of gharanas as urban sociocultural phenomena see Neuman (1978a).

2. My own collected data in this historical summary are supplemented by Khan (1959) and Sen (1972). Deshpande (1973) is the most comprehensive account of the styles of vocal gharanas, but see the foreword to his book by B. R. Deodhar, who furnishes an important corrective to Deshpande's interpretation. Also see Gupta (1973) on the musical history of Gwalior.

3. Like the similar story of Haddu and Hassu Khan, surreptitious learning seems to account for a bridge between an old and what is afterwards perceived as a new tradition.

4. Perhaps this is not so strange an origin after all if one considers somewhat similar occurrences in the West. Beethoven was deaf at the time he composed his most innovative music and the father of ethnomusicology, Alexander John Ellis, was himself tone-deaf (Hood 1963:227).

5. Indeed the controversies surrounding claims and counterclaims enter even the general public domain. After a National Program of Music broadcast, featuring a prominent artist, in which the names of his ustads were announced, a letter to the editor appeared in a newspaper, claiming that one of the ustads mentioned was not the artist's teacher and that All India Radio was mistaken in announcing him as such. In response to my queries, other musicians said it was a well-known fact that he had studied with the ustad mentioned on the program, but did not want to acknowledge his discipleship because of a break in his relationship with his teacher.

6. For a discussion of tabla "gharanas," reflecting the modern usage of this term for tabla styles, see Ghosh (1972).

7. Part of the difference can be attributed to an error I made in the earlier version of Table 7 (Nettl 1978a:190) where Nathan Khan, the father of Haddu and Hassu Khan is shown as a brother of Haider Khan and Bahram Khan. Other significant alterations are: (1) The phrase "Dagar family occasionally known as Saharanpur Gharana" in the earlier version has been eliminated because Z. M. Dagar claims this is not the case. The family is listed as such by Trikha (1967), but he is far from reliable

since there are several other errors in his otherwise valuable compilation. (2) Bande Ali Khan's mother is now shown as a sister of Bahram Khan, whereas earlier she had been shown as his daughter. (3) The father of Bande Ali Khan, although reported as Sadiq Ali Khan, is, according to Z. M. Dagar, Ghulam Jaffar Sahib, who was himself descended from a lineage of Sufi musicians, originally from Barnawa near Saharanpur. Trikha presumably thought that the Dagar family should be known as the Saharanpur gharana because Bahram Khan originally came from Ambaitha, which is in the district of Saharanpur.

Chapter 6

1. For a more extended treatment of this point, see Neuman (1978a).
2. "I have been told more than once that the congressmen at Washington are not interested in Music. I refuse to believe it, for I know it for certain that even snakes and beasts are interested in, and influenced by, Music" (Roy 1919).
3. The data on the following pages are from an unpublished list of musicians at the Delhi station, in 1969. For information about musicians in radio in South India see L'Armands (1978).
4. Taken from *Akashvani* (formerly *The Indian Listener*), August 24, 1969. For the whole week from Sunday, August 24, to Saturday, August 30, 1969, there was an average of 204 minutes of classical music programming (excluding commercial recordings) per day. The National Orchestra was heard for a total of 75 minutes during the week.
5. This was the information as of 1973. Since that time there have been a number of changes which I am so far unable to document. I believe that the whole system has been upgraded, allowing many more musicians to enter the "top-class" category. I have also been told that the B grade no longer is used for classical musician. It may be of interest to know that at about the same time, the third-class rail compartment designation was abandoned and there is now only air-conditioned, first and second class. This suggests an official strategy to eliminate India's proverbial hierarchical system by lifting the bottom to the top.
6. This section of the chapter is based on my personal observations. All names are fictitious, and several deliberate distortions have been introduced to the data to keep identities anonymous. The distortions are not substantive and do not alter my interpretations.
7. The mandatory retirement age is now fifty-five years for government servants, a classification which includes staff artists at All India Radio.
8. The practice of using Khan Sahib as a form of address for traditionally low-ranked Muslim accompanists is said to have been introduced by B. V. Keshkar when he was Minister for Information and Broadcasting, and is partly responsible, many say, for the rise in rank of these musicians. Silver suggests that the use of *ustad* for Muslim musicians generally is also recent (1976).
9. Mullick goes on to relate a story of some interest. Apparently one of the station directors was upset at the ban and by the order that all harmoniums were to be auctioned. He assembled the eleven harmoniums to look like a bier and, along with other senior colleagues, formed a party of "pall-bearers," who were followed by a "funeral procession" of other staff members. The group went out of the station and lowered the bier into a "grave." After the final rites, the person who had bid the highest at the auction earlier in the day claimed his property. This event, complete with photographs, was reported in the newspapers the following day. What gives this account historical interest is that there is a similar, very famous story repeated in virtually every history of Indian music: when the last great Mughal ruler, Aurangzeb,

banned music, pallbearers carrying "Music" appeared before him in an effort to change his mind. His response was, "Bury it deep."
10. To be exact, twice in ten years.
11. Rs. 7/50 to the dollar was the official exchange rate. It is now approximately Rs. 8/50 to the dollar. However, it would not be unrealistic to assume a rough equivalence, e.g., Rs. 400/- is about the same as $400, as its value is "felt" in India.
12. The artist's name is fictional, and he is a composite of several musicians. Parts of this section have been published in my article, "Journey to the West" (1978b), in somewhat different form.
13. By 1974, five years later, good tabla players were, however, demanding a straight 25 percent plus expenses. They had perceived correctly that their role in the West was not an unimportant one.
14. One possible exception, which I have been unable to verify, is Ram Narayan teaching sarangi at the newly established Performing Arts Centre in Bombay.

Chapter 7

1. The only exception known to me is the Katthak dance master Birju Maharaj.
2. Jennifer Post has written a number of articles on the role of women in Indian music, and it is to be hoped that they will soon be made available in published form. A brief essay on women in the performing arts by Kapila Vatsayayan can be found in Devaki Jain's book *Indian Women* (1975).
3. Silver (1976) provides an illuminating glimpse into what it means to be an ustad and how this conception has both persisted and undergone changes in the twentieth century.
4. I have been informed that the use of advertising in what is in India almost always a seller's market is subsidized indirectly because it can be used as a tax write-off.
5. For example, the opening paragraph of the Constitution for the Sangeet Natak Akademi (the National Academy of Dance, Drama, and Music), states: "Whereas it is considered expedient to establish an organization to foster and develop Indian dance, drama (including films) and music and to *promote through them the cultural unity of the country,* it is hereby resolved . . . " (Then follows the resolution establishing the Academy [Sangeet Natak Akademi Report: 1953–1958, emphasis mine]).
6. To my knowledge there are virtually no available data on the recording industry in India. A study which can be considered a model for India will be found in Jihad Racy's work on the history of recording in Egypt (1976, 1977).
7. For a discussion about the importance of preserving the musical tradition through the medium of recordings, see the comments by various musicians and musicologists (Various Authors 1974) brought together under the title "Canned Concerts: Comments on the Subject." It should be noted that this humorous title is not intended to be perjorative although it gives that impression, a fact one of the respondents (B. C. Deva) noted.
8. As of this writing, one student (Sharon Woodruff of Brown University) is doing research in Calcutta on misra rāgs and their implication for Hindustani music change.
9. "Metaphor, we have observed, is nonsense, though nonsense of a special kind. Not every incongruous coupling, then, is a figure, but every such structure may be thought of as a potential figure awaiting an actualizing environment" (Leondar 1970:384). Barbara Leondar's discussion of metaphor in the article just cited is highly suggestive for ideas concerning musical creativity, although she is concerned essentially with poetry.

Glossary

The definitions provided here do not necessarily include all possible connotations, but rather are restricted to the way the words are used by musicians within the context of Hindustani music culture. Words followed by an asterisk are not included in the Chaturvedi-Tiwari dictionary.

alāp	The introductory section of a musical performance. In the instrumental style it consists of three major parts, the first one of which is also called alāp, and characterized by free rhythm. It is followed by jōr and jhālā. In the dhrūpad form the alāp can include fifteen or more divisions, distinguished from each other essentially by tempo.
antārā	The second part of a vocal or instrumental composition, following the asthāī. It stresses the upper tetrachord of the rāg scale and is usually performed in the upper octave.
asthāī	The first part of a composition, preceding the anatārā. It is usually focused on the lower part of the rāg scale and performed in the middle and lower octaves.
auliyā	A Muslim holy person; saint.
bandish	The general term for a composition in Hindustani music, conventionally including both the instrumental composition (gat) and the composition of khayal vocal music (chīz).
bānī	A musical style (of which there are four types) preceding the development of gharānās as styles.

bānsrī	The bamboo flute of North Indian music.
bāj	Musical style technique. Related to the verb *bājna* ("to strike") and used only where music is produced by some kind of strike, as in playing the paired drums (tabla) or in plucked instruments such as the sitār and sarod. Also a distinctive technical approach to an instrument leading to a differentiation in style (e.g., Delhi bāj).
besur	Out of tune.
bhāī	Brother. Used also as a form of address by relatives, friends, and in certain instances between strangers.
bhajān	A Hindu devotional song type.
bhakti	Devotion.
bīṛī	Indian cigarette.
bīn	The North Indian stick zither. It is considered the most ancient and revered of musical instruments in India. It is also called vīna.
bīnkār	One who performs on the bīn.
birādarī (birādrī)	Brotherhood. Among Muslim occupational groups this is often the endogamous unit. It is a territorially defined social category, which is also often the largest effective social group in North Indian villages.
bol	Music "word." Each of the characteristic timbres produced on drums and plucked instruments. Also, text of a song.
Brāhman	Member of the caste of priests, the highest of all Indian castes. There are numerous and distinct subcategories and, when relevant, qualifiers are added to distinguish these more particular social units (e.g., Chitpāvan Brāhman).
chelā	Disciple, pupil, student. In the Delhi area *chelā* is more commonly used than *shishya*, which I have adopted in the text for purposes of consistency.
chillā	The state of pursuing a strict regimen during a period of forty days.
chikārī	The side strings on the sitar and sarod used to provide a drone as well as a rhythmic pulse.
chīz	Vocal composition; also other musical elements when unspecified.

chaudharī (chaudhrī)	The headman of a birādarī.
dādrā	A light classical vocal form; also the rhythmic cycle of six beats (mātras) in which it is performed.
darbār	The royal court.
darshān	View, especially of something sacred or special.
deredār*	A male musician, son of a courtesan performer.
Dhārī	Community (and most probably category) of musicians, said by some to be the oldest such community in India.
dhrupad	The oldest extant form of classical music in North India. Also a composition in that style.
dhun	A light classical song type.
dilrubā	A fretted, bowed long-necked lute, similar to the sitār: from Panjab.
drut	The fast movement in a performance.
esrāj*	A bowed instrument, similar to the dilrubā; from Bengal.
gamak	An embellishment or ornamentation of a note; a "shake."
gaṇḍa bandhan	*Lit.,* "tying the thread." The ceremony marking the initiation of the candidate as a disciple.
gandharva (gandharv)	One of Imam's categories of musicians. Also a celestial musician.
gat	A set instrumental composition fit to a particular rhythmic cycle. Also a composition for the tablā.
gawaiyā	Vocalist.
gāyakī*	Performance style of an individual vocalist or of his gharana.
gāyakī-ang*	Vocal style, with reference to instrumental styles imitating vocal performance style.
gīt	Song.
gharānā*	*Lit.,* "of the house." Family tradition; a stylistic school and/or the members of that school.
gharānadār*	A hereditary member of a gharana, in contrast to a non-hereditary disciple.
ghazal (gazal)	A genre of light classical song based on Urdu poetic forms of the same name.
guru	Master, teacher, preceptor.
hathauṛī	The hammer used to tune the tablā.

huqqā pānī
band   *Lit.,* "smoking and drinking stopped." The phrase used in villages in North India to refer to social ostracism.

izzat   Respect, honor, dignity.

jajmānī*   A hereditary patron-client relationship.

jaltarang   An instrument consisting of porcelain bowls which are filled with water differentially to fix the pitch and which are struck with two sticks.

jāti   The general Hindustani term for caste. Also generally connotes species, type, etc., including musical types.

jhālā   The third section of the instrumental alāp, also played at the end of a composed section where it is known as gat-jhālā. Musically it is characterized as a rhythmic section in which a main melody is played against pulse patterns plucked on the chikarī. It is performed only on plucked instruments.

jī   An honorific added to a name or term of address as a sign of respect. Alone usually translated as "sir."

jinn   A capricious spirit.

jor   The second part of the instrumental alāp, characterized by an increase in tempo and a rhythmic pulse.

jugalbandī   A duet, usually of instrumentalists.

Kalāwant   A musician whose pedigree includes no sarangi or tabla players. Also a title that Tansen is said to have conferred on four outstanding musicians of his court.

Katthak   A caste of musicians in eastern Uttar Pradesh. Also the classical Hindustani dance form.

khalīfā   The preceptor of a musician lineage and its gharānā.

khāndān   Lineage; lineal descent group; extended family.

khān sāhib   Respectful term of address for a Muslim musician.

khās khān-
dānī   A speciality of the khāndān.

khayāl*   The major vocal form of Hindustani music.

laharā*   Recurrent melodic accompaniment to a drum solo.

laya (lay)   Rhythm; tempo.

layakārī
(laykārī)   The aspect of a performance style in which rhythmic elaboration is prominent.

lok gīt   Folk music.

mehar   In Muslim marriage the money amount due the wife from the husband in the event of divorce or his death.

mānd*	Rajasthani folk song type.
maqām	The mode of Arabic music.
mātrā*	One beat in a rhythmic cycle.
masītkhānī gat*	A composition set to tīntāl in slow tempo, played on the sitar or sarod.
mīr	A slide or glide from one tone to another, equivalent to the portamento of Western music.
mehfil	An intimate gathering for performance of and listening to music.
Mīrāsī	A category and caste of musicians.
misra rāg	Mixed rāg; taking elements from two rāgs to make a third rāg.
muhallā	An urban ward, locality, or neighborhood, usually with fairly explicit boundaries.
Muharram	The first month of the Islamic lunar year. Also the holiday celebrating the martyrdom of Hussein and his family.
Musalmān	The Hindustani term for Muslim.
mūsīqār	An Urdu term for musician.
muquam	*See* maqām.
namaste	The Hindu greeting.
nāyak	Musicians most learned in theory and practice.
Pachhāos*	Branch of the Seniyas who migrated to western India, principally Rajasthan.
Pachwāllā*	Pachhāos.
pakhāwaj	The double-headed barrel drum now used principally to accompany dhrupad style music.
pān	Betel nut and leaf of numerous varieties, chewed and eaten as a stimulant in India.
panchāyat	Caste council.
paṇḍit	Learned one. Used as a respectful form of address (*paṇḍitjī*) or reference and as an honorific for Hindu musicians.
paramparā	Line; lineage; tradition.
peshkār	The introductory part of a tabla performance.
pīr	A Muslim holy man or saint.
Purabiyā (Purbiyā)	The branch of the Seniyas who migrated to the eastern part of India.

qāydā	A fixed or improvised developmental section of a tabla solo.
qauwall*	*See* qawwāl.
Qawwāl (Qavvāl)	A singer of qawwālī. Also a member of the Qawwāl community.
qawwālī (qavvālī)	Muslim devotional song.
Qawwāl Bachchhe	*Lit.,* "children of qawwāl." Persons who traced their descent from the time of Amir Khusrau, sometimes considered a gharana. Now extinct.
Quraishī*	Descendants of Muhammad's tribe.
rāg	The "mode" of Indian classical music.
rāgmālā	A "medley" of rāgs.
ras	The affective state generated by an aesthetic performance. In classical theory each rāg (sometimes each tone) is thought to characterize, embody, and generate particular emotional states.
rabāb*	A gut-stringed/plucked lute, unfretted. There are two major types, known as the Afghani and the Indian rabāb.
rishtedār	Relative.
salām	The Muslim greeting.
sam	The first beat of a rhythmic cycle. The point where the soloist and tablā player are often supposed to meet.
samajhdār log	*Lit.,* "people who understand"; connoisseurs.
sangīt	Music.
sārangī	The Indian bowed fiddle.
sārangiyā	Sārangī player.
Saraswatī	The goddess of learning and music. Also the name of Tansen's daughter.
sargam	The Hindustani equivalent of the solfège.
sarod	Unfretted long-necked lute.
sawāl-jawāb (savāl-javāb)	*Lit.,* "question-answer." A call and response pattern between two musicians, usually soloist and tablā player.
Seniyā*	One who claims descent from Tansen. More specifically, those who claim descent from Tansen's son, Bilas Khan.
shāgird	The Urdu-Persian word for disciple.

Shaikh (Shekh)	A social category of Muslims.
shahnāī (shehnāī)	Hindustani musical instrument similar to the oboe.
shishya (shishy)	Pupil, disciple.
sitār	A fretted, long-necked lute.
sthāī	*See* asthāī.
surbahār*	A bass version of the sitār.
sursringār*	A bass version of the sarod. Also called swarsringār.
tabalchī	Tabla player (mildly pejorative).
tablā	The set of two drums, called dāyān for the right hand and bāyān for the left. The dāyān is tuned to the ground note (sa) and the bāyān is not tuned. *Tablā* is also used to refer to the dāyān only.
tabliyā	Tabla player (respectful term).
tāl	Rhythmic cycle.
tālīm	Training.
tānpūrā	The four-, sometimes five- or six-stringed, unfretted lute used to provide the drone.
tān	A musical phrase.
ṭappā	A type of light classical song, originally said to be a Panjābī camel driver's song.
tarab*	Sympathetic strings.
tarānā	A vocal form using meaningless syllables.
tawāif (tavāyaf)	A courtesan performer, dancer or singer.
tīntāl	The most prominent tal, consisting of sixteen beats.
ṭhekā	The basic rhythmic framework of a tal, defined by the particular combination of bols.
ṭhumrī	The least constrained form of classical music, typically used to finish a performance. Originally a romantic vocal genre, it is now also performed by instrumentalists.
urs	The death anniversary in honor of a saint or other important person.
ustād	Master. Used as a respectful form of address (ustādji) or reference and as an honorific for Muslim musicians.
Vadya Vrindan (vāddya vrind)	The National Orchestra of All India Radio.

vamsha-param-parā	The line of descent from father to son.
vichitr vīnā	Unfretted stick zither, the strings of which are stopped with a smooth ball.
vilambit	The slow movement of a musical performance.
vīnā	The South Indian fretted lute. In North India *vīna* is used interchangeably with *bīn*.
zamīndār	Landlord.
zanānā	The women's apartment or room in a household.

References

Abraham, Gerald
1974 *The Tradition of Western Music.* Berkeley: University of California Press.
Aggarwal, Vinay K.
1966 *Traditions and Trends in Indian Music.* Meerut: Rastogi & Co.
Ahmed, Aziz
1969 *An Intellectual History of Islam in India.* Edinburgh: Edinburgh University Press.
Ahmed, Imtiaz, ed.
1973 *Caste and Social Stratification among the Muslims.* New Delhi: Manohar Book Service.
Ahmed, Nazir, trans.
1956 *Kitab-I-Nauras* of Ibrahim Adil Shah. New Delhi: Bharatiya Kala Kendra.
Alavi, Hamza A.
1976 "Kinship in West Punjab Villages" in T. N. Madan, ed., *Muslim Communities of South Asia.* New Delhi: Vikas. First published in *Contributions to Indian Sociology,* n.s., Vol. 6, 1972.
Ansari, Ghaus
1960 *Muslim Caste in Uttar Pradesh.* Lucknow: Ethnographic and Folk Culture Society, U.P.
Archer, William Kay
1964 "On the Ecology of Music." *Ethnomusicology* 8(1):28–33.
Bachmann, Werner
1969 *The Origin of Bowing.* New York: Oxford University Press.
Bailey, F. G.
1957 *Caste and the Economic Frontier.* New York: The Humanities Press.
Bake, Arnold A.
1960 "The Music of India." In *The New Oxford History of Music.* Vol. I, ed. Egon Wellesz. New York: Oxford University Press.
Barnett, Elise
1975 *A Discography of the Art Music of India.* Society for Ethnomusicology, Special Series No. 3.
Basso, Keith H., and Henry A. Selby, eds.
1976 *Meaning in Anthropology.* Albuquerque: University of New Mexico Press.
Basu, Salil K., and Shibani Roy
1972 "Change in the Frequency of Consanguineous Marriages among the Delhi Muslims after Partition." *The Eastern Anthropologist* 25(1):21–28.

Bateson, Gregory
1972 *Steps to an Ecology of Mind.* New York: Ballantine Books, Inc.
Benjamin, Walter
1969 *Illuminations.* Translated by Harry Zohn. Edited by Hannah Arendt. New York: Schocken Books.
Bhatkhande, Pandit V. N.
1974 *A Short Historical Survey of the Music of Upper India.* Baroda: Indian Musicological Society. First published 1943.
Blunt, E. A. H.
1931 *The Caste System of Northern India: With Special Reference to the United Provinces of Agra and Oudh.* Oxford University Press.
Brahaspati, Acharya
1975 "Mussalmans and Indian Music." *Journal of the Indian Musicological Society* 6(2):27–49.
Briggs, George W.
1953 *The Doms and Their Near Relations.* Mysore: Wesley Press and Publishing House.
Briggs, John, trans.
1966 *History of the Rise of the Mohammedan Power in India till the Year A.D. 1612.* By Mahomet Kasim Ferishta. Vols. I to IV. Calcutta: Editions Indian. First published 1829.
Brown, Robert E.
1965 "The Mrdanga: A Study of Drumming in South India." Ph.D. dissertation, University of California, Los Angeles. Unpublished.
Brown, Robert E.
1970 "India's Music." In Joseph W. Elder, ed., *Indian Civilization,* Vol. II, pp. 137–76. Dubuque: Kendall/Hunt Publishing Co.
Bryant, Kenneth
1978 *Poems to the Child-God: Structure and Strategies in the Poetry of Surdass.* Berkeley: University of California Press.
Burton, Sir Richard F.
1973 *Sindh and the Races That Inhabit the Valley of the Indus.* Karachi: Oxford University Press. First published 1851.
Carriuolo, Ralf E., and Neuman, Daniel M., eds.
1977 "American Ethnomusicology." *Essays in Arts and Sciences* 6 (1, Special Issue).
Census of India
1931 *Census Reports,* U.P., 1931. Table, p. 531.
Census of India
1961 "Beliefs and Practices Associated with Muslims Pirs in Two Cities of India" (Delhi and Lucknow), Vol. I, pp. 28–31. Monograph Series, Part VII-B, Monograph No. 1.
Chaubey, S. K.
1945 *Indian Music Today.* Allahabad: Kitab Mahal.
Choudhury, M. L. Roy
1957 "Music in Islam." *Journal of the Asiatic Society* (Bengal), Letters, Vol. XXIII, No. 2, pp. 46–102.
Clebert, Jean-Paul
1963 *The Gypsies.* Translated by Charles Suff. Baltimore: Penguin Books.
Crooke, William
1896 *Tribes and Castes of the North-Western Provinces and Oudh.* 4 vols. Calcutta, Office of the Superintendent of Government.
Crooke, William
1897 *The North-Western Provinces of India.* London: Methuen & Co.

279

Crooke, William
1907 *The Native Races of the British Empire.* London: Archibald Constable & Co., Ltd.
Curtiss, Marie J.
n.d. *Kathak: Classical Dance of India.* Albany, N.Y.: The University of the State of New York, Center for International Programs and Comparative Studies.
Danielou, Alain
1974 *The Situation of Music and Musicians in Countries of the Orient.* An International Music Council Publication. Florence: Leo S. Olschki.
Deodhar, B. R.
1973 *Thor Sangitkar.* Bombay: Akhil Bharatiya Gandharva Mahavidyalaya Mandal.
Deshpande, Vamanrao H.
1971 "Harmonium as Accompaniment for Hindustani Classical Music." *Journal of the Sangeet Natak Akademi* (20):15–19.
Deshpande, Vamanrao H.
1972 *Maharashtra's Contribution to Music.* New Delhi: Maharashtra Information Centre.
Deshpande, Vamanrao H.
1973 *Indian Musical Traditions: An Aesthetic Study of the Gharanas in Hindustani Music.* Bombay: Popular Prakashan.
Deshpande, Vamanrao H.
1974 "Mogubai Kurdikar" (program notes). Reprinted from *Satyakatha,* July 1974.
Deva, B. C.
1967 *The Psychoacoustics of Music and Speech.* Madras: Music Academy.
Deva, B. C.
1975 "Tradition and Non-Conformity in Indian Music." *Journal of the Indian Musicological Society* 6(4):27–30.
Deva, B. C.
1977 *Musical Instruments.* New Delhi: National Book Trust, India.
Deva, B. C.
1978 *Musical Instruments of India.* Calcutta: Firma KLM Private Ltd.
Dumont, Louis
1970 *Homo Hierarchicus.* Chicago: University of Chicago Press.
Edwardes, Michael
1960 *The Orchid House.* London: Cassell.
Elder, Joseph W., ed.
1970 *Lectures in Indian Civilization.* Dubuque, Ia.: Kendall/Hunt Publishing Co.
Erdman, Joan
1978 "The Maharaja's Musicians: The Organization of Cultural Performance at Jaipur in the 19th Century." In *American Studies in the Anthropology of India.* Edited by Sylvia Vatuk. New Delhi: Manohar Publications.
Fazl, Abu'l
1948 *The Ain-i-Akbari.* Translated by Colonel A. S. Jarret. Revised by Sir Jadunath Sarkar. Calcutta: Royal Asiatic Society of Bengal.
Fazl, Abu'l
1965 *The Ain-i-Akbari.* Translated by H. Blochmann. Delhi: Aadiesh Book Depot. First published 1871.
Fox-Strangways, A. H.
1965 *The Music of Hindostan.* London: Oxford University Press.
Fryer, John
1698 *New Account of East-India and Persia in Eight Letters.* London: Printed by R. R. for R. Chiswell, at the Rose and Crown in St. Paul's Church-Yard.
Gaisberg, F. W.
1942 *The Music Goes Round.* New York: The Macmillan Co.

References

Geertz, Clifford
1972 "Deep Play: Notes on the Balinese Cockfight." *Daedalus* 101:1–37.

Ghosh, Nikhil
1972 "Different Gharanas in the Field of Tabla Art." *Journal of the Indian Musicological Society* 3(1):5–10.

Gladwin, Francis
1965 "On the Vina or Indian Lyre." In S. M. Tagore, *Hindu Music from Various Authors*. Varanasi: Chowkhamba Sanskrit Series Office. First published 1875.

Goffman, Ervin
1961 *Encounters: Two Studies in the Sociology of Interaction*. Indianapolis: Bobbs-Merrill.

Gottlieb, Robert S.
1977 *The Major Traditions of North Indian Tabla Drumming*. Munich: Musik Verlag Emil Katzbichler.

Gould, Harold
1970 "Is the Tradition-Modernity Model All Bad?" *Economic and Political Weekly* (29–31, Special Number).

Gupta, B. L.
1973 "The Gwalior School of Music." *Journal of the Indian Musicological Society* 4(1):5–15.

Haq, Abdul
n.d. *The Standard Urdu-English Dictionary*. Delhi: J. S. Sant Singh & Sons.

Higgins, Jon
1976 "From Prince to Populace: Patronage as a Determinant of Change in South Indian (Karnatak) Music." *Asian Music* 7(2):20–26.

Hood, Mantle
1963 "Music, the Unknown." In Frank U. Harrison, Mantle Hood, and Claude V. Palisca, eds., *Musicology*. Englewood Cliffs, N.J.: Prentice-Hall.

Hood, Mantle
1971 *The Ethnomusicologist*. New York, McGraw-Hill.

Husain, Imtiaz
1967 *Land Revenue Policy in North India: The Ceded and Conquered Provinces, 1801–33*. New Delhi: New Age Publishers Private Ltd., Calcutta.

Husain, Yusuf
1957 *Medieval Indian Culture*. Bombay: Asia Publishing House.

Ibbetson, Sir Denzil Charles Jeff
1970a *Glossary of Tribes and Castes of the North-West Frontier Province*, Vol. III. Edited by H. A. Rose. Punjab: Languages Department. First published 1883.

Ibbetson, Sir Denzil Charles Jeff
1970b *Panjab Castes*. Punjab: Languages Department. First published 1916.

Imam, Hakim Mohammad Karam
1959a "Melody through Centuries." Translated by Govind Vidyarthi. *Bulletin, Sangeet Natak Akademi* (11–12):13–26.

Imam, Hakim Mohammad Karam
1959b "Effect of Ragas and Mannerism in Singing." Translated by Govind Vidyarthi. *Bulletin, Sangeet Natak Akademi* (13–14):6–14.

Jafri, S. N. A.
1931 *The History and Status of Landlords and Tenants in the United Provinces (India)*. Bombay: The Pioneer Press.

Jain, Devaki, ed.
1975 *Indian Women*. New Delhi: Publication Division.

Jairazbhoy, Nazir A.
1971 *The Rags of North Indian Music: Their Structure and Evolution*. Middletown, Conn.: Wesleyan University Press.

References

Jairazbhoy, Nazir A., with Stone, A. W.
1963 "Intonation in Present-Day North Indian Classical Music." *Bulletin of the School of Oriental and African Studies* 26, Pt. 1:119–32.
Joshi, Baburao
1963 *Appreciating Indian Music.* New York: Asia Publishing House.
Joshi, Nirmala
1959 "Compositions of Ustad Zahoor Khan." *Bulletin, Sangeet Natak Akademi* (13–14):15–18.
Kailasapathy, K.
1968 *Tamil Heroic Poetry.* Oxford: The Clarendon Press.
Karnani, Chetan
1976 *Listening to Hindustani Music.* Bombay: Orient Longmans.
Kaufmann, Walter
1967 *Musical Notations of the Orient.* Indiana University Humanities Series, No. 60. Bloomington: Indiana University Press.
Kaufmann, Walter
1968 *The Ragas of North India.* Calcutta: Oxford & IBH Publishing Co.
Keshkar, B. V.
1967 *Indian Music: Problems and Prospects.* Bombay: Popular Prakasham.
Khan, Hazrat Inayat
1973 *The Sufi Message of Hazrat Inayat Khan.* Vol. II. London: Barrie & Jenkins.
Khan, Muhammad Safdar Hussain
1871(?) *Qanun-e-sitar.* Lucknow, no pub.
Khan, Vilayat Hussain
1959 *Sangitagyon-ke-Samsmaran.* New Delhi: Sangeet Natak Akademi.
Kramrisch, Stella
1956 "Artist, Patron, and Public in India." *Far Eastern Quarterly* 15:335–42.
Krishnaswami, S. Y.
1968 *Tyagaraja, Saint and Singer.* Bombay: Orient Longmans.
Kubler, George
1962 *The Shape of Time.* New Haven: Yale University Press.
Lambert, Richard D.
1967 "Review of *New Lamps for Aladdin: Mass Media in Developing Societies,* by J. D. Mathur." *Journal of Asian Studies* 26(2):315–16.
Leondar, Barbara
1970 "Metaphor in the Classroom." In Ralph A. Smith, ed., *Aesthetic Concepts and Education.* Urbana: University of Illinois Press.
L'Armand, Kathleen and Adrian
1978 "Music in Madras: The Urbanization of a Cultural Tradition." In Bruno Nettl, ed., *Eight Urban Musical Cultures.* Urbana: University of Illinois Press.
Levi-Strauss, Claude
1969 *The Raw and The Cooked.* New York: Harper & Row.
Levy, Reuben
1957 *The Social Structure of Islam.* 2d ed. New York: Cambridge University Press.
Lomax, Alan
1968 *Folk Song Style and Culture.* Washington: American Association for the Advancement of Science.
McAllester, David
1954 *Enemy Way Music.* Papers of the Peabody Museum, Harvard University, Vol. 41, No. 3.
McClain, Ernest G.
1976 *The Myth of Invariance.* New York: Nicholas Hays.
MacMunn, Sir George
1933 *The Underworld of India.* London: Jarrolds Publishers Ltd.

Madan, T. N., ed.
1976 *Muslim Communities of South Asia.* New Delhi: Vikas Publishing House. First published in *Contributions to Indian Sociology,* n.s., Vol. 6, 1972.

Marriott, McKim, and Inden, Ronald
1974 "Caste." In *Encyclopedia Britannica,* 15th edition.

Mathur, J. C.
1965 *New Lamps for Aladdin.* Calcutta: Orient Longmans, Ltd.

Mathur, P. N.
1969 "Tansen." *Illustrated Weekly of India,* February 2, 1969.

Mattoo, J. L.
1965 "Education in Music." *Bharatiya Sangeet* 1:15–22.

Menon, Narayana
1963 "The Music Public in India." *The World of Music,* Bulletin of The International Music Council 5(1–2):17–19.

Merriam, Alan
1964 *The Anthropology of Music.* Evanston, Ill.: Northwestern University Press.

Mirza, Wahid
1974 *The Life and Works of Amir Khusrau.* Delhi: Idarah-I Adabiyat-I Delli. First published 1935.

Misra, Susheela
1955(?) *Music Profiles,* n.p.

Mookerji, Radha
1951 *Ancient Indian Education.* London: Macmillan & Co., Ltd.

Mujeeb, M.
1967 *The Indian Muslims.* London: George Allen & Unwin Ltd.

Nettl, Bruno
1964 *Theory and Method in Ethnomusicology.* New York: Free Press of Glencoe.

Nettl, Bruno, ed.
1978 *Eight Urban Musical Cultures.* Urbana: University of Illinois Press.

Nettl, Bruno
1979 "Musical Values and Social Values: Symbols in Iran." *Journal of the Steward Anthropological Society* 10(1) (forthcoming).

Neuman, Daniel M.
1976 "Towards an Ethnomusicology of Culture Change in Asia." *Asian Music* 7(2):1–5.

Neuman, Daniel M.
1977 "The Social Organization of a Music Tradition: Hereditary Specialists in North India." *Ethnomusicology* 21(2):233–45.

Neuman, Daniel M.
1978a "Gharanas: The Rise of Musical 'Houses' in Delhi and Neighboring Cities." In Bruno Nettl, ed., *Eight Urban Musical Cultures.* Urbana: University of Illinois Press.

Neuman, Daniel M.
1978b "Journey to the West." In *Contributions to Asian Studies* 12:40–53.

Neuman, Daniel M.
1979 "Country Musicians and Their City Cousins: The Kinship of Folk and Classical Music Culture in North India." In *Proceedings of the XIIth Congress of the International Musicological Society.* Kassel: Barenreiter Verlag (forthcoming).

Owens, Naomi
1969 "Two North Indian Musical Gharanas." Unpublished M.A. thesis, University of Chicago.

Pandey, K. C.
1959 *Indian Aesthetics.* Varanasi: Chowkhamba Sanskrit Series Office.

Peters, Emrys
1960 "The Proliferation of Segments in the Lineage of the Bedouin of Cyrenaica." *Journal of the Royal Anthropological Institute,* part 1, 90:29–53.

Platts, John T.
1965 *A Dictionary of Urdu, Classical Hindi and English.* London: Oxford University Press.
Popley, Herbert
1971 *The Music of India.* 4th edition. New York: Oxford University Press. First published 1921.
Powers, Harold
1979 "South Asia." In *Grove's Dictionary of Music and Musicians,* 6th edition (in press).
Prajnanananda, Swami
1960 *Historical Development of Indian Music.* Calcutta: Firma K. L. Mukhopadhyay.
Prajnanananda, Swami
1965 *A Historical Study of Indian Music.* Calcutta: Anandadhara Prakashan.
Racy, Jihad
1976 "Record Industry and Egyptian Traditional Music: 1904–1932." *Ethnomusicology* 20(1): 23–48.
Racy, Jihad
1977 "Commercial Recording in Egypt, 1904–1932." *Essays in Arts and Sciences* 6(1):58–94.
Raghavan, V.
1966 *The Great Integrators: The Saint-Singers of India.* Delhi: Publications Division-6.
Rahman, M. L.
1970 *Persian Literature in India During the Time of Jahangir and Shah Jahan.* Baroda: M. S. University of Bander.
Ratanjankar, S. N.
1965 "Music as a Career or Profession" in *Bharatiya Sangeet* 1(1):13–14.
Ratanjankar, S. N.
1971 "Harmonium and Indian Music." *Journal of the Sangeet Natak Akademi* (20):11–14.
Raynor, Henry
1972 *A Social History of Music.* New York: Schocken Books.
Risley, Sir H. H.
1891 *Tribes and Castes of Bengal.* 2 vols. Calcutta: Bengal Secretariat Press.
Rizvi, S. N. Haider
1941 "Music in Muslim India." *Islamic Culture* 15:331–40.
Roach, David
1972 "The Benares Baj: The Tabla Tradition of a North Indian City." *Asian Music,* 3(2): 29–41.
Row, Peter
1977 "The Device of Modulation in Hindustani Art Music." *Essays in Arts and Sciences* 6(1):104–20.
Row, Peter
1978 "The Role of the Non-Khandani Musician in the Shaping of Musical Change in North India." Delivered at the Xth International Congress of Anthropological and Ethnological Sciences, New Delhi.
Roy, Basanta K.
1919 "Patronage of Music in India." *The Musical Observer* 18(6):9–10, 15.
Roy, Hemendra Lal
1937 *Problems of Hindustani Music.* Calcutta: Bharati Bhanan.
Rudolph, Lloyd I., and Susanne H.
1967 *The Modernity of Tradition: Political Development in India.* Chicago: University of Chicago Press.
Russell, Ralph, and Islam, Kurshidal
1968 *Three Mughal Poets.* Cambridge, Mass.: Harvard University Press.

Ruswa, Mirza Mohammad
   n.d.. *The Courtesan of Lucknow (Umrao Jan Ada)*. Translated by Kushwant Singh and M. A. Husaini. Delhi: Hind Pocket Books.
Sachs, Curt
   1940 *The History of Musical Instruments*. New York: W. W. Norton.
Sakata, Lorraine
   1976 "The Concept of Musician in Three Persian-Speaking Areas of Afghanistan." *Asian Music*, 8(1):1–28.
Sambamoorthy, P.
   1959 *Dictionary of Music and Musicians*. Vol. II. Madras: Indian Musical Publishing House.
Sambamoorthy, P.
   1971 *Dictionary of Music and Musicians*. Vol. III. Madras: Indian Musical Publishing House.
Sangeet Natak Akademi Report
   1953–1958
Sarmadee, Shahab
   1975 "Musical Genius of Amir Khusrau." In *Amir Khusrau* (Memorial Volume). New Delhi: Publication Division.
Schneider, David M.
   1976 "Notes Towards a Theory of Culture." In Keith H. Basso and Henry A. Selby, eds., *Meaning in Anthropology*. Albuquerque: University of New Mexico Press.
Sen, Sharmistha
   1972 "The String Instruments of North India." Ph.D. dissertation, Visva-Bharati University. Unpublished.
Shankar, Ravi
   1966 "Listening and Learning." *Indian Music Journal* (6):44–48.
Shankar, Ravi
   1968 *My Music, My Life*. New Delhi: Vikas Publications.
Sharar, Abdul Halim
   1975 *Lucknow: The Last Phase of an Oriental Culture*. Translated and edited by E. S. Harcourt and Fakhir Hussein. London: Paul Elek.
Sharma, B. L.
   1971 "Contribution of Rajasthan to Indian Music." *Journal of the Indian Musicological Society* 2(2):32–47.
Sharman, Gopal
   1970 *Filigree in Sound*. New Delhi: Vikas Publications.
Shepard, Francis A.
   1976 "Tabla and the Benares Gharana." Ph.D. dissertation, Wesleyan University. Unpublished.
Sherring, M. A.
   1872 *Hindu Tribes and Castes, as Represented in Benares*. Calcutta: Thacker, Spink & Co.
Silver, Brian
   1976 "On Becoming an Ustad: Six Life Sketches in the Evolution of a Gharana." *Asian Music*, 7(2):27–58.
Silverberg, James, ed.
   1968 *Social Mobility in the Caste System of India: An Interdisciplinary Symposium*. New York: Humanities Press.
Singer, Milton
   1972 *When a Great Tradition Modernizes*. New York: Praeger.
Singer, Milton, and Cohn, Bernard S.
   1968 *Structure and Change in Indian Society*. Viking Fund Publications in Anthropology, No. 47. Chicago: Aldine.

References

Sinha, Purnima
1970 *An Approach to the Study of Indian Music.* Calcutta: Indian Publications.
Slobin, Mark
1976 *Music in the Culture of Northern Afghanistan.* Viking Fund Publications in Anthropology, No. 54. Tucson: University of Arizona Press.
Spear, Percival
1951 *Twilight of the Mughuls: Studies in Late Mughul Delhi.* Cambridge: Cambridge University Press.
Srinivas, M. N.
1976 *The Remembered Village.* Delhi: Oxford University Press.
Stewart, Rebecca
1974 "The Tabla in Perspective." Ph.D. dissertation, University of California, Los Angeles. Unpublished.
Tagore, S. M.
1965 *Hindu Music from Various Authors.* Varanasi: Chowkhamba Sanskrit Series Office. First published 1875.
Tagore, S. M.
1963 *Universal History of Music.* Varanasi: Chowkhamba Sanskrit Series Office. First published 1896.
Tandon, Prakash
1961 *Punjabi Century.* New York: Harcourt, Brace & World, Inc.
Taylor, Meadows
1872 *The People of India.* Edited by J. Forbes Watson and Sir John William Kaye. Vol. VI. London: India Museum.
Tewari, Laxmi G.
1974 "Folk Music of India." Ph.D. dissertation, Wesleyan University. Unpublished.
Todd, James
1965 "Music." From his *Annals and Antiquities of Rajasthan,* Vol. I, pp. 538–40. In S. M. Tagore, *Hindu Music from Various Authors.* Varanasi: Chowkhamba Sanskrit Series Office. First published 1875.
Trikha, S. N.
1967 *A Glimpse of Hindustani Music and Musicians.* New Delhi: published by the author.
Various Authors
1974 "Canned Concerts: Comments on the Subject." *Journal of the Indian Musicological Society* 5(2):37–46.
Vreede-Desteuers, Cora
1968 *Parda: A Study of Muslim Women's Life in Northern India.* Assen: Van Gorcum & Co. N. V.
Weber, Max
1958 *The Religion of India.* Glencoe, Ill.: Free Press.
Weber, William
1977 "Mass Culture and the Reshaping of European Musical Taste, 1770–1870." *International Review of the Aesthetics and Sociology of Music* 8:5–22.
Who's Who of Indian Musicians
1968 New Delhi: Sangeet Natak Akademi, Rabindra Bhavan.
Willard, N. Augustus
1965 "A Treatise on the Music of Hindoostan." In S. M. Tagore, *Hindu Music from Various Authors.* Varanasi: Chowkhamba Sanskrit Series Office. First published 1875.

Index

Daniel M. Neuman is assistant professor of anthropology at Dartmouth College and visiting professor, 1978–79, at the School of Music of the University of Washington. He has contributed to journals of Asian studies and ethnomusicology and is associate editor of the journal *Ethnomusicology*.

The Life of Music in North India developed from the author's two-year stay in India, 1969–71, and several shorter visits, in 1973–74, 1976–77, and 1978.

The book was designed by Richard Kinney. The typeface for the text and display is Garamond, which is based on a design by Claude Garamond in the 16th century.

The text is printed on International Bookmark text paper and the book is bound in Holliston Mills' Kingston cloth over binder's boards. Manufactured in the United States of America.